THE SHAPING OF CHRISTIANITY

The History and Literature of Its Formative Centuries (100–800)

Gérard Vallée

PAULIST PRESS
New York/Mahwah, N.J.

Cover design by Nick Markell. The image is based on "Emperor Constantine and his mother Helena holding the 'true cross.'" Fresco of the Yilanli Church (Snake Church) in Göreme, Cappadocia (Turkey).

Copyright © 1999 by Gérard Vallée

Library of Congress Cataloging-in-Publication Data

Vallée, Gérard, 1933–
    The shaping of Christianity : the history and literature of its formative centuries (100–800) / Gérard Vallée.
        p.   cm.
    Includes bibliographical references and index.
    ISBN 0-8091-3867-0 (alk. paper)
    1. Church history—Primitive and early church, ca. 30–600. 2. Christian literature, Early—History and criticism. 3. Church history—Middle Ages, 600–1500. I. Title.
BR165.V35   1999
270.1—dc21   99-24386
                                                                                        CIP

Published by Paulist Press
997 Macarthur Boulevard
Mahwah, New Jersey 07430

www.paulistpress.com

Printed and bound in the
United States of America

Contents

Acknowledgments

Over the years many colleagues and friends expressed encouragement for the present enterprise, and some were generous enough to read drafts of chapters at various stages and comment on them. I remain particularly thankful to Howard Jones, Travis Kroeker, Eileen Schuller, and Peter Widdicombe for sharing their expertise and making this book far richer as a result. But I must single out the substantial contribution I received from Michel Desjardins in the completion of this book; at a crucial time in its preparation he generously sifted the entire manuscript, suggested changes in form and content, corrected imbalances; his tact and competence made the book ready to sail on high seas. I am greatly in his debt for doing so and for rekindling my confidence.

Collaboration with Paulist Press has been most pleasant and stimulating. I wish to thank first Father Kevin Lynch, who was kind enough to welcome a manuscript that a less exercised eye perhaps might have rashly dismissed as trite and conventional. I appreciated his openmindedness and generous hospitality. In that he was well seconded by Donald Brophy. For her encouragement and fine suggestions I owe a considerable debt to Kathleen Walsh, my in-house editor at Paulist; she showed a high level of acumen and diligence, and did not shirk going the extra mile to make the manuscript coherent and transparent. She was competently assisted by the keen attention of Glorieux Dougherty as copy editor. I am grateful to all for making the Paulist house feel like home to me.

Abbreviations

ACW   Ancient Christian Writers series. Westminster, Md.: Newman Press/New York: Paulist Press, 1946–.

Adv. Marc. Tertullian, *Against Marcion*. Translated by E. Evans. 2 vols. *Oxford Early Christian Texts*. Oxford: Clarendon Press, 1972.

AH   Irenaeus, *Against Heresies*. In A. Roberts and J. Donaldson, eds., The Ante-Nicene Fathers, vol. 1. Grand Rapids, Mich.: Eerdmans, 1989 (repr.).

ANF   The Ante-Nicene Fathers series. Edinburgh, 1867. Repr. Grand Rapids, Mich.: Eerdmans, 1989.

ANRW   Aufstieg und Niedergang der Römischen Welt/Rise and Decline of the Roman World. Berlin/New York: de Gruyter, 1972–, especially II. 16–28.

Apol.   Justin, *Apology*. Translated by L. W. Barnard. Ancient Christian Writers, vol. 56. New York: Paulist Press, 1997.

C. Cels.   Origen, *Against Celsus*. Translated by H. Chadwick. Cambridge: Cambridge University Press, 1953.

Conf.   Augustine, *Confessions*. Translated by H. Chadwick. *Oxford World's Classics*. Oxford: Oxford University Press, 1991.

De pr. haer. Tertullian, *On Prescription Against Heretics*. In A. Roberts and J. Donaldson, eds., The Ante-Nicene Fathers, vol. 3. Grand Rapids, Mich.: Eerdmans, 1989 (repr.).

De princ. Origen, *On First Principles*. Translated by G. W. Butterworth. New York: Harper & Row, 1966.

Dial.   Justin, *Dialogue with Trypho*. In A. Roberts and J. Donaldson, eds., The Ante-Nicene Fathers, vol. 1. Grand Rapids, Mich.: Eerdmans, 1989 (repr.).

HE   Eusebius, *Ecclesiastical History*. Translated by K. Lake and J. E. C. Oulton. Loeb Classical Library. 2 vols. Cambridge, Mass.: Harvard University Press, 1926, 1932.

Life   Athanasius, *The Life of Antony*. Translated by R. C.
                Gregg. Classics of Western Spirituality, vol. 16. New
                York: Paulist Press, 1980.

NPNF   A Select Library of Nicene and Post-Nicene Fathers of
                the Christian Church. Buffalo/New York, 1887–1892.
                Repr. Grand Rapids, Mich.: Eerdmans, 1982.

NPNF   A Select Library of Nicene and Post-Nicene Fathers of
2nd Ser.   the Christian Church. Second series. New York,
                1890–1900. Repr. Grand Rapids, Mich.: Eerdmans, 1961.

PL   Patrologia latina. Edited by J.-P. Migne, 221 vols. Paris,
                1844–1864.

Praep. ev.   Eusebius, *Preparation for the Gospel*. Translated by E.
                H. Gifford. 2 vols. Oxford: Clarendon Press, 1908.

Str.   Clement of Alexandria, *Stromateis*. In A. Roberts and J.
                Donaldson, eds., The Ante-Nicene Fathers, vol. 2. Grand
                Rapids, Mich.: Eerdmans 1989 (repr.)

———

Note to the Reader: All bibliographical information and technical material can
be found in appendices 1–7. Most ancient Christian writings referred to in the text are
listed in appendix 3.

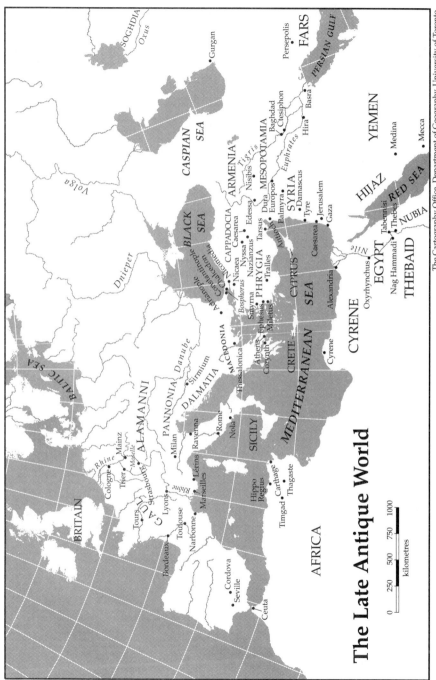

The Late Antique World

The Cartography Office, Department of Geography, University of Toronto

ROMAN EMPERORS

98–117	Trajan		238–244	Gordian III
117–138	Hadrian		244–249	Philip the Arab
138–161	Antoninus Pius		249–251	Decius
161–180	Marcus Aurelius		253–260	Valerian
180–193	Commodus		260–268	Gallienus
193–211	Septimius Severus		268–270	Claudius II
211–217	Caracalla		270–275	Aurelian
218–222	Elagabalus		276–282	Probus
222–235	Alexander Severus		282–283	Carus
235–238	Maximinus Thrax			

WEST			**EAST**	
283–285	Carinus		283–284	Numerian
284–286	Diocletian		284–305	Diocletian
286–305	Maximian			
305–306	Constantius		305–311	Galerius
307–324	Constantine		308–324	Licinius
		324–337 Constantine		
		337–361 Constantius II		
		361–363 Julian		
		363–64 Jovian		
364–375	Valentinian		364–378	Valens
375–392	Valentinian II			
367–383	Gratian		379–395	Theodosius I
383–388	Maximus			
395–423	Honorius		395–408	Arcadius
			408–450	Theodosius II
423–455	Valentinian III		450–457	Marcian
455–456	Avitus			
457–461	Majorian		457–474	Leo I
461–465	Libius Severus			
467–472	Procopius		474	Leo II
475–476	Romulus		474–491	Zeno
			491–518	Anastasius I
			518–527	Justin I
			527–565	Justinian I
			565–578	Justin II
			578–582	Tiberius II
			582–602	Maurice
			602–610	Phocas
			610–641	Heraclius
			641–668	Constantine III
			668–685	Constantine IV
			685–695	Justinian II [1st reign]
			695–698	Leontius
			698–705	Tiberius III
			705–711	Justinian II [2nd reign]
			711–713	Philippicus Vardan
			713–715	Anastasius II
			715–717	Theodosius III
			717–741	Leo III
			741–775	Constantine V
			775–780	Leo IV
			780–797	Constantine VI
			797–802	Irene

LEADING FIGURES OF

Apostolic Fathers (1st half of 2nd century)

Clement of Rome   –101
Ignatius of Antioch   69–112/125

Greek Apologists (2nd half of 2nd century)

Justin Martyr   100–165

Hegesippus   175/180
Athenagoras of Athens   177–
Irenaeus of Lyons   130–202
Theophilus of Antioch   180–

Greeks of 3rd Century

Clement of Alexandria   150–215 (220/231)
Origen   185–254
Hippolytus of Rome   170–235/250

Alexandrians of 4th–5th Centuries   *Cappadocians of 4th Century*

Arius   256–336
Gregory of Nazianzus   330–390
Basil of Caesarea   330–379

Athanasius   299–373

Gregory of Nyssa   331–393

Evagrius Ponticus   345–399

Cyril of Alexandria   372/376–444

End of Patristic Period
(5th–8th Centuries)

Leo the Great   400–461
Boethius   480–524
Gregory the Great   540–604
Dionysius (Pseudo-Areopagite)   500–
Isidore of Seville   560–636
Maximus Confessor   580–662
John of Damascus   675–749

THE PATRISTIC PERIOD

(Qumran)

Gnostic Teachers

Simon Magus

Marcion ca.   85–160

Valentinus ca.   100–160   Basilides   120/145

Montanus   172–

Theodotos   Bardaisan
Carpocrates

Celsus   179–
(Mishnah)

Latins of 3rd Century

Tertullian   160–225
Cyprian   210–258

Plotinus   205–270
Mani   216–277

Antiochene-Syrians of 4th–5th Centuries   ### Latins of 4th–5th Centuries

Eusebius of Caesarea   265–340

Ephrem   306–373   (Nag Hammadi Libary)
Ambrose of Milan   337–397

Epiphanius of Salamis   310/320–403
John Chrysostom   345–407   Rufinus of Aquileia 345–410
Theodore of Mopsuestia   350–428   Jerome   347–420
Nestorius   380–451   Pelagius   350–425
Augustine of Hippo 354–430

(Muhammad 570–632)

Introduction

The purpose of this small book is to whet the appetite of its readers for a dish they have presumably not yet tasted, and to invite a sampling of its pleasures. It is not designed for the regular and confident customers of a familiar establishment. Hence acquaintance with the subject matter, Christianity in its formative period, is not presupposed nor is it even desired. The only prerequisite the reader is expected to hold, besides a common level of literacy, is a guileless interest in the early development of the Christian movement as it is made manifest in historical and literary sources, and an interest in how modern scholarship goes about discharging its function in this field.

In what follows, every effort is made to use transparent and non-technical language, and to explain theological ideas when they turn up. To that end the available material is organically rearranged, subtle details are bypassed and left to experts, didactic concerns are generously honored, and a number of appendices handle difficulties generally experienced by students unfamiliar with the period. It is hoped that beginners will find here the basic information presupposed for a successful encounter with primary sources. My wish is to prepare readers for such an undertaking, the "main course" on the menu of early Christian studies.

Clarity does not mean oversimplification. The narrative that follows includes the description of a complex historical process at the same time that it incorporates the main results of recent research. A double concern for substantial information and lucid communication thus informs the intended objective of this book: to convey the excitement that comes from the study of those centuries, and to invite further explorations. I do not claim to improve on the numerous excellent presentations of the development of early Christianity that already exist. However, experience has taught me that a different, simpler guide is needed to accompany the first steps in that study, to tour the "dining room" and to provide the primary knowledge, not expected from the reader, of the history and literature of the early Christian movement. Originality is not directly sought; if it is achieved here and there, it is to be traced to my good fortune. What is sought is unimpeded communication based on realistic assumptions.

It will easily be granted that my presentation cannot deal with all the important issues that emerged during those centuries. The "Select Bibliography" (see appendix 7) lists works particularly relevant to a more comprehensive study or referred to in more than one chapter; the "Readings" at the end of each chapter provide sources used in the chapter.

The Patristic Period

It has become usual to call the first centuries of the Christian tradition the "Patristic Period." It is indeed the period of the founders of the church, of the "fathers" *(patres)* who did pioneering work in turning the Christian movement into a self-assured religious, social, and intellectual force. In the course of various feats of self-presentation and self-defense the church leaders—not all were men—gave shape to the essential contours of what became a well-circumscribed entity, Christian life and thought.

The time span covered by the Patristic Period is variously delimited. It is generally agreed that its beginning follows on the life and work of Jesus' immediate followers and thus starts with the so-called postapostolic times, roughly 100 of the common era (C.E.). As for its end and term, there is less agreement. Various dates are proposed. While the Protestant tendency is to have the Patristic Period end, and the Middle Ages begin, with Constantine (306–337), Catholic historians traditionally have preferred a much later date, as late as the eleventh century. Those who wish to count Augustine among the medieval writers have the Patristic Period end around 400; others opt for 476, the death of the last emperor of the West; or for 604 in the West, the year of the death of Gregory the Great; or 749 in the East, the year of the death of John of Damascus; or 787, the year of the seventh general council. Still others choose 632, the year of Muhammad's death, because of the radical change brought about by the Muslim irruption around the Mediterranean. The year 800, in my view, makes room for all those opinions and underlines the European import of Charlemagne's crowning. With the year 800 a new age is dawning and a new kind of intellectual output begins to emerge, while Christianity's center of gravity decisively shifts away from the Mediterranean to northwestern Europe, marking the end of a world; at the same time, Eastern Christianity begins to turn northward to the Slavic populations.

Periodization is always subjective, especially, as in the present case, when one is faced with a conjunction of historical and literary perspectives. The formative Christian period traditionally called "the age of the fathers" designates a certain segment in time but also a certain kind of literary production. Allowing for flexibility in determining the limits of the period is quite apropos. One encounters the same flexibility, for instance, in setting the parameters to the "medieval" or "modern" periods.

Christianity

The formative Christian period can be approached from various angles, depending on one's major interest or on what one considers central to the development of the Christian tradition in those centuries. Thus writers interested in the emergence of a mainstream institution, the church, study the period in the framework of "church history." Those concerned with the gradual construction of normative tenets talk about "history of dogma." Similarly, we can explore those centuries with an interest, for instance, in the history of doctrine, the history of Christian thought, the history of theology, and the history of Christian practice. Far from being mutually exclusive, all those various aspects complement each other and constitute an object that is best called "Christianity" and is most extensively dealt with in the context of history of religions or religious studies. By opting for the expression history of Christianity, I choose the formulation that is most comprehensive and least conducive to isolation from the historical and social context.

The present study of Christianity in its early history is conducted from a perspective that is not necessarily that of the church; it aims to respond to a twentieth-century detached interest in the development of Christianity as a social and religious movement, coupled with the desire to understand how and why that development took the directions it did. Given the nature of that development, readers may at times feel painfully taxed; it should then be kept in mind that challenge is also a familiar incitement to learning.

The term Christianity used in this most inclusive manner also serves to indicate that my interest goes to the many facets of the Christian movement as a historical, social, and religious process. Such an understanding of the term should not be seen as an innovation. As early as the second century, the term *khristianismós* itself, which became in translation Christianity, referred first of all to the concrete way of life of the Christians in opposition to that of the Jews and the Greeks; that usage is significant for its empirical connotations, akin to this book's perspective.

The historical development of Christianity can be explored through the usual scholarly means without the assumption of a faith commitment on the part of the explorers. Elements of institution, doctrine, and piety are thereby inserted into a presentation, as devoid as possible of willful partisanship, of the history and literature of the period. This approach simply reflects the migration of patristic studies out of its clerical cradle into the secular university, which has taken place particularly in the wake of the Second World War.

Patristics as a Field of Research and Study

As a scholarly enterprise, patristics cannot be defined with any satisfactory precision. The main reason is that patristic studies, investigating the history and literature of the first centuries of the common era, have always been practiced in connection with other academic disciplines such as philosophy, biblical studies, classical studies, theology, philology, history, literary theories. As a field of research and study, patristics is essentially interdisciplinary. While this fact makes the field more attractive, it also makes for a fragile or tenuous definition of its territory and method. We have here not an autonomous discipline but a conglomerate of disciplines around a focal interest: the development of a religious movement as it reverberated in the surrounding social history and was reflected in its literature. For our purpose there is no need for a more clear-cut subject matter or for any further description of its scope. The overall intent of my presentation remains the critical retrieval of the historic foundations of Christianity through the careful sifting of an array of available sources.

Sources and Tools

The last century and a half have witnessed a massive influx of fresh material to study classical antiquity and the Patristic Period. Ancient sources of all kinds, including Christian sources, are more readily accessible through new collections and editions. Previous centuries were often satisfied with written testimonies and built their reconstructions of the past almost exclusively on textual remains. The situation is different today. Other sources and tools come to the help of the textual approach: archeology with its wealth of material remains, epigraphy and papyrology, iconography and artistic representations are some of the main ways unpublished or fresh information is put at our disposal. Anthropology and sociology have also provided fruitful hypotheses and conceptual tools often yielding fresh understanding of the historical and intellectual processes. The evidence gathered as a result of those expanded sources and instruments, submitted to a critical assessment, is now used in the reconstruction and interpretation of the past.

Topicality of Patristic Studies

The spectacular blossoming of patristic studies in the past two centuries is arguably due to a double cause. First, the spirit of criticism that characterized the eighteenth century Enlightenment, especially in its German branch, could not bypass the need for assessing the extent to which contemporary Christianity had developed away from its original features. The names of G. E. Lessing (1729–1781) and A. von Harnack (1851–1930) mark two important moments in the enterprise of critique of dogma. In his attempt to find out the extent to which Christianity rests on solid rational grounds, Lessing turned to the church fathers and found their ideas and positions, especially about the "rule of faith," totally at odds with those current in recent theology, for which the written letter of the Bible was the exclusive norm.

Second, the emergence of historical consciousness, signaled by such names as G. W. F. Hegel (1770–1831) and F. C. Bauer (1792–1860), provided the definitive driving force in the development of patristic studies. It became clear that the historical perspective was now essential to an understanding of the present. The study of ancient sources was seen as offering vital elements in the search for Christian identity in the contemporary situation. In fact, the proximity of the fathers to the origins of the Christian movement gives them a unique worth as regards the interpretation and understanding of Christianity. The current interest in beginnings finds in their writings a privileged voice of authenticity, most helpful in the task of retrieving a concept of Christianity that antedates the strictures of European cultural self-importance.

The interest in ancient Christian literature has now reached the entire Christian community across confessional borders. For instance, regardless of an interpreter's denominational context, it is no longer possible to do Christian theology today without a close look at the writings of the fathers. These are no longer drawn on as providers of isolated statements likely to buttress one's position; works are studied as integral wholes and in context so that their specific understanding of Christianity is manifested and can serve as a marker in today's theological enterprise.

Obviously the interest in beginnings has ecumenical implications. By looking together at ancient witnesses, scholars of all confessional backgrounds take a firm step toward overcoming Christian divisions. The discovery of the lush diversity that characterized the early centuries is conducive to greater tolerance and mutual understanding. For some, it is simply one step further to pass from this form of Christian ecumenism to a wider ecumenism that is willing to recognize and act on what is valid in other religious traditions.

Trends in Recent Research

The wider horizon to which I have just pointed characterizes much of the recent work in the study of Christianity in Late Antiquity. Increasingly this work is carried out in the context of European and world history, whose past traditions it wishes to recover. It is a fact that Western religious thought is rooted in both Semitic and Indo-European cultures. The Hebrew Bible and cognate writings on the one hand, and the New Testament along with Greco-Roman traditions (incorporating important elements coming from Persia/Iran and perhaps India) on the other, are the two offshoots of the Semitic and Indo-European streams that merge in the writings of the fathers. After the fifth century, the heritage of the "barbarians" (Celts, Germans, Franks, etc.) is added and is also reflected or refracted in the selfsame writings. Contemporary study of early Christian literature is thus conscious of being in touch with quasi-universal movements of thought and practices; it is conducted in the awareness that ancient Mediterranean culture included innumerable riches still to be identified.

A second trend characterizes recent work in patristics: that work is performed in the broader context of the history of religions. For a long time the investigation of the Patristic Period was conducted exclusively in connection with the study of Christian origins and Judaism. For Jews and Christians the early fourth century marked the definitive split between the two religious traditions; the march toward that split was documented in patristic literature, valued for that precise reason. Today the religious context is expanded. Patristic literature is seen to incorporate or reflect more elements coming from indigenous Near Eastern and Mediterranean origins that have to be taken into consideration; these are likely to yield a better understanding of Europe's birthplace in the culture of the late Roman Empire.

This wider context for the study of patristic literature is aided by a third trend, one that might claim the place of honor in the eyes of an outside observer: Current work is characterized by a direct, resolute, and extensive dealing with sources. New discoveries and editions of sources have made this situation possible. It is with primary sources that the patristic scholar is working, not with second-hand presentations or anthologies. To be sure, work with sources characterized much of the serious scholarship of the past, but the current expansion of sources and instruments makes their use still more desirable and has rendered research a still more exacting activity. Present-day scholarship demands expertise in history, philology, and philosophy, and it increasingly appeals to social-scientific aids. Whenever this quality of research is sought, a high level of production can be expected.

Finally, present-day patrologists are generally not inclined to pursue apologetic interests. Increasingly their work is carried out within secular institutions. Their contributions are judged by the value of their scholarship, not by its usefulness to interest groups or clerical ghettos. This is a major shift when one considers how scholars in previous centuries were inclined to put their research at the service of confessional, sectarian, or other vested interests. Patristics has hooked up with general literature and reentered the public domain.

The field of patristic studies presents all the features of a lively building site. Since the Second World War it has been the object of an accelerated interest similar to the previous interest in things medieval, and paralleled only by biblical studies.

History and Literature

This book does not investigate the formative Christian period as representing the period of the establishment of enduring beliefs and practices, which is a justifiable perspective in a theological context. Rather, I consider that period one in which Christianity evolved as a religious and social movement, one that exhibits that development mainly through its literary and historical remains. I consult the early Christian writers in order to construct a narrative of the many turns taken by Christianity in those centuries.

In doing this I do not claim an impossible objectivity and detachment whereby I could pretend to a neutral standpoint or to no standpoint at all. I only try to let the sources speak. Occasionally those sources will have nonliterary partners, such as epigraphic and iconographic resources. All will be interrogated for the light they can throw on the development of the Christian movement. The literary evidence, however, receives pride of place: Early Christianity is marked out among religions by the quasi-natural tendency with which, from the start, it took to writing. Texts mattered to Christians of the first centuries; they enjoyed a special status. That initial propensity was to be confirmed by Christianity's later history.

READINGS

G. F. Chestnut	*The First Christian Histories: Eusebius, Socrates, Sozomen, Theodoret and Evagrius.* Paris: Beauchesne, 1986.
F.-C. Fredouille and R.-M. Roberge, eds.	*La documentation patristique: Bilan et prospective.* Québec: Presses de l'Université Laval, 1995.
W. H. C. Frend	*Archeology and History in the Study of Early Christianity.* London: Variorum Reprints, 1988.
W. H. C. Frend	*The Archeology of Early Christianity.* Minneapolis: Fortress Press, 1996.
J. de Ghellinck	*Patristique et moyen-âge*, 2 vols. Gembloux: Duculot 1946–1947 (review of publications up to 1940).
C. Kannengiesser	"Fifty Years of Patristics." *Theological Studies* 50 (1989): 633–656 (review of publications for 1940–1990).
C. Kannengiesser	"The Future of Patristics." *Theological Studies* 52 (1991): 128–139.
M. Simon	"Histoire des religions—Histoire du christianisme—Histoire de l'Eglise: Réflexions méthodologiques." *Le christianisme antique et son contexte religieux. Scripta varia*, vol. 2, 390–403. Tübingen: Mohr, 1981.

1

Christianity in the Roman World (70–120)

Christianity was born along the shores of the Mediterranean Sea; its birth took place in the early decades of the Roman Empire. Those two factors must first be registered, for they constitute the background against which Christianity was to make its start and from which it took over many a feature; like any historical movement it could not possibly operate on an entirely clean slate.

The Mediterranean Region

The Mediterranean Sea, "mare nostrum" (our sea) as the Romans called it, presented all the appearances of a lake of arresting dimensions, providing one of the world's most natural highways on which circulation from shore to shore was relatively easy. Its lands were blessed with a friendly climate and prevailingly clear skies. Scattered around the sea lived populations of varied character and talent, most able to exploit the resources of land and sea. It can be said that geographic, climatic, and human features combined to give an impetus to some of humankind's highest cultural achievements. So in the course of centuries Egyptians, Greeks, and Romans took turns at promoting that choice commodity: civilization. The turn of the era saw Greek towns of Asia Minor experience a remarkable boom while North Africa continued to attract notice as the intellectual powerhouse of the Latin populations.

Advent of the Roman Empire

When Rome took over from Athens, it found itself to be a bilingual composite; Latin in the West took its place beside Greek, mainly located in the East. Rome then developed a literature of its own while at the same time transmitting Greek culture to future generations.

By 100 B.C.E., after conquering Italy and the main areas around the Mediterranean and having considerably augmented its population, the Roman Republic seemed to have reached a state of lasting stability. Yet two civil wars between 88 and 45, and the excessively large role of the army, boded ill for its tranquillity and preluded an imminent disintegration. Indeed in 44, having extended the Roman boundaries as far as the Rhine and assumed a kind of perpetual dictatorship, Caesar made no secret of his distrust of the senatorial aristocracy and of his intention of ending the republic. His assassination in the same year led to further troubles until Octavian picked up the pieces of the republic, was declared "Augustus" ("he who rules by divine approval") by the Senate, and assumed the modest status of "Princeps" (First Citizen), which, in fact, made him "imperator" or supreme chief of the military forces and of the entire estate.

The "Roman Peace"

Under the firm hand of Augustus (27 B.C.E.–14 C.E.) the Mediterranean world was submitted to a comprehensive administrative reform that led to stability, security, and peace (the famous *pax romana*). Army and Senate were brought under control. Frontiers were rectified and made easily defensible. The existing seaways and an extended network of paved roads over land effectively bound the empire together.

The early emperors were intent on consolidating the huge territory entrusted to them, with its western extensions and eastern conquests, comprising over thirty-five provinces, a territory the size of the United States. They were also intent on maintaining and developing the system of government they had inherited. There was no civil war after 69 although frontier provinces (e.g., Syria-Palestine) were often on the brink of open revolt. Second-century emperors were generally good rulers.

The cumulative effect of centuries of Roman hegemony left its mark on Western history and amounted to a considerable advance in the domains of culture and civilization. In particular, Romans bequeathed to generations to come eminent achievements as administrators, jurists, and engineers.

Society and People in the Second Century

One hundred years after Augustus, Christians were beginning to make a certain mark on the Roman world. Yet they were still close to being invisible in the huge crowd. How big was the Mediterranean crowd at the beginning of the second century? Obviously general agreement is not the strong point of demographic studies when applied to ancient history. Nonetheless the Roman practice of regular census for fiscal and military uses along with literary, epigraphic, and archeological evidence (mainly limited, though, to upper classes in cities) can help us figure out the demography of the empire. The most serious bets have been able to estimate the population of the empire at 54 million at the death of Augustus in 14 C.E. Then demographers conjecture 60 to 70 million for around 110, although we ought to keep in mind that the small size of the population always remained one of the great weaknesses of the empire. There might have been some 4 to 5 million Jews, of which some 2 million lived in Palestine, and about 50,000 Christians by then, soon to span most of the Mediterranean region and to reach the frontiers of the empire. Imperial Rome had a population of at least 600,000 (but only 200,000 according to some), slightly larger than that of Alexandria, followed by Antioch, Ephesus, and Carthage. In the fourth century the population of Rome was to decrease relative to that of Constantinople. Cities were generally overcrowded within their precincts, and insalubrious, offering a welcoming ground to recurrent epidemics.

It has been noted that 90 percent of Roman society lived in the countryside, and that 2 percent were wealthy and 8 percent middle-class, while the rest lived in poverty and, in cities, counted on the free distribution of grain and meat, the food banks of the time. Although it is not possible to determine the precise ratio of free and unfree persons, this was a slave society in which the major source of energy was human labor, in which patronage and clientage were crucial for protection and well-being, and in which those compelled to work in order to live as well as the "plebeians" generally were held in contempt. Health was rather poor and women were almost invisible. All the same, material prosperity among the "patricians," well-born, and notables seems to have been on the rise; city life was growing; and the population was increasingly mobile, especially at the frontiers, thus making possible the diffusion of Greco-Roman culture in the provinces.

The empire was run by the urban nobility. After 190/200 a period of stagnation set in, making the "barbarians" who still lingered outside the frontiers think perhaps of looking south beyond the Rhine and the Danube. They were all the more invited to do so as emperors increasingly assumed the obsolete power of Oriental despots and displayed the debilitating pomp of Asiatic satraps in their courts. An aggravating circumstance was that the general population of the empire, after reaching a ceiling of about 95 million, began to decrease due to a lower birth rate and a marked waning in the recruitment of slaves. This decrease was coupled with military overgrowth and anarchy, pestilence, soil abandonment under excessive fiscal burden, and general economic regression. The decline of the empire had started. It was thought that the barbarians were called in order to offset the shrinking population of the empire. Indeed, the overall population of the empire might have reached its lowest level by 400 (some 45 million). Despite this fact, Augustine and Jerome thought that the population was big enough, perhaps too big; hence there was no necessity for all to get married.

The Religious Menu of the Romans

It could hardly be argued that Romans took to religion more than other peoples did. Yet they cherished, along with astrology and magic, a plethora of gods, old and new. A large pantheon had made room, beside the native Roman gods, for most of the renamed Greek deities; they served the main purpose of attending to various human activities. Rituals and ceremonies were performed with scrupulous precision by appointed personnel (priests, augurs, vestals) in sanctuaries, temples, and homes. Festivals and sacrifices were duly practiced, their observance being commended for the soothing effect they produced.

The Roman conquests had a double impact on the religious makeup of the region. Wherever Romans established a colony, they introduced their trinity—Jupiter, Juno, and Minerva. But they also brought home new cults. Meanwhile the state religion that had emerged at the end of the republic was revitalized by Augustus; pride of honor was given to Apollo and Artemis, and the formality unsuitably called "emperor cult" (it showed only weak religious features, if any) was introduced.

The decisive development following the reign of Augustus relates to the spread of Oriental cults over the empire and in Rome itself. They answered needs unfulfilled by traditional religion, above all those relating to the afterlife and to soteriology. More will be said about them in chapter 4.

Parallel to the appearance of the monarchical system of government, a certain trend toward monotheism can be perceived: More and more local deities were seen as mere manifestations of a single power. The educated Romans, skeptical as to official ceremonies and popular beliefs, and not too inclined to believe in the gods of the pantheon, generally believed in Providence.

Prophetic Religions of the Book

Greek and Roman religions had oracles, providing a much sought-after orientation to life (a function first of all discharged by philosophy). Judaism, Christianity, and Islam were to have prophets and scriptures, the latter an innovation in the Greco-Roman world. Prophets receive a message from God for the people, remind them of their commitment to a personal God, insist that moral codes flowing from faith be adhered to, and act as social critics.

The situation of the Jews in the empire presented special features. A double lot befell them on account of their religion. On the one hand, they were allowed to live according to their laws and enjoyed various privileges. Though under Roman control, they were prospering in many near eastern and western areas and formed important colonies, especially in Alexandria and Rome where they had synagogues and schools. On the other hand, their uncompromising monotheism, certain features of their practices, and their reluctance to participate in public life met with total incomprehension. Nevertheless they possessed a clear identity, listened to their past prophets and present teachers who vigorously denied the existence of all deities but one, and held their scriptures and traditions in great reverence. Family bonds were sacred; Jews, it was generally thought, reproved abortion and exposed none of their children but (as Egyptians and Germans also did) they raised them all, an oddity in the Roman world where female and malformed infants were often abandoned.

The early Christian communities initially shared the ambivalent lot of the Jews. Soon, however, they were harassed and denied exemption from public rituals. Like the Jews, and even more, they were considered "atheists" and became objects of malevolent gossip. All that was publicly known about them was that they followed the Galilean prophet Jesus, who had talked about a new kingdom before being ignominiously crucified. They revered their own writings in addition to the Hebrew scriptures, and held meetings mainly at night. After difficult beginnings in Palestine, the early Christians had turned to the Mediterranean world, had opted for the Greek language (emblem of civilization in that Hellenized culture), and were soon found in major centers of the empire (Rome, Alexandria, Antioch, Ephesus). They opened the doors to the Gentiles, mainly thanks to the influence of Paul, a former Pharisee with Roman citizenship. At the beginning they recruited considerably from the lower classes of society, but gradually members of higher strata also joined, all of them at their own risk since their illicit "name" (or membership in the group) made them virtual outlaws.

Religious Faith

Paganism with its ancient and new cults was alive and well when Christianity arose. What singled out Judaism and Christianity among the many religious groups was that these religions required personal dedication to the one God and imposed on their adherents ethical demands as essential to that religious dedication. To the Jewish faith in God and obedience to his commands Christians added a personal devotion to their founder. The linkage of an ethical code with religious faith was practically unknown to most contemporary religions, which rarely went beyond the opinion that the gods liked virtue. Some pagan philosophies (see chapter 3), however, unlike pagan religions, had developed high standards of morality and it is not surprising that Christianity was to seek an alliance with such philosophies. Soon true piety came to be seen as residing in faith and good conduct, over above mere practices; it aimed to mobilize the entire domain of the self in obedience to God's will.

Christianity Around 100 C.E.

It would doubtless be an exaggeration to state that the empire had been shaken by the appearance of the new religious force. Three generations after the death of its founder, Christianity represented a barely visible minority (some 50,000 members at most). Yet that minority was rather diverse (they did not seem to agree on the real meaning of the gospel) and remarkably dynamic. Christians seemed to want to take on the entire inhabited world. First excited by the imminent establishment of the kingdom of God on earth, they progressively formed themselves into a less apocalyptic congregation, and went on teaching ways of virtuous life appropriate to various callings in a civilized society. Harassed in Palestine, they moved in all directions, intent on gathering the Gentiles into the "new Israel." They were soon found in Asia Minor, Egypt, Syria, and Rome, where they suffered sporadic persecutions.

At a time when the great majority of people lived a rural life, Christians appeared in cities, recruiting first of all among artisans and tradesmen and their households, that is, among humble persons. In Rome and Corinth, though, they had wealthy patrons, and converts included some people of substance. Outside Palestine they first used the Greek language in its international form called *koine* (common tongue); in the second century in Rome and Africa they adopted the Latin language and remade it into an instrument suited to their needs.

Very early they had leaders—bishops, presbyters/elders, and deacons, all insisting that they had received their mandate from Jesus through the "apostles." Leaders presided at the worship of the community, cared for the well-being of its members, encouraged them by words and letters to lead a good life and—a shock to the "respectable pagan"—to shun distinctions between Jew and Gentile, Greek and barbarian, slaves and freemen, men and women.

The first half of the second century saw the first writers appear, who, distinct from the authors of both the "canonical" books of the New Testament and the Christian "apocryphal" literature, were to be called "fathers," in the present case "apostolic fathers," because they were in a position to have known personally some of the apostles. Ignatius of Antioch (about 69–112/125) is the most typical among them. As bishop of Antioch, he wrote a series of letters of encouragement to various communities when he was taken as a prisoner to Rome, where he was to be put to death early in the second century.

One important role of the apostolic fathers, traditionally seven in number, must be emphasized. They reflect the first developments beyond the New Testament writings in matters of church order, life practices, language, and theology. Beyond insisting on obedience to the leaders of the community and warning against heresies and schisms, they offer an initial delimitation of normative Christianity as regards its faith and its literature. They witness to the reception of certain "apostolic" writings as particularly treasured and deserving the name of "scripture": authentic holy books held to be depository of Christian truth and worthy to be used in the public proclamation of the church. Initiated at that time, the process toward the fixation of the canon of New Testament writings was to be essentially completed by the end of the second century, prompted by the controversies of the period; yet the final determination of the canonical list of twenty-seven books constituting the New Testament took place only in the fourth century, which explains minor variations encountered in various communities or regions.

Other Christian writings of the first centuries (gospels, letters, stories and legends, secret revelations), which, though received by groups as authoritative and apostolic yet were denied inclusion in the canon, came to be called "apocryphal," that is, secret and not quite reliable. All the same, because of their form, content, and intention of supplementing the canonical works, they are also relevant to an understanding of the faith of the early Christians. More precisely, on the basis of their proximity to the New Testament writings, their study belongs to biblical studies, but to the extent that they were used by the church fathers, they fall under patristics.

Taken together, the New Testament books, apocryphal writings, and the first patristic works are our main sources of information on the manifold diversity of early Christian piety and thought.

The Roman Perspective on Christians

Still more than the Jews, Christians were a puzzle to the Roman world. Officials did not know too well how to deal with these eccentrics who refused to adhere to the Roman way of life. The general populace resented their very difference and was quick to hold them responsible for any untoward happening. In fact, the Christian community presented all the features of an "alternative society"; as such, Christians posed a threat to Roman society and were feared for their vague power. They managed very well to irritate the traditionalists who governed and peopled the empire, by the "abomination" of their practices and their refusal to participate in the prescribed religious rituals. Roman administrators of the second century were perceptive enough to differentiate between Jews and Christians and usually treated them differently. For instance, Nero in 64 saw Christians as a group distinct from Jews and acted against them; then Nerva (96–98) exempted Christians from the capitation tax imposed on ordinary Jews as a punishment for the revolt of 66–70. Rulers were often quick to impose the death penalty on Christians.

Intellectuals of the time did not hide their contempt for the new believers and their strange doings, and were prone to think of them according to firmly fixed stereotypes. Their beliefs were deemed irrational, their "scriptures" of poor quality, their behavior disrespectful of honorable conventions. They were accused of "hatred of the human race"[1] due to their repressive morality, their imputed neglect of civic duties (e.g., their reserve concerning military service and their unreserved encouragement of procreation), and their lack of fear before violent death. Christians were generally perceived as scorning respect for the ancestral customs.

On the other hand, and this could have counted in their favor, Christian groups offered definitive analogies with other groups or associations that indeed were tolerated, such as burial societies, philosophical sects, various confraternities of like-minded people pursuing a common interest (be it trade, worship, or even drinking), voluntary associations and clubs. Nevertheless Christian communities were labeled "unauthorized" clubs. Tacitus thought he was in the right in branding Christianity a "deadly superstition";[2] others kept denouncing the "execrable" practices of Christians. All approved of the treatment meted out to their founder and his disciples. Throughout the second century Christians complained that their actual behavior and doctrines were never really examined; presumably they would have been found quite unobjectionable.

The Jewish Perspective on Christians

Having started as a Jewish sect among other Jewish sects, Christianity eventually followed a separate course. Prior to 70, that gradual

---

1. Tacitus, *Annals* 15.44.6, in J. Stevenson, *A New Eusebius.* London: SPCK, 1987, p. 2.
2. Ibid., 15.44.4.

parting of the ways met with only mild irritation on the part of the Jews: Christians were brothers who had gone astray by believing in Jesus; they were estranged relatives. Bitterness mounted in the late first century as some of the Christian traditions concerning Jesus and the apostles had just been recast in an anti-Jewish spirit (e.g., John's gospel) and as it became clear that the Christian group had been moving step by step away from Pharisaic Judaism. It was then natural for Jews not only to see Christianity as a rival twin, but also to look at Christians as unrepentant renegades and tainted heretics *(minim)*. The claims of Jesus had already been stamped blasphemous and his followers had to fall under the same verdict. Those transgressors, those separatists, were not to be assisted. They had used "our" synagogues only to end up proclaiming themselves the "true Israel";[3] they had applauded the fall of Jerusalem and were inclined to dignify the Roman Empire as an instrument of divine will. Christians were henceforth cursed or at least scoffed at in the synagogues, and they had to be denounced; to that effect malicious gossip and gibes were often resorted to. Some popular Jewish pamphlets of the second century onward contain nasty talk about Christians and tend to malign Jesus, Mary, Paul, the apostles, and, generally, the new believers. Clement, in apparent agreement with Tacitus, noted that "jealousy"[4] bred and fed Jewish resentment and verbal assaults. But then, extreme rhetoric in disputes was a practice common to all in the ancient world; in that regard Jews and, later, Christians were no exception.

An Ambiguous Start

By 100 c.e., Christianity seemed to have little to recommend itself in the eyes of the world. Often caught in in-fighting, Christians constituted a weird flock and clearly had bad press. Some of their beliefs (e.g., the belief in resurrection), some of their practices (e.g., the "cannibalistic" eating of "flesh" and "blood"), and some of their attitudes (e.g., their exaltation of virginity and continence) inspired repulsion and verged on the scandalous. Their books were odd and could certainly not match the great productions of Greco-Roman culture. Keeping aloof from society while deploying an unavailing aggressive-

---

3. Dial. 123.

4. Clement of Rome, *First Epistle to the Corinthians* 5.2, in Stevenson, *A New Eusebius,* p. 4.

ness, those aliens seemed to have no positive contribution to make. Hence labeling, name-calling, and stereotyping were soon to be the easy way of dealing with the early Christians.

As it entered the second century, the Christian movement had to assert and define itself in relation to the surrounding world; otherwise its identity threatened to fade into invisibility. In the process it was exposed to a double challenge. On the one hand, its relation to Judaism, which it was gradually abandoning, remained still largely unreflected on and had to be explicitly worked out. On the other hand, its relation to Hellenistic culture and especially to the more or less popular moral philosophy, which seemed to offer it support and expression, still had to be clarified. This double relationship must now be examined.

READINGS

J. Beloch	*Die Bevölkerung der griechisch-römischen Welt.* Roma: L'Erma di Bretschneider, 1886. Repr. 1968.
J. H. Charlesworth	"Research on the New Testament Apocrypha and Pseudepigrapha." ANRW II.25.5 (1988): 3919–3968.
R. Doran	*Birth of a Worldview: Early Christianity in its Jewish and Pagan Context.* Boulder, Colo.: Westview Press, 1995.
E. Ferguson	*Backgrounds to Early Christianity.* Grand Rapids, Mich.: Eerdmans, 1993.
R. M. Grant	*Early Christianity and Society: Seven Studies.* San Francisco: Harper & Row, 1977.
W. Haase, ed.	"Pre-Constantinian Christianity: The Apostolic Fathers." ANRW II.27.1 (1992): 3–762.
G. La Piana	"Foreign Groups in Rome During the First Centuries of the Empire." *Harvard Theological Review* 20 (1927): 183–403.
R. MacMullen	*Enemies of the Roman Order.* Cambridge, Mass.: Harvard University Press, 1967.
H. O. Maier	*The Social Setting of the Ministry as Reflected in the Writings of Hermas, Clement, and Ignatius.* Waterloo, Ont.: Wilfrid Laurier University Press, 1991.
W. L. Westermann	*The Slave Systems of Greek and Roman Antiquity.* Philadelphia: American Philosophical Society, 1955.
R. L. Wilken	*The Christians as the Romans Saw Them.* New Haven, Conn.: Yale University Press, 1984.

2

The Jewish Legacy (50–150)

Christianity was linked to Judaism by an umbilical cord, so to speak, and after the early decades of essential dependence on Judaism it never evolved in total isolation from it. Nascent Christianity took shape within the matrix of Jewish sectarian and apocalyptic groups that had been flourishing during the previous two centuries. Those groups in turn were rooted in ancient Israelite soil. This shared history and shared culture was a fact that belonged to the substance of Christianity in its relation to Judaism, but also a fact that had to be publicly emphasized for its strategic potential, for it was vitally important to Christianity to affirm and to hold to its Jewish roots because in doing so it scored a winning argument in favor of its own venerable antiquity. An examination of its Jewish roots is therefore necessary to an understanding of early Christianity.

Biblical and Jewish History

By including the creation narratives in its pre-history, Israel attested to an acute awareness of a divine design on her. But the truly founding events were to belong to the historical period. The call of Abraham (ca. 1850 B.C.E.), the activity of Moses and the Exodus from Egypt (ca. 1250) followed by Yahweh's manifestation at the Sinai, the migration through the desert and the occupation of the land that was to become home—those were the events that created Israel as a nation and were kept alive in the collective memory.

Lending reality to a wish his father, King David, had entertained, Solomon built a dwelling for his God, thus inaugurating the period that is now called First Temple Judaism (ca. 950–586). Although distinct, the two kingdoms of the post-Solomonic period—Judah in the south and Israel in the north—generally considered Jerusalem and its Temple their religious and national center. Before long, political turmoil and foreign interventions hit the nation. The kingdom of Israel fell to Assyria in 722 and many of its inhabitants were deported. Then the fall of Judah in 597/587, culminating in the destruction of the Temple in 586, shocked the nation (and the approximately 150,000 inhabitants of the land) at its roots and sent more deportees to Babylonia or fugitives to Egypt, inaugurating what came to be known as the *Diaspora* (dispersion).

The period known as the Exile lasted from 597 to 538/537. The edict of Cyrus in 538 allowed Jews to return to their land. Few returned (around 520 the population of Judea approximated 20,000, rising to some 50,000 by 440), the rest remaining in Babylonia, Egypt, and Asia Minor. Those who returned began rebuilding the Temple, which was rededicated in 515. Henceforth vast sums of money from the Diaspora made their way every year to the Temple, which acted as a bank for projects, employment, and improvements of the capital. Ezra restored the Mosaic law and is credited with laying the foundations (ca. 450) for the Judaism of the future centered on Torah. The name Second Temple Judaism is given to the religious and national entity that lasted from 520/515 B.C.E. to 70 C.E., successively going through a Persian period (520–332), a Hellenistic period (332–363), and a Roman rule (63 B.C.E.–395 C.E.). Second Temple Judaism is the soil out of which both Rabbinic Judaism and Christianity grew in the first century C.E.

The Second Temple (or Second Commonwealth) era saw the domination of the Jewish people by a succession of foreign powers, except for eighty years of relative independence (141–63) at the time of the Hasmonean dynasty (152–37). With the restoration of the sacrificial ritual after the return from Exile, the Temple began again to function as a religious center with its own court (the Sanhedrin); high priests were discharging temporal and religious functions in a kind of power sharing with foreign rulers that constituted a fragile equilibrium and, in the eyes of some, a risky compromise. That equilibrium was in fact shaken in 167 when the Syrian/Seleucid ruler, Antiochus IV Epiphanes, launched a campaign of all-out Hellenization and made the Temple the seat of Zeus Olympios or, according to some, the seat of the Syrian Baal Shamen. This was too much. Against the deadly threat of assimilation with Hellenism a revolt broke out under the leadership of Judah the Maccabee, who was able to rededicate the Temple in 164 and inaugurated the century of Hasmonean rule. More groups emerged then (e.g., the Qumran community), questioning the legitimacy of the high priests.

Jewish resistance was steadily fanned among the people by messianic and apocalyptic yearnings: It was hoped that a leader would soon come to bring redemption to all and free the Jewish people from foreign domination. After the Roman takeover in 63 and the seizure of Jerusalem by Pompey, in the course of which many Jews were taken to Rome as slaves, things somehow seemed to quiet down and a kind of regime of self-rule was established under procuratorial supervision. Jews enjoyed rights based on treaties with Rome and were eventually exempted from the duties of the imperial cult; patriarch (from ca. 20), high priests, and Sanhedrin found accommodation with the occupants. Unrest persisted among the population, though, and was exasperated by the excesses of King Herod (37 B.C.E.–4 C.E.), whose rebuilding of the Temple, of which only the west wall remains today, could hardly provide an excuse for his follies. Those circumstances favored the activity of charismatic teachers and created the background against which his followers could see in Jesus the expected messiah.

Unrest culminated in the first Jewish revolt (66–70 C.E.), in Alexandria and, above all, throughout Palestine. The Roman reaction was both harsh and restrained: Qumran was wiped out (68), Jerusalem burned (70), and the Temple destroyed; repression, deportations, and executions followed. The resistance ended at Masada in 74. The end of the sacrificial cult seemed to sound the knell of Judaism. But the Romans allowed Judaism to reconstitute itself around the Academy (a group of rabbis and sages dedicated to the study of Torah) at Yavneh/Jamnia about 75. Thus it can be said that Roman permissivity provided the occasion for the rise of the formally organized Rabbinic Judaism, successor to both Pharisees and the Sanhedrin. Those years saw the increased activity of the Tannaim (sages) in adapting religious practices to post-temple times and in fixing the threatened traditions of the nation, activity that led to the codification of the Mishnah. With the destruction of the Temple, Sadducees lost their power base. Other sects were decimated, deprived of their centers or no longer viable.

Most revolutionaries slipped out but resistance to the Roman rule persisted among nationalist Jews in the Diaspora (115–117) and in Palestine. When Emperor Hadrian decided to rebuild Jerusalem, now to be called Aelia Capitolina, and the Temple, now dedicated to Jupiter (130), passions rose again at the similarities with the Maccabean predicament. Bar Kokhba, acclaimed in messianic terms by the venerable Rabbi Akiba, led what was to become the second Jewish rebellion (132–135). Christians were harassed for refusing to join in and thus the revolt had a significant impact on the way Jews and Christians henceforth viewed each other. The rebellion ended with Judea reduced to the status of a Roman colony forbidden to Jews, the Temple transformed into a sanctuary of Zeus and Hadrian, and many rabbis martyred. The harsh decrees of repression were rescinded a few years later and the patriarchate reconstituted in Galilee in 140 as a self-governing body to head the communal rabbis and represent the Jews before the imperial authorities. It flourished especially between 150 and 210 and was to last until 425/429. Henceforth religious freedom, not national independence, was sought. The center of Jewish life in Palestine moved from Jerusalem and Judea to Galilee until 870/900, at which time it became mainly concentrated in Babylonia.

Rabbinic Judaism arose out of those historical circumstances. Without the Temple as a powerful sign of God's presence and rule, and without the possibility of sacrificial ritual, religious life and leadership patterns had to be readjusted. Thanks to the activity of the Tannaim, the process of recasting was completed about the year 200. The center of cult is relocated in the home and local assembly, and focused on communal and private prayer. Study and practice of the Torah define the essence of the new cult, with the major festivals transferred to the synagogue (the synagogue was already in existence in the mid-first century; see Mk 1:21; Lk 4:31–37; Mt 7:28f.) or to meals and prayers at home. The transition from Temple to synagogue, all at once house of study, house of prayer, meeting house, and guest house, and from priest to rabbi was completed early in the second century. This momentous development included a reinterpretation of certain elements of the covenantal relationship with God in the aftermath of the destruction of the Temple and the demise of the priestly cult, at the same time that it forced a new assessment of both the meaning of national suffering and the theology of redemption/atonement. Those revisions found lasting expression in the Mishnah.

Biblical and Jewish Literature

Christianity started as a Jewish splinter group and marginal sect during that period of history when Judaism was experiencing the just-mentioned transition from the Judaism of the Hebrew Bible to what became known as Rabbinic or Talmudic Judaism. Hence the transition to that form of Judaism serves as backdrop for an understanding of the rise of Christianity.

Early Christians laid claim not only to shared Hebrew history, but also to the Hebrew scriptures and to the distinctive identity that had developed on the basis of the sacred writings. In that respect they strongly felt that they had more in common with the Jews than with the pagans, although their belief that they were the authentic successors of the biblical Hebrews obviously was challenged by the Jews and created tensions with emergent Rabbinic Judaism.

The Hebrew Bible, in the form given it by the Greek translation known as the *Septuagint* (Latin for seventy, referring to the supposed seventy translators who produced it, abbreviated as LXX), produced in Alexandria about 270 B.C.E., was the holy book of the first Christians, serving as the basis of their teaching and thinking. The canon of the Hebrew Bible had been fixed over the centuries: the Pentateuch (the first five books of the Bible) around 500 B.C.E., the Prophets (possibly) about 400–332, the Writings about 150 (some say ca. 90 C.E.). "Torah" came to designate the Pentateuch and also, according to the rabbis, the "oral law," presumably given to Moses along with the written law (the Oral Torah is referred to as the "tradition of the elders" in the gospels, e.g., in Mk 7:3).

Commonly known to and used by Jews and Christians alike were the so-called apocrypha (works found in the LXX but not in the Hebrew Bible) and the pseudepigrapha (works attributed to biblical figures and not found in the LXX), many of which included apocalyptic writings. After 70, Judaism and Christianity each added something different to their shared (Hebrew) scriptures: Rabbinic literature and the New Testament (twenty-seven writings along with the Christian additions and expansion of Old Testament pseudepigrapha, and their own apocryphal literature). Apocrypha and pseudepigrapha saw the light between 200 B.C.E. and 200 C.E.

The scrolls found at Qumran near the Dead Sea since 1947 give us an idea of the kind of Judaism out of which Christianity sprung. Whether or not it can be identified with the Essenes, the Qumran community represented an alternative community to official Judaism, suspicious about the authenticity of the high priest of Jerusalem. Its members withdrew from the political scene and entertained messianic/apocalyptic hopes that found expression in many of their writings.

Jewish authors of the Hellenistic age, whose works were preserved mainly by Christian writers, reflect the situation in which the rise of Christianity took place. Among them Philo (20/15 B.C.E.–50 C.E.), a leading figure of the Jewish community in Alexandria, represents the Greek Diaspora; he recast the biblical narrative in the idiom of Plato and the Stoics, making wide use of the allegorical interpretation that the Alexandrian fathers and Ambrose were to develop with such gusto. The historian Josephus (ca. 37–100 C.E.), for his part, at home in Palestine, produced writings that are crucial for the understanding of the Herodian period and of the first revolt.

The body of Jewish literature produced after the first century is no longer shared by Christians, although the latter occasionally refer to it. This is the Rabbinic literature, a huge output of Jewish sages made up of the following: the Mishnah ("instruction"), a legal collection due to the work of the Tannaim ("teachers") from 25 B.C.E. on, incorporating the core of the Oral Torah and finally compiled in 200/220 C.E. thanks mainly to the work of Rabbi Judah the Prince; the Tosephta, a supplement to and elaboration on the Mishnah by Tannaim, put together from about 400 on; the Palestinian Talmud (edited ca. 400) and the Babylonian Talmud (ca. 500), made up of the text of the Mishnah and commentaries on it (Gemara) by Amoraim ("explainers") between the third and the sixth centuries; Midrashim or interpretive rewritings of scripture by rabbis, collected mainly in the fifth century and, among other things, trying to show the unity of the dual Torah. All those collections of traditions are characterized by a vivid sense of their continuity with the early stages of Judaism while they serve as the permanent basis for Jewish life, thought, and scholarship. When they are taken as a whole, their emergence signals the transition from Torah to Talmud.

When Christianity wishes to identify the Jewish element in its own makeup, such extensive literature has to be considered along with the New Testament writings themselves and also the few allusions to Jewish affairs in Greek and Roman sources (e.g., Tacitus, Pliny, Juvenal, Polybius). The Jewish literary production provides the evidence that Judaism was following its own path, while Christianity increasingly detached itself from its original milieu. After over a century of common history, cold war, rapprochements, and open conflict, what emerged around the year 200 were the classical Judaism of the rabbis and the Christianity of the fathers.

Messianic Dreams and Apocalyptic Visions

Two movements, or two wings of the same movement, at once socioreligious and literary, mark the course of Second Temple Judaism. The first one, messianism, had its roots in ancient Judaism and the prophetic tradition; it expressed yearnings for a redeemer who would appear in the end of days to restore the monarchy, destroy the wicked, and liberate the land from foreign domination. The second trend, apocalypticism, developed toward the end of the biblical period and intensified around the turn of the era; it expected the advent of the messiah as immediate and imminent at the same time that it sketched graphic scenarios for his coming. Such scenarios included the revelation of other-worldly secrets about God, the upper world, the last days, and the bodily raising of the dead. Apocalyptic movements, then as now, were generally suspected of being subversive by assuming the termination of present-day secular rule.

The expectation of divine intervention to usher in a new age was acute in the first century C.E. It can be seen both as the by-product of a national situation exasperated by repeated frustrations, and as the expression of the vivid hopes that God would decisively steer the course of history. John the Baptist and Jesus based their preaching on those beliefs when they called people to awake to the dawning new age. The earliest Christian authors were also to appeal to those expectations, thus making apocalypticism, with its sweeping vistas of a universal history oriented toward an ultimate goal, into the mother of Christian theology.

Paul provides a lively illustration of the seminal impact of apocalypticism on theological reflection. He passed from an imminent expectation of the Parousia (the return of Christ to end history), to the assertion of a delay, and finally to a sort of accommodation with an indefinite length of worldly existence. John completes the evolution when he affirms that the Spirit, not Christ, is coming (Jn 14–16, and perhaps also 2 Cor 3:17: "Now the Lord is the Spirit").

As for the fate of those two movements within Judaism, it appears that the two Jewish revolts brought lasting discredit to messianic-political rebellions and to extreme forms of apocalypticism. After 200,

Torah in the form of the Mishnah tends to replace the remnants of messianism; the messiah will not come before Israel has attained the level of sanctification required by Torah.

Palestinian and Diaspora Judaism

In the first century Judaism existed in two geographical areas, with such distinct features as to lead some scholars to talk, with some exaggeration, of two types of religion. On the one hand, Palestinian Judaism, better called Rabbinic Judaism because both Palestine and Babylonia constituted its homeland, took over the tradition of the Pharisees after 70 when the rabbis emerged as a distinctive group. The leader of the rabbis was the patriarch, with the school and the judicial court as the major rabbinic institutions. As a group the rabbis concentrated on biblical interpretation in the form of Midrash, emphasizing first of all legal discussions *(halakhah),* secondarily ethical teachings and stories about biblical or rabbinic figures *(aggadah).* Aramaic and then Hebrew were the languages used, but some Greek influence and knowledge of the language are also discernible (e.g., the historian Josephus could write Greek). By the end of the first century, some 2 million Jews lived in Palestine itself.

On the other hand, Diaspora Judaism, found since 586 in Egypt, Asia Minor, Syria, Cyrene, and Greece, attempted an interpretation of the biblical tradition for Greek-speaking Jews. Naturally it showed a higher degree of assimilation to Greek culture and thought than did Palestinian Judaism. We know very little about the kind of communication that went on between those two Jewish groups. It appears that Second Temple Judaism saw Jews thrive in major places around the Mediterranean basin and in the Near East (there were about 4 million Jews in the empire toward the end of the first century, i.e., 7 percent of the total population; they made up one-third of the population in Alexandria), constituting an eastern and a western Diaspora. The evidence shows that Judaism was an attractive religious alternative for many and enjoyed an extraordinary success in proselytism. Repeated influx of exiles from Palestine, however, led to a gradual hebraizing of the Greek-speaking synagogue and to the spread of tannaitic Judaism in the Diaspora.

After 120 C.E., the Greek-speaking Diaspora entered a period of decline. Babylonian Jews had already turned to Aramaic; more rabbis from the land of Israel took residence in Babylonia after 135 and made Rabbinic Judaism flourish. Elsewhere Hellenistic Christianity absorbed most of the Gentiles who had been attracted to Judaism (proselytes who had converted to Judaism and God-fearers or sympathizers who had adopted some Jewish practices only), as well as a fair number of Hellenized Jews, perhaps already drawn to Greek mysteries. Hellenistic Judaism finally withered away for lack of survival power.

Features common to both Rabbinic and Diaspora Judaism must not be overlooked. For both the law of Moses with its essential demands retained undisputed primacy; both were submitted to Hellenistic influences, although they yielded to various degrees of assimilation to Greek culture.

Jewish Groups and Sects

In spite of the fragmentary character of the evidence and the disparateness of the literary sources, it can be said that the Second Commonwealth saw the multiplication of Jewish groups or tendencies mostly differentiated, on the basis of their common Judaism, by their various ways of relating Jewish religious concerns to the political situation of Greco-Roman Palestine. The phenomenon intensified and gave rise to grave tensions during the Hasmonean period, when issues debated related to the very interpretation of Torah and to the alternatives defined by assimilation/Hellenization or separatism. The ensuing malaise grew and reached a climax in 63 B.C.E. when the Romans awarded the high priesthood to their favorite, Hyrcanus II, and imprisoned the legitimate candidate, Aristobulus II.

The Pharisees, so much and so unjustly caricatured in Christian literature, developed from about 150 B.C.E. as a loose association of pietists from the middle and lower classes, holding the ancient traditions of Israel as solely authoritative but accepting a whole set of "traditions of the fathers," which were to be referred to as the "Oral Torah" by later rabbis. They distinguished themselves by their careful observance of the law as well as by their flexibility in adapting the law to new circumstances. In the process, two schools emerged among the Pharisees: the rigid school of Shammai and the more lenient school of Hillel. Their central teachings were to be incorporated in the rabbinic tradition—ideas concerning the soul's immortality and the resurrection of the dead, Providence, retribution, angels. As the Hasmonean leaders and their supporters became increasingly Hellenized, Pharisees dissociated themselves from them, thereby ceasing to be a political force and constituting themselves as a group of purely religious leaders, thus passing from politics to piety. Eventually the Pharisee merged with the rabbi, and the Tannaim inherited the Pharisaic approach to Judaism, especially the approach characteristic of the school of Hillel.

The high priestly office was under the control of the Sadducees, who claimed some continuity with the times of Solomon. They belonged to the aristocracy. Like the Samaritans, they did not appeal to the traditions of the fathers and they favored a sort of literalism in interpreting scripture. Sadducees thought that purity laws did not apply to the daily life of all people but only to the Temple and its priests. They consistently denied the central teachings espoused by the Pharisees and were more open to Hellenization. When a Hasmonean leader took over the high priesthood sometime between 152 and 140 B.C.E. many of the Sadducees, out of resentment, seem to have moved to Qumran. Thus the priestly Sadducees lost their influence in favor of the learned Pharisees, and indirectly contributed to the later shift from Temple to Torah.

Two further important groups, possibly identical, rounded off the backdrop against which Christianity arose. They developed ascetic practices and mystical ideas, and perhaps encouraged the messianic visions that led certain activists to the two revolts against the Romans. The Essenes were described by Philo, Josephus, and Pliny as a sect entered through initiation; practicing collective ownership, frugality, and asceticism; keeping its distance from the Temple but emphasizing ritual purity. Some scholars recognize in them Pythagorean features. They disappeared after 73 C.E. Philo also mentions a Jewish sect in Egypt, the Therapeutae, similar to the Essenes.

The Dead Sea Sect (Qumran) presented basically the same features as the Essenes with the addition of sharp messianic and apocalyptic overtones. They actively prepared for the coming age when a clear distinction would emerge between temporal and priestly authority. They were prone to castigate the priest officiating in the Jerusalem Temple. Their relation to the Sadducees and to the Essenes is still debated but seems to have been real in view of their common anti-Hasmonean bent.

Another group, called the Zealots by Josephus, opted for an activist, even military solution to the national predicament. Either recruiting from all the previously mentioned factions, significantly perhaps from among the Shammaite Pharisees, or made up of a mere coalition of brigand bands from the countryside pushed out of their lands by the Roman advance in the late sixties, they made the headlines for a short while. Sporadic outbursts of activity culminated in the first revolt of 70. The Zealots vanished definitively after 135, as did numerous sects, while the legacy of the Pharisees, as pointed out above, survived in Rabbinic Judaism.

It must be emphasized that all these groups, and these are only the most important ones, were sharing a common history and the common experience of election, covenant and law, Temple, and exile and return, in addition to the accumulated frustrations under foreign rule. They were parties (*haireseis,* according to Josephus) holding different views and practices within the same ethnic and religious group. It is mainly in the kind of response to common frustrations that they differed between themselves and slid into factionalism. Popular discontent and religious expectations combined to create those associations espousing various options, some encouraging activism, others withdrawal, yet others collaboration. The constellation they constituted represented the nourishing soil for both Rabbinic Judaism and early Christianity, while the various interpretations of Jesus, encountered from the start among the Christian community, doubtless reflect various tendencies within the Jewish Palestinian society itself.

Jewish-Christianity

Modern scholarship is still taking uncommon pains over determining the character and history of the early Christian grouping called Jewish-Christianity or Judaeo-Christianity. Besides the New Testament writings, the Christian reworkings of older Jewish legends (apocrypha and pseudepigrapha), and the witness of the church fathers, our sources for understanding of the group are quite limited and complex; they are based on the literature connected with the Pseudo–Clementine writings *(Homilies* and *Recognitions),* elements of Theophilus of Antioch, and, the so-called Jewish-Christian gospels known only in fragments: the gospels of the Hebrews, of the Nazoreans, of the Ebionites. The wide variety encountered at all levels of the primitive church is found here as well. Jewish-Christianity seems to have taken a plethora of forms.

It was only step by step that Christianity was identified as a distinct religion by its own members, by the Jewish community, and by the Roman rulers. The Jewish influence on Christianity was obviously seminal in a literal sense and there is a Jewish element to Christianity that is essential and permanent. If almost everything in Christianity could, in that way, be called Jewish-Christian, this communality is certainly not what is meant when reference is made to the precise phenomenon of Jewish-Christianity and to the group of early Christians wearing that name.

It goes without saying that the earliest Christians came from among ethnic and religious Jews. They were Christian Jews or Judean Christians, and here we think first of all of the Jerusalem community gathered around the twelve apostles. The name "Nazarene" or "Nazorean" encountered in Acts 24:5 and in the church fathers sometimes designates those first Jewish believers in Jesus; they somehow survived the destruction of Jerusalem (by fleeing to Pella?) and were found in Palestine and Syria until late in the fourth century according to some, although in decreasing numbers. The New Testament authors were mainly Judean Christians or Christian Jews, that is, Christians of Jewish descent.

Paul was a Christian Jew in this sense. But the first Christians, by the mere fact of their "regular going to the Temple" (Acts 2:46), were not strictly Jewish-Christians. To justify that statement, we must proceed carefully. After Gentiles, mainly thanks to the influence of Paul, were accepted into the church in increasing numbers without being asked to maintain the Mosaic prescriptions (Acts 15), the ethnic Jews who had joined the church were forced to reconsider or relax the binding character of the Jewish practices (circumcision of males, dietary laws, refusal of table-fellowship, Sabbath and festival observance), a development discernible in the Jerusalem community led by James, the brother of the Lord, called the Just,[1] and indeed in Antioch. And here we come closer to the Jewish-Christians proper.

Some Christians, Greek-speaking Gentile converts—some of whom may have been previous proselytes or God-fearers—as well as ethnic Jews, were reluctant to give up Jewish observance; critical of Paul and his letters, they assumed that it was preferable to uphold legal

---

1. HE 2.23.4–7.

observance along with the church requirements, thus in a way combining the Jewish and the Christian religions. Such is the group properly called Jewish-Christianity, still quite visible within the church around the middle of the second century, distinct from all heretical groups mentioned by Justin[2] and rather considered with tolerance by him. The name does not refer to race anymore, nor does it to thought categories and literary forms borrowed from Judaism and surviving within Christian theology, nor to patterns of worship inherited from the synagogue service. It is only in a general, even improper sense that all those factors can be called Jewish-Christian.

Thus recent research clearly tends to restrict the meaning of the term Jewish-Christianity and to apply it only to the enforced maintenance of Jewish practice among Christians everywhere in the church and not exclusively in the Jerusalem or Palestinian community (e.g., the Ps.-Clementine romance exemplifies Jewish-Christianity although it originates in Greek-speaking Syria).

Jewish-Christians were gradually forced out of the church mainstream. They first split into two branches, so to speak, and became alienated from the church in quite different circumstances. First, Christians who merely wished others to uphold the practice of Jewish law or favored a return to it could be called "Judaizers"; echoes of their activity are found in the New Testament "circumcision party" (Acts 11:2, 15:5) and in Ignatius's letters. They were censored. Second, Christians who not only wished others to keep the law but were intent on compelling all converts to continue with the practice of the law of Moses were called "Ebionites" (the "poor") by the church fathers from Irenaeus on.[3] They insisted that those who embraced Christianity also embraced Judaism as a fuller way of imitating Jesus, a Jew who had come to fulfill the Jewish law, not to abrogate it. With time, Ebionites became sectarians, seeking not only to preserve or reintroduce Jewish practice but also to add their own theological idiosyncrasies; they ended up propounding views no longer acceptable to the church, for example, that Jesus was prophet or messiah, yet not the son of God, or that he was merely "adopted" as son; they were then labeled heretics.

Still in the third and fourth centuries Judaizers are encountered in

---

2. Dial. 35, 46–48.
3. AH 1.26.

the church. They are the Christians, probably Gentiles, whom Origen, Ephrem, and John Chrysostom criticized for their continued flirting with Jewish practices; they were urged to refrain from attending the synagogue on Saturday and the church on Sunday, from sharing Passover meals with Jews and participating in the still highly attractive and popular Jewish festivals. Did they also maintain contacts with rabbis? Possibly. At any event, the church fathers enjoined them to stay away from Jewish practices; they never warned Christians, however, against using the Jewish scriptures or Jewish conceptual categories, expressions, and ideas. Those belonged forever to Christian thought and culture. Jewish-Christianity, as described, receded by the end of the second century in the West and in the fourth century in the East when it became identified as Ebionism. But Jewish practice and ritual remained for many an object of fascination.

In contrast with Jewish-Christian tendencies, a movement developed in the opposite direction in the second century. Perhaps prompted by the excesses of the Bar Kokhba revolt, it wanted a Judaism-free Christianity and reacted to what it took to be an overemphasis on the Jewish element even in the Gentile church. Besides some Gnostic teachers, its main spokesman was Marcion. He not only agreed with Justin that Gentiles had replaced Jews in the covenant with God; he wished to expunge everything Jewish from the Christian church. He rejected the entire Hebrew Bible, retained of the gospels only a mutilated Luke, and extolled the teachings of Paul critical of the law. In his unrealistic grumbling at everything Jewish, Marcion can be compared only with another extremist, Tatian, who vituperated against everything Greek.

From Coexistence to Hostility

The disappearance of Jewish-Christianity illustrates the growing deterioration of the relationships between Judaism and Christianity from the first to the second century. Prior to 70, the ex-Pharisee Paul from the Diaspora did not think he had to deny his Jewishness in order to proclaim that the law was transcended by the gospel; for him God's benevolent attitude toward Israel had turned now also to the Jesus movement. In his missionary activity Paul used the synagogue as a stepping-stone for his proclamation; in many ways the Judaism he knew helped the spread of Christianity. His disagreement with the synagogue receded behind his main interest in the Gentiles.

The Christian writings produced after 70 attest to the beginning of an escalation in negative feelings and rhetoric. The Synoptics, after affirming that the prophecies had been fulfilled in the new Israel, retrojected in their narratives a situation of steady confrontation between Jesus and the Jews. They emphasized the dissociation from nationalist groups and began to shift the blame for the interruption of Jesus' career from the Romans to the Jews. For John the rupture with the synagogue is a fact. Correspondingly, the first anti-Christian polemics among Jews are registered before the end of the first century.

The confrontation became antagonism when it was claimed that Christianity supersedes Israel, being the authentic heir to Israel's traditions (see Barnabas, Epistle to Hebrews) and fulfilling its messianic prophecy (Justin in 140/155). Clear hostility emerged in Melito of Sardis (ca. 160), who through his misreading of the gospels still more bluntly than Justin held the Jews responsible for the death of Jesus, inaugurating a fateful tradition of interpretation that was to be reinforced in the fourth century (Ephrem, John Chrysostom). Anti-Jewishness had already reached a summit with Marcion's rejection of everything Jewish in Christianity; his stance was not condoned by the church, but the anti-Jewish mood remained, ignoring Christianity's essential indebtedness to Judaism and acquiescing in the anti-Jewish legislation of the fourth and fifth centuries. Thus the stage was set for the tragic history of Jewish-Christian relations in medieval and modern times.

As a result, from the second century on, while Christian leaders like John Chrysostom did their best to contain and isolate the Jewish community, Jews themselves were inclined to see in Christianity the arch-enemy. Antipathy was mutual and "the rabbinic maledictions are perfectly balanced by the imprecations of Christian anti-Semitism."[4]

The Bible in Christianity

From the start, the Jewish scriptures in the LXX version were the Bible of the Christians: They were seen as a Christian book, pointing to the new era opened up by the activity of Jesus and his followers.

---

4. M. Simon, *Verus Israel.* New York: Oxford University Press, 1986, p. 201.

The New Testament writings teem with paraphrases and citations from Old Testament scriptures. Christians were not only to rely permanently on the canon of Jewish scriptures; they also were to learn methods of interpretation from scholars like Philo, and exegetical techniques from the traditions embodied in the Rabbinic schools. The first great Christian exegete, Origen, does not hide his borrowings, while Jerome follows Jewish predecessors in his work as translator. Both are said to have consulted learned Jewish rabbis in the course of their literary activity.

Old Testament scriptures continued to be part of Christian worship and patristic writers wrote as many commentaries on the Old Testament as they did on the distinctively Christian scripture, the New Testament.

> Christians studied the history of ancient Israel, told and retold the stories of its holy men and women, set the lives of patriarchs and prophets before the eyes of fellow Christians as models to emulate, and sought within the Jewish scriptures signs pointing to Jesus as the Christ. Christian clergy and monks learned the Psalms by heart, and in Christian worship the Psalms became the Christian prayer book par excellence. Where Christians established churches, they carried with them the books of ancient Israel.[5]

It could perhaps be argued that the two Christian schools of interpretation that were to be attached to the names of Alexandria and Antioch (see chapter 8) witness to an enduring influence of the Jewish methods of reading the Bible. Philo, living in a Gentile context, had exploited the allegorical interpretation in order to make the Jewish Bible understandable or acceptable. The Alexandrian school developed that form of exegesis along with its "high" Christology. In Palestine the sages were rather inclined to the sounding of the literal meaning; not only did Jewish-Christianity with its concern for the maintenance of the law take over that stance, it was also promulgated by the Antiochene school of interpretation with its emphasis on the literal sense, its dependence on Jewish haggadic literature, and its "low" Christology.

In any event, by adding to the Hebrew corpus the twenty-seven

---

5. R. L. Wilken, *John Chrysostom and the Jews.* Berkeley: University of California Press, 1983, p. 69.

writings of the New Testament as completing the scriptures considered inspired and authoritative, and by propounding an emphatic christological interpretation of the Old Testament, the church introduced an essential tension between the two canons that was to create both insight and resentment. Jews naturally take exception to having their scriptures (Tanakh) referred to as the "old" testament in opposition to the second part of the Christian Bible, the "new" testament. In using the name *Old Testament* then, it should be stressed that, though different in the order (and sometimes in the number) of the books, the Old Testament and the Hebrew Bible substantially overlap; but it cannot be ignored that that very overlapping is a cause of uneasiness on the Jewish side, the Christian use carrying with it the assumption of a superseding of their tradition.

READINGS

H. W. Attridge and G. Hata, eds.	*Eusebius, Judaism and Christianity.* Detroit: Wayne State University Press, 1992.
J. D. G. Dunn	*The Partings of the Ways Between Christianity and Judaism and Their Significance for the Character of Christianity.* Philadelphia: Trinity Press International, 1991.
E. Ferguson, ed.	*Early Christianity and Judaism.* New York: Garland, 1993.
D. Flusser	*Judaism and the Origins of Christianity.* Jerusalem: Magnes Press, 1988.
R. A. Horsley	*Jesus and the Spiral of Violence: Popular Jewish Resistance in Roman Palestine.* San Francisco: Harper & Row, 1987.
A. F. J. Klijn and G. J. Reinink	*Patristic Evidence for Jewish-Christian Sects.* Leiden: Brill, 1973.
R. Pritz	*Nazarene Jewish Christianity.* Leiden: Brill, 1988.
E. P. Sanders	*Judaism: Practice and Belief 63 B.C.E.–66 C.E.* London: SCM Press, 1992.
E. P. Sanders with A. L. Baumgarten and A. Mendelson, eds.	*Jewish and Christian Self-Definition*, vol. 2: *Aspects of Judaism in the Greco-Roman Period.* London: SCM Press, 1981.
J. T. Sanders	*Schismatics, Sectarians, Dissidents, Deviants: The First One Hundred Years of Jewish-Christian Relations.* London: SCM Press, 1993.
H. Shanks, ed.	*Christianity and Rabbinic Judaism: A Parallel History of Their Origins and Early Development.* Washington: Biblical Archeology Society, 1992.
M. Simon	*Verus Israel: A Study of the Relations Between Christians and Jews in the Roman Empire 135–425.* New York: Oxford University Press, 1986.

J. C. VanderKam   *The Dead Sea Scrolls Today*. Grand Rapids, Mich.: Eerdmans, 1994.

R. L. Wilken   *John Chrysostom and the Jews*. Berkeley: University of California Press, 1983.

S. G. Wilson   *Related Strangers: Jewish-Christian Relations 70–170*. Minneapolis, Minn.: Fortress Press, 1995.

3

The Greek Legacy (50–170)

To examine the Jewish and Greek factors in the rise of Christianity in two separate and successive chapters is certainly artificial, though inevitable. Much as we wish to maintain the concomitance of the impact of the two factors on the Christian movement, we are bound to advance only one step at a time. The very subject matter calls for some distinction and ordering. Judaism was the native soil of early Christianity and that is why Judaism had to be treated in the first place. But now it must be emphasized: The Judaism that concerns us here was in a state of more or less advanced Hellenization.

For over a century scholars tended to neglect the Jewish roots of Christianity and to spend most of their concerted energies tracking down non-Jewish influences on the nascent movement; Greek, Hellenistic, Syrian, Oriental, or Roman parallels were itemized and deemed sufficient to account for the birth of the movement in the context of religions other than Judaism.

That situation changed around 1950. Because our knowledge of Judaism had improved (thanks to archeology, epigraphy, and spectacular finds like Qumran, but also after the horrifying uncovering of the Holocaust) and had successfully managed to overcome the ruts of academic prejudice, it became widely recognized that Hellenistic influences on Christianity had been chiefly mediated through the variously tinted Greek-speaking Judaism thriving in the Diaspora and in Palestine itself. Even elements that until then were thought to have directly shaped Christianity (pre-Gnostic tendencies, aspects of Hellenistic mystery religions, and popular philosophy) appeared now to have largely reached the young movement via their various Jewish embodiments. A consensus developed then that Hellenistic Judaism, both in Palestine and in the Diaspora, exercised the greatest influence on the rise of the church. This must be kept in mind when dealing with the Greek legacy.

The Hellenistic Period

"Hellenism" first designates a historical period, the Hellenistic age ushered in by the Macedonian Alexander the Great (whose tutor had been Aristotle) and extending from 332 B.C.E. onward. It followed on the classical (Hellenic) age (sixth to fifth centuries) and overlapped with the most creative period of Greek cultural history, 500 to 200. Spreading from India to Spain and including Persian, Semitic, and Egyptian tracts, Alexander's empire made possible the universalization of Greek culture. On his death three dynasties divided the realm, though, and put a check on his dream of unification: The Antigonids in Macedonia were of little import; the Ptolemies (304–230) ruled from Egypt and its recent foundation, Alexandria; the Seleucids (312–295) governed Babylonia, Syria, and Palestine from their main center, Antioch. Ptolemies and Seleucids were most of the time at swords' point with each other. For over two centuries and a half, Palestine appeared as a toy in the hands of Egypt and Syria. It has been observed that at least 200 campaigns were fought in or across Palestine during that period. Rivalries between the two main dynasties spawned various alignments in the land and gave the native religious parties a distinctly political slant.

Hellenistic Culture

Above all, Hellenism refers to a specific cultural phenomenon, a world culture that permeated the western and eastern parts of the Mediterranean world; it extended well into Roman times. In fact, although the Romans were the ones who helped Greek culture to its victory, the Greeks' influence around the world was already felt prior to the Hellenistic period and the Roman takeover, and remained dominant in the East up to the fourth century C.E.

Mentioned for the first time along with "Judaism" during the Hasmonean period (2 Mc 2:21, 4:13), "Hellenism" received, from scholars in the nineteenth century, an extended meaning. It now denotes that blend of Greece and the Orient arising in the wake of Alexander's conquests and embracing all aspects of life. Beyond the command of the Greek language, it came to mean the adoption of Greek education and its ideals in matters of administration, warfare, trade, commerce, sport, rhetoric, literature, philosophy. Greek culture thus understood exercised a pervasive influence and shaped all forms of life and thought among the people who came in contact with it.

Hellenistic culture was dominated by two figures: Alexander the Great, who dreamed it, and Augustus, who Hellenized the most important regions of the realm and made Romans the patrons of Greek culture. Claiming to originate from the Aeneas of the Homeric epic, the Romans took over the political and cultural heritage of Alexander, without properly initiating a new culture; along with Latin, Greek was to be the really effective language. The prestige of Greek culture in second-century society is well illustrated by the gesture of the Roman emperor Hadrian, on his grand imperial tour in 131/132 C.E., dedicating the temple of Zeus Olympios at Athens as a symbol of the religious and cultural unity of the Greco-Roman world. The consolidation of the empire rested on his panhellenic program, buttressed by a revived emperor cult and carried out under Greek auspices.

Hellenism in Palestine

The process of Hellenization in Palestine began with Alexander's conquest in 332 and was intensified thereafter. Greek became the language of commerce, government, and literature in the cities and in the upper levels of society. Aramaic and Hebrew continued to be used in other areas of life, so that a truly bilingual (or trilingual) society emerged, especially in cities like Jerusalem. From 250 on, all Judaism, scholars tell us, must be called Hellenistic, be it the Greek-speaking communities in the West or the Aramaic/Hebrew-speaking Jews in Palestine and Babylonia. All were under the spell of the ascending culture.

Palestinian Judaism stood in a situation of uneasy tension between acceptance and rejection of the Hellenistic zeitgeist. It was clear to mobile strata of society that, were they to climb the social ladder and share in the "blessings of civilization," they had to invest in better education, that is, Greek *paideia,* and multiply contacts with the non-Jewish world. A movement appeared around 175 B.C.E., predominantly made up of well-to-do aristocrats of Jerusalem around the high priest Jason, that espoused the so-called Hellenistic reform; it was symbolized by the construction, due to the same Jason, of a gymnasium at the foot of the temple mount. Encouraged by the Seleucid ruler Antiochus IV Epiphanes, it sought to transform the largely international

Jerusalem into a Greek polis, to alter the traditional way of life, and to bring about what was perceived by some as an excessive Hellenization of the land, even as an attempt to abolish Torah.

Against the penetration of that alien spirit the Maccabees revolted (168–164) and led a movement of self-assertion to overcome cultural and religious assimilation, and to counter the policy of alienation sponsored by the Jewish reform party. In spite of the success of the nationalistic revolt, the Hasmoneans did not stop nor even really slow down the process of Hellenization in Palestine; as soon as they themselves came to power they pursued it. In fact, with the passing of time, Jewish faith felt less and less threatened by Hellenization. Greek models were imitated without inhibition; a good example can be seen in the *gerousia,* made up of principal priests, rich lay nobility, landowners, and heads of clans, from Herod's time called the Sanhedrin. It was a borrowed Greek institution. With Herod and the Herodians the process reached a new climax. Jerusalem was then a Hellenistic city through and through. In Judea in the first century C.E., and still more in Galilee, epigraphic evidence shows that a strong minority spoke Greek as the mother-tongue; most inscriptions connected with the Temple and Jewish burials in the first century are in Greek. Paul, some of Jesus' disciples, the seven "Hellenists" of Acts 6, Josephus and the house of the patriarchs, all were conversant with Greek language and culture. It is likely that Jesus himself spoke some Greek. All of them were no less "Jewish" or "native" for that fact. Thanks to Hellenism and imperial rule, the rather fluid identities blossomed and actually became crystallized.

Jewish Break with Hellenism

Owing to the failure of the Roman procurators and their administration in the 50s C.E., the radical anti-Roman forces, at one and the same time anti-Hellenist, began again to gain ground and precipitated the final catastrophe. The Jewish wars between 66 and 135 had as a sequel the destruction of a flourishing Jewish-Hellenistic culture that involved a major segment of the population. That segment, made up of various interest groups (Herodians, high-priestly families, Jews returning from the Diaspora, well-to-do proselytes, landowners, merchants, etc.), joined the moderate Pharisees of the Hillel school and the Jerusalem middle class, and stood up to the Jewish revolutionaries. To no avail. Their attempts to integrate Judea into the Roman Empire by encouraging Greek education and life-style had miscarried. The Roman repression bitterly put an end to their designs of a shared culture. Henceforth Judaism would be more concerned with its own difference; fixed on the letter of Torah, it would gradually renounce the dream of becoming a world religion.

That reaction did not prevent Talmudic and Midrashic literature from displaying a wide knowledge of Gentile language and literature, seen, for instance, in the abundance of loan words. Greek contacts could never be totally severed; the Hasmonean experience of over two centuries earlier, for all its nationalistic emphasis, remained a lasting reminder to that effect. The late Hebrew literature of the Old Testament produced during their rule had shown incontrovertible echoes of the influence of Greek enlightenment. At that time affinities with Greek views had even led some to claim that Greek philosophers of old had borrowed from Moses, a view that not few early Christian writers were to take up. In its turn, Rabbinic literature itself was not to be entirely immunized against Greek thought.

Two Opposite Reactions

It remains that the final attitude toward Hellenism espoused by Jews and by Christians came to a distinctive branching off in the second century C.E. In spite of sporadic hesitations (seen, for instance, in the writings of Irenaeus and Tertullian), Christianity was not prepared to follow Judaism in publicly breaking with Hellenism. On the contrary, it made a bid for a quasi-uninhibited use of Greek culture. It chose to put the Greek heritage to work in the task of shaping its own beliefs into a system fittingly stowed to travel on high seas.

Ultimately that evolution owed much to basic differences affecting Christianity's relationships to Judaism and to Hellenism. The relation of Christianity to Judaism had been one of dependence and, for that reason, it followed a one-way path. The rise of Christianity left Judaism quite unaffected. Not so with respect to Christianity and Hellenism. Here the relation was one of interaction by virtue of which each party appropriated elements of the other and sought mutual accommodation. For Christianity the reception of Greek culture was evidently to be fraught with historic consequences, usually beneficial, though at times uncomfortable.

The First Christians and the Gentiles

It is not only the separation of nationalism and religion, which it favored, that gave Christianity an edge over other religious movements. Indeed, Christianity was greatly aided in its beginnings and expansion by the extensive Hellenization of Judaism in the first century. The roots of "the Greek-speaking Jewish community in which the message of Jesus was formulated in Greek for the first time clearly extend back to the very earliest community in Jerusalem."[1] Even before Paul and his associates deliberately turned to the Gentiles, Jesus' message, very early rendered in Greek, had attracted not only Palestinian Jews acquainted with the imperial culture but also Diaspora Jews in Jerusalem itself along with proselytes and God-fearers of Gentile descent. For a while Christian Hellenists and Christian Jews held separate worship in their respective languages, but it is significant that the former seem to have been there from the start.

The first bearers of the Christian proclamation are said to have come from the Palestinian creative middle class open to Hellenism, although their literary and philosophical education appeared rather superficial. At any event, it was natural, in the work of gathering all nations into a "new Israel," that the apostles first turned to Hellenized Jews in Palestine and abroad, and to those Gentiles in Palestine and abroad who had been already touched by the influential Jewish communities, and that they reaped special success among those groups.

Thus the Greek language in the form of *koine* (common Greek spoken in the Hellenistic and Roman periods) was the natural vehicle for the Christian proclamation in Hellenized Palestine, in Syria, Asia Minor, the Aegean, and Rome. In the Diaspora, besides native Gentiles, missionaries encountered Jews who, as mercenaries, slaves, peasants, craftsmen, or merchants, had long been established in their new lands. Jewish names are found in Greece itself in the fourth century B.C.E. Hellenized from birth, those Jews appear to have made

---

1. M. Hengel, *The "Hellenization" of Judaea in the First Century After Christ.* Philadelphia: Fortress Press, 1989, p. 18.

common cause with Greek culture, rejecting only the surrounding polytheistic currency.

Encounter with the Real Gentiles

When confronted with more sophisticated Hellenists among Gentiles, for example, in Athens and Ephesus, the missionaries were apparently shaken and certainly made aware of the limitations of their own education. The overcoming of such limitations on the part of Christian spokesmen would be the decisive event of the second century.

In the meantime, the first confrontation with real Gentiles revealed a quality of Hellenism unfamiliar to the Palestinian apostles. Here we can look at the example of Paul, one of the better educated members of the community. His education in the Hellenized Semitic Tarsus and in Jerusalem ("at the feet of Gamaliel": Acts 22:3) had certainly included training in rhetoric and pharisaic exegesis, sprinkled with a shimmer of apocalyptic worldview. In philosophy his education seems to have been confined to its popular form. What else could be expected? After all, what gave impetus to the mission was less the level of culture of the missionaries than their vivid expectation of God's impending action.

Paul's education had ill prepared him for an encounter with the "real Gentiles," that is, those who had imbibed Greek education from birth and had noticeable knowledge of the philosophical tradition. They were the ones who posed the most disquieting challenge to the mission. To approach them and their views of the world was an invitation to an intellectual venture within the overall religious campaign.

The Challenge of Greek Thought

To turn to those Gentiles, then, was to turn to a world of thought that, to be sure, had already affected Judaism to some extent (there were Hellenized poets and philosophers of the Stoic and eclectic brand in Palestine). That world of thought, however, went beyond what the Jews had generally perceived of it; it had its own history and vitality. Christianity had now to define itself in relation to the culture that had been shaping the Mediterranean world for centuries.

In the first and second centuries the philosophical ground, difficult to reconnoiter with total clarity, was mainly occupied by the conglomerate called Middle Platonism. After the mid-third century, Neoplatonism took its place. How had it come to the philosophy of the day called Middle Platonism in the first place?

Philosophical Schools

For centuries there had been widespread talk about "schools" *(haireseis)* to designate loose associations of like-minded people espousing the way of life recommended by a particular philosopher. Judaism itself had been referred to by the Jew Aristobulus (ca. 175 B.C.E.) as "our school of philosophy."[2] From the fourth century B.C.E. what the various philosophical schools had in common was a keen interest in virtue and happiness, and a flaunted dissatisfaction with the human condition. Philosophers taught people to turn from a life of luxury, self-indulgence, and superstition to a life of discipline, freedom, and wisdom. They promised tranquillity and happiness to those who did. To those general concerns each school added its own specific ingredient and offered "differing ways of deliverance from the uninformed and mentally footloose life."[3] Teachings and life-style of the schools are particularly relevant to an understanding of early Christianity.

The Cynics, of either mild or austere allegiance, appealed to many in the Mediterranean world. They were dogged critics of those received ideas and customs that encouraged falsity in society and religion. Yet they had nothing to do with our popular label cynical, but were deeply concerned with how to live a better life. Making use of philosophical anecdotes of the kind that marks Jesus' sayings and style and the life of the first desert ascetics, Cynics insisted on a conduct based on frugality, simple demeanor, and personal decision. The notion of world-citizenship was also one of their leitmotivs. The Skeptics, for their part, shared the Cynics' attitude toward ancient dogmas. Ironically, they came to be located mainly among the traditional Platonic Academy.

---

2. See Praep. ev. 13.12.7f.

3. A. D. Nock, *Early Gentile Christianity and Its Hellenistic Background.* New York: Harper & Row, 1964, p. xv.

The Stoics had a lasting impact on Christian ethics and conceptuality. In many matters quite close to the Peripatetics, the followers of Aristotle, the Stoics recommended the virtuous life and a life according to nature, an ideal wrought by mental discipline and *apatheia* (a kind of active indifference), and they insisted that one's worth is to be judged by the canons of virtue, not by one's descent. Stoicism came close to constituting a religion. At least it represented a philosophy of life that, in addition to the attention given to one's conduct and to self-mastery, enjoins people to see the divine reality in everything and to detect a Providence at work in the world. Stoicism was to fade into the kind of Christianity represented by Clement of Alexandria or into the resurgent Platonism.

Seeking, as the Stoics also did, to liberate humans from fate and from dependence and reliance on externals, the Epicureans were well known for their unrelenting critique of religious fear. They formed highly organized communities *(collegia),* taking an oath of obedience to their founder and teachers. Their ideal in ethics was summarized in *ataraxia* (tranquillity) and expressed itself in the concern to free oneself from illusory anxieties and false needs. With the Christians they were to share the same suspicions of presumed atheism, misanthropy, social irresponsibility, and sexual immorality.

Nothing prevented one from picking left and right bits of philosophical wisdom for the conduct of one's life. Around the turn of the era all thinkers had a good dose of eclecticism, well illustrated by Cicero, who was hard pressed to decide between Plato and the Stoic Cleanthes; he personally came up with an unbinding blend of disparate wisdom and, as a true Roman, finally reverted to the traditional religion of the ancient gods. Eclecticism certainly satisfied his intellectual curiosity although it seems to have been of little use in his personal life. Others were able to make a better use of the "philosophical supermarket."

The major trends of centuries of philosophical debate and search came together in Middle Platonism, seasoned by a contemporary revival of Pythagorean lore. Here we find Plato and Aristotle to a large extent reconciled, and allied to Stoic ethics and Neopythagorean metaphysics. Such amalgamation was intended to express better what Plato was assumed to have really meant. Reflections on God's transcendence and immateriality moved to the center of the philosophical quest; as normative life, "likeness to God" replaced the traditional "conformity with nature."

Philosophical conflicts in the second century led to the triumph of mysticism and prepared the way for Neoplatonism, which was to evolve in the direction of a religious philosophy and thereby itself become a serious rival of Christianity. When church fathers refer to the "Platonists" they usually mean the "modernized" Platonic tradition as it appeared from the second century, eclectically enriched, among the Middle Platonists, before it became embodied mainly in the Neoplatonism of Plotinus and Porphyry.

Philosophy, a Competitor

These are some of the formidable constructions the still tiny community of second-century Christianity hit on; it was tempting for a group described by the critic Celsus as an ill-educated plebeian rabble to develop an inferiority complex that would express itself in an aggressive denigration of philosophy. Denunciation of Greco-Roman culture and its arrogance occurred occasionally among the church fathers, for instance in the Syrian Tatian. On the whole, however, admiration prevailed, then emulation. The initially ambivalent attitude toward philosophy might be attributed to the perception that Hellenistic philosophy, much as it criticized traditional religions, constituted a rival religion of sorts. As encountered in the various schools, it had all the appearances of a religion, proposing a way of life based on specific beliefs and practices, offering a coherent worldview along with practical guidance. Schools were like sects (*hairesis* means school and sect) with their gurus, holy men, rivalries, conversion stories, promises of rewards such as tranquillity of mind and happiness. Philosophers "preached" by word and example, their exterior trappings (life-style, coarse cloak, long and ill-kempt beard) reinforcing their message. It is significant that concepts such as "conversion," "virtue," "dogma," and "heresy," which became central to Western religion, were first coined by philosophical sects and it is as a nag to them that Clement of Alexandria proclaimed Christianity to be the best *hairesis*.[4]

Very little of the philosophical tradition is reflected in the New Testament writings and in the apostolic fathers. Besides references to popular philosophy (Acts 17) and attacks on pagan learning, little attention was paid to philosophy per se. Because philosophers were predominantly addressing an elite, their doctrines did not seem, at first,

---

4. Str. 7.15.

to be of concern to the first missionaries, but this is precisely the situation that Christianity was going to alter. Moral exhortation, the core of philosophical culture, was appropriated by the Christian fathers of the second century and firmly rerouted to address all classes. Through that redirection the philosophers' upper-class culture became democratized, and a truly universalist morality, based on the equality of all before God's law, was now proposed to all. Writing on private life in Late Antiquity, P. Brown asserts:

> Anyone who reads Christian writings or studies Christian papyri...must realize that the works of the philosophers...had drifted down, through Christian preaching and Christian speculation, to form a deep sediment of moral notions current among the lower classes in those regions: Greek, Coptic, Syriac and Latin.[5]

Alliance with Greek Thought

It therefore became natural for Christian writers to show interest in the moral teaching of the philosophers and to associate themselves with them—in fact Christianity made few innovations in morality—in order to involve the masses and thereby try to alter the moral texture of the Roman world. Current religions (see chapter 4) did not offer to Christianity that kind of promise. Morality was quite without interest to Greco-Roman cults, not known for proposing codes of ethics. This, admittedly, was the reason why "pagan philosophy had often been very cool towards popular religion."[6] Seemingly aware of the double meaning of "Hellenism" (paganism, Greek culture), the church fathers made a clear distinction between pagan religion and Greek philosophy. They generally chose to make common cause with philosophy and to oppose pagan cults with the same energy they displayed from the second century in their opposition to "heresies" (now understood as doctrines at variance with prevailing "orthodox" beliefs). Both cults and heresies, in the end, will be traced back to demonic origins.

The option in favor of philosophy, its ethical seriousness and its

---

5. P. Brown in P. Veyne, ed., *A History of Private Life,* vol. 1. Cambridge, Mass.: Harvard University Press, 1987, p. 251.

6. R. A. Markus, *Christianity in the Roman World.* London: Thames & Hudson, 1975, p. 41.

intellectual resources, is best illustrated by the work of second-century Apologists in their efforts to defend, prove, and recommend Christianity. Justin Martyr was eminent among them and shows eloquently the kind of problems the Apologists had to wrestle with. Apologists often described Christianity as a philosophy and were in general inclined to see a convergence between the Bible and Greek philosophy, provided the Bible was interpreted correctly (allegorically, according to the Alexandrians, but typologically, according to Justin).

Justin Martyr (100–165) and Greek Philosophy

Born in Palestine, a descendant of Greek or Roman colonists settled in Samaria since 72 C.E., Justin, he tells us in a stylized account, embarked on a spiritual pilgrimage in search of "the knowledge of reality and a clear understanding of truth."[7] That quest for the sources of religious and moral knowledge took him through the main philosophical schools of the time: Stoic, Peripatetic, Pythagorean, Platonist. Having exhausted what philosophy could offer him and still unsatisfied, he came into contact with the writings of the Jewish prophets and finally those of the Christian church. There he found the end of his philosophical pursuit, convinced that Christianity was the true philosophy. He converted (probably in Ephesus) and then became a philosophy teacher in Rome—wearing the philosopher's cloak and looking much like a Cynic philosopher—where he was martyred for his faith around 165, after having repeatedly confessed that as a Christian he was atheist "so far as gods of this sort (i.e., pagan gods) are concerned, but not with respect to the most true God."[8]

In his extant writings, the largest set of writings from one single Christian author until the middle of the second century, Justin addresses a double audience. (A lost writing, the *Syntagma,* dealt with heresies and had a Christian audience.) First in his *Dialogue with the Jew Tripho* (a Hellenized Jew!), Justin musters all the resources of typological exegesis to convince the Jews that their scripture, the Old Testament, is superseded, that Judaism has been replaced or crowned by Christianity, that the Old Testament promises have been fulfilled in the career of Jesus

7. Dial. 3.4.
8. Apol. 1.6.

and the life of the church. (Note that Justin is not able to call on a book called the New Testament, which does not yet exist; he can appeal only to the "memoirs" of the apostles.) Christians constitute a "third race" between or beyond Greeks and barbarians (Jews). They have begun to gather all people into the new and true Israel and they invite the Jews to recognize the signs of the times. Justin hoped to win over more cultured Jews, encouraged by the fact that around 155 there were still a good number of Jews in the Christian ranks.

It is in his *Apology,* a petition addressed to the emperor Antoninus Pius, the Roman senate, and the Roman people on behalf of the maligned Christians whose civic loyalty and reliability he wishes to vouch for, that Justin conducts the most searching interpretation of Greek philosophy from a Christian perspective so far, and thereby offers what might be the first instance of a real encounter with pagan culture. Perhaps prompted by Polycarp's death at the stake in 156, Justin is eager to respond to current prejudices and slanders affecting the Christians. In doing so, he is led to make quite daring claims for Christianity; the critic Celsus seems to have taken Justin's arguments seriously enough to try in his turn to discredit them in his work, the *True Logos.*

Justin's main argument is this: Among Christians is found Christ the universal Logos, who is divine Reason and embodies the whole truth; but teachings similar to Christian teachings are also found, right or distorted, in various forms of pagan thought. To account for this state of affairs Justin offers three theories that were to keep recurring in the history of Christian thought.

1. The agreements with Greek philosophical tenets are due to the fact that philosophers read or "borrowed from the prophet Moses"[9] and the Old Testament, a bizarre argument already put forward by Aristobulus in 175 B.C.E. and taken over by Philo. (It is interesting to note that Celsus thought the opposite—that the prophets had stolen from the Greeks!) This is the "loan theory"; its purpose was to vindicate the antiquity of Christianity. It was to become, in the hands of Justin's disciple Tatian, the "theft theory"; without too much regard for ethical niceties, Clement of Alexandria was to add that the thief genuinely possesses what he steals.[10]

---

9. Apol. 1.44.4.
10. Str. 1.20.100.5.

Perhaps surprisingly to us, a contemporary of Justin, the philosopher Numenius of Apamea, agreed with Justin on that score and used to ask: "What else is Plato but Moses in Attic Greek."[11]

2. Distortions of the truth encountered, for instance, in Greek mythology with its immoral stories, but also in philosophical aberrations, are the works of the demons' "wicked disguise."[12] This is the "demons theory"; it explains both the disagreements with Christian views and those among philosophical schools.

3. More valuable is the *logos* or "*logos spermatikos* theory," in which *logos* refers both to Christ the Word and to human reason, and which says: The whole of *logos* is in Jesus Christ, the sowing *Logos,* but portions of it are also found among Jews and Greeks, in the words of prophets and philosophers. These are seeds of truth implanted in human hearts, being the formative principle of right knowledge and right living. Thus Christ was "known by Socrates, for He was and is the *Logos,* who is in every man."[13]

Being the first substantial attempt at articulating the problem of the relationship of revelation to reason, of Bible to Middle Platonism, the *logos* theory was to have a long and distinguished career. It is to Justin's credit, drawing on Philo, the Bible, and Stoicism, to have been able to see not only that Christianity adds something crucial to philosophy but also that philosophy had a contribution to make to Christian thought. His positive reception of elements of philosophical systems— for his theory does not grant a character of revelation to philosophical systems in their entirety but only to some elements such as selected ideas of God, the critique of idolatry, and basic moral notions—led to the optimistic view that the God of the Old Testament and the God of the New Testament are identical. Still more, and this shows Justin's courage and open-mindedness, it holds that the God of the Bible and the God of the philosophers are one and the same God.[14]

A searching exploration, his position has been variously assessed by theologians—applauded by most, seen by some as a case of naive harmonization and by others as a melding of Christianity into Platonism (i.e., Middle Platonism), by still others as a dangerous contamination of

11. Ibid., 1.21.150.3.
12. Apol. 2.13.1.
13. Ibid., 2.10.8.
14. Ibid., 1.46.3.

Christianity by philosophy, which, under the cover of a clumsy camouflage, was able to make inroads into Christianity and ended up rendering a fatal disservice to Christian thought.

However Justin's contribution is judged, it ought to be maintained that thanks to the work of second-century Apologists Christianity raised itself to the level of respectability that was up to then the exclusive preserve of philosophy. Pagans soon began to acknowledge that promotion. For instance, it has been noted that Galen (131–201) is "the first pagan author who implicitly places Greek philosophy and the Christian religion on the same footing."[15] The way was thus prepared for philosophical theology and, we might say, for theology altogether.

The Threat of All-Out Hellenization

Over the centuries it has been a recurrent criticism of Paul, mainly in Jewish circles, that as he turned to the Gentiles he succumbed to Hellenism and that he was rightly censored for his presumed apostasy to Hellenistic syncretism. Paul is sometimes blamed for having begun a process that would result in people's thinking they converted to a religious faith when in fact they were merely embracing a new philosophical position. Some scholars see a similar ambiguity even in Augustine's conversion. Affirmations of that kind, however, tend to short-circuit a complex process that still is in need of greater exploration and remains an object of research. As for Justin and the Apologists, in their impassioned effort to make Christianity understandable and acceptable to well-educated people in particular, one would be hard pressed to demonstrate how they have unduly watered down the religious element. They were rather involved in a novel contest and fought expressly for the cause of Christ; the sincerity of their commitment was paid for by many with their lives.

But the danger of excessive Hellenization was there and it is a sign of its potential noxiousness that, when it was not resisted, it led to marginality in relation to the mainstream church, as will appear below. In principle Christianity intended to interact with Hellenism, not to be subordinated to it. But the debate continues and it remains a valid and

15. R. Walzer quoted by R. M. Grant, *Greek Apologists of the Second Century*. Philadelphia: Westminster Press, 1988, p. 110.

creative query to investigate the extent to which Christianity was Hellenized as well as the extent to which Hellenism was Christianized.

The Burden of Greek Categories

The move to an alliance of Christianity with Greek *paideia* was an imperative one, if Christianity wanted to gather all the nations into a single community. Greek culture in the early centuries C.E. helped Christianity become a universal movement. The rapid expansion of Christianity after the second century showed the validity of the option for the Greek medium. Nevertheless it is one of those ironies of history that, in the long run, the imprint of Greek thought has ended up making Christianity seem a parochial movement when native traditions in the West and non-Western traditions abroad are taken into account. What had been an instrument of cosmopolitan reception could possibly become later an obstacle to a wider acceptance. Christianity transcended its condition of being a mere Jewish sect and became a world religion thanks to the creative use it made of Greek thought. But after that initial adaptation to the Mediterranean world, Christianity had to be on its guard against refusing further inculturation; it had to resist privileging Greek culture one-sidedly to the detriment of other cultures and at the risk of its own downfall into provincialism.

READINGS

H. Chadwick	*Early Christian Thought and the Classical Tradition.* Oxford: Oxford University Press, 1966.
J. Dillon	*The Middle Platonists: Study of Platonism 80 BC to AD 220.* London: Duckworth, 1977.
F. G. Downing	*Cynics and Christian Origins.* Edinburgh: T. & T. Clark, 1992.
E. Ferguson, ed.	*The Early Church and Greco-Roman Thought.* New York: Garland, 1993.
R. M. Grant	*Greek Apologists of the Second Century.* Philadelphia: Westminster Press, 1988
J. Gregory	*The Neoplatonists.* London: Kyle Cathie, 1991.
W. Haase, ed.	*"Philosophy, Science, Technology."* ANRW II.36.1–7 (1987–1994).
W. Haase, ed.	*"Pre-Constantinian Christianity: The Apologists."* ANRW II.27.2 (in prep.)
M. Hengel	*The "Hellenization" of Judaea in the First Century After Christ.* Philadelphia: Fortress Press, 1989.
M. Hengel	*Jews, Greeks and Barbarians.* Philadelphia: Fortress Press, 1980.
R. Holte	"Logos spermatikos: Christianity and Ancient Philosophy According to St. Justin's Apologies." *Studia theologica* 12 (1958): 109–168.
H. Jones	*The Epicurean Tradition.* New York: Routledge, 1989.
A. A. Long and D. N Sedley, eds.	*The Hellenistic Philosophers*, 2 vols. Cambridge: Cambridge University Press, 1987.
A. J. Malherbe	*Paul and Popular Philosophers.* Minneapolis, Minn.: Fortress Press, 1989.

B. F. Meyer and E. P. Sanders, eds.	*Jewish and Christian Self-Definition*, vol. 3: *Self-Definition in the Greco-Roman World*. London: SCM Press, 1982.
M. C. Nussbaum	*The Therapy of Desire: Theory and Practice in Hellenistic Ethics*. Princeton: Princeton University Press, 1994.
J. M. Rist	*Stoic Philosophy*. London: Cambridge University Press, 1969.
W. Schoedel and R. L. Wilken, eds.	*Early Christian Literature and the Classical Intellectual Tradition*. Paris: Beauchesne, 1979.

4

Varieties of Syncretism (120–220)

It has become received wisdom among historians of Christianity to hold that, from the start, many distinct internal alternatives competed in the shaping of the Christian movement. Variety and even division are exemplified, for instance, by diverging tendencies allied with the three names Peter, Paul, and James, or by the views respectively expressed by the Synoptics and John. From the mid-first century the small Christian communities were involved in a struggle to determine the real meaning of Jesus' career and gospel; questions relating to the nature of salvation and community, to the conduct of life and jurisdiction, to eschatology, all found particular answers depending on persons and places. It was not easy to interpret the sense the movement was to take and to discern where "periphery" and "center" were to be found. In the process, some early options were bound to lose out. No doubt, tensions most religiously relevant (e.g., the place of Torah and the debate reflected in Gal 1–2) generally found a resolution intended to be peaceful and to harmonize differences (Acts 15). But otherwise fluidity prevailed and some pluralism in doctrine and practice was admitted as inescapable, even legitimate.

Syncretism

Pluralism of that sort, however, does not qualify as syncretism. The latter no longer has to do with internal options; it results from a movement's relationship to religious factors deemed external to the original vision and tradition. Now from the point of view of its prehistory Christianity, like all religions for that matter, was syncretistic; it could not begin and grow without incorporating elements coming from the "outside," especially from the not particularly monolithic Judaism and from Hellenism. From its inception, Christianity was never a pure and pristine entity totally alien to its surroundings. The syncretist content appears doubly compounded when it is recalled that Hellenistic and Roman times are themselves labeled by historians "the age of syncretism." It is no surprise that the debate became incontrovertible in the second century as to the limits of the admissibility of syncretism.

The term *syncretism* is derived from a metaphor relating to chemical processes (such as mix, alloy, compound, amalgam) but its meaning remains fluid. For some it connotes decline and fall in regard to presumed pure beginnings; then it designates an artificial mix of sundry and incompatible things, and implies an illicit contamination or compromise. In that sense it easily becomes a term of abuse. For others (and it is the way the term is used here) it does not carry a value judgment; it simply refers to a universal cultural phenomenon, common to the formation of all religions in their very first stages and resulting naturally from sociohistorical placing, population movements, and/or explicit religious propaganda. Religious forms are taken over but placed in a new whole that lends them a new signification. Widespread in the Hellenistic age, syncretism was particularly to affect second-century Christianity.

Hellenistic syncretism was based on the belief that gods are known among different peoples by different names; consequently deities can be fused, and religious attributes and tenets merged. In the formative period of Christianity, three great religious constellations fully deserve the strict epithet *syncretist:* mystery religions, Gnosticism, and Manichaeism. Thanks to the abundance of recent finds, the three can no longer be relegated to "the lost outermost bounds" (Renan's "confins perdus") of Hellenism and Christianity, or of our knowledge of them. Rather they appear to us today as being close to the center of ancient religious life; hence they have moved to the center of present-day research, along with their multiform accompaniments catering to psychological-religious needs: explorations in magic, revelation literature, cult associations, oracles, divination, astrology, healing clubs, and other paraphernalia of religion.

Oriental Cults and Mysteries

Most Greek cults and mystery religions were based on the agrarian cycle. Great gods and nature spirits were celebrated at festivals related to agriculture and fertility. This became true also of the Roman religion from the third century B.C.E. when its deities were identified with Greek deities (the famous *interpretatio romana*) or new cults were introduced to satisfy the religious needs of the individual. Gradually some ancient deities received a universal role: Apollo, Demeter, and their like assumed an eminent place in the maintenance of the order of things, marginalizing Zeus, Poseidon, Hades. That order of things, which tradition had made readily accessible to the masses through the scrupulous observance of rituals and respect of ancestral customs, and to the learneds through philosophy, in the course of time began to be made accessible only by initiation, as in the case of mysteries, or through revealed knowledge, as in the case of Gnostic schools.

Variety of Mysteries

"Mystery" refers to a secret rite performed in a ceremony of initiation that allowed certain individuals to enter into a privileged relation with a god/goddess and receive certain benefits therefrom. Along with the Syrian sophist Pausanias, Apuleius's *Metamorphoses* (or *Golden Ass*) written around 150 C.E. is our principal source of information here, summing up the epoch with its multiple alternatives in thought and religion.

The main mysteries of Hellenistic and Roman times included the Greek mysteries of the grain-goddess Demeter at Eleusis, appealing mostly to rural populations; the originally Egyptian, then Hellenized mysteries of Isis and Osiris/Sarapis, more urban in character; those of the Syrian goddess Atargatis, of the Phrygian Cybele (the "Great Mother" of the gods) and Attis, of the Phoenician Astarte and Adonis. Those cults moved around the Mediterranean and, through transfer of personality traits, identifications (e.g., Astarte was successively identified with Atargatis, then with Cybele, finally with Aphrodite and Demeter), and combinations, received an international stamp. This evolution applies also to the religious transformations of the cult of Dionysus (the Roman Bacchus); to Orphism, often allied with Pythagorean ideas; even to Judaism in its Hellenistic form with the new role accorded to Wisdom, almost seen as a consort of Yahweh. The mysteries had in common that, not heavily syncretist at first, they became so once transplanted into a new social context and welcoming novel additions. Through assimilation and mingling, imported gods went indigenous. They all promised a happy afterlife or at least a transformed life in the company of the gods, whose friendship made an arbitrary fate appear as divine Providence or "good fortune."

Innovations

At the turn of the era, the cult of Asclepius the Healer went through a revival, ascending to new heights of popularity. But this was not really a new cult. At that time two religious movements appeared that were real innovations. The first one was indeed very much like the cult of Asclepius, related to the search for personal salvation and healing: Mithraism. It is generally argued that, originating in Persia centuries earlier and centered on the Persian Sun-god Mithras, the cult was especially strong among soldiers of the frontier garrisons, among Roman sea-merchants and city dwellers. Reserved to males, it displayed a certain anti-Greek bent, accounting for its being virtually absent from Greece, Asia Minor, and Palestine. Its profound solar symbolism made it a more or less formidable competitor of Christianity as well as a close kin of its infancy: Mithras's birth was celebrated on December 25; a sacred meal with bread and drink commemorated a pact with Sol/Sun; Mithras was believed to have ascended to heaven in a chariot; the seven grades of initiation symbolized the passing through the seven life conditions or the seven planetary spheres to paradise. Mithraism finally was the only cult clearly to offer a supernaturally sanctioned ethic, basically Stoic, comparable to Judaism and Christianity—usually moral conversion was the domain of philosophy, as mentioned earlier.

The second innovation was Christianity itself. And here the question arises: Did "this ordered multitude of mysteries"[1] help or hinder the progress of Christianity? It is certain that they constituted "one of the most tenacious foci of resistance to Christianity."[2] But in turn Christianity "succeeded in depriving the old religion of its power,"[3] if not of its attraction, by absorbing and, more or less consciously, adopting pagan symbols and customs. Yet we must keep in mind that, while the ancient culture continued to live in a new guise,

1. J. Geffcken, *The Last Days of Greco-Roman Paganism*. New York: North Holland, 1978, p. 13.

2. Ibid.

3. Ibid.

what it really had to say had already been said when Christianity gained the dominant position.

Similarities between mysteries and Christianity are undeniable. Yet they should not blind us to the point of reading Christian elements back into mysteries only then to see mysteries as the source of Christianity. Once parallels have been identified (need of healing, quest for blessedness beyond the grave, dying and rising of a savior, a ruler of the dead, salvific meaning of initiation, solar and light imagery, in some cases moral earnestness and, generally, religious symbols such as vine, fish, lamb, anchor, dove, palm, bread, good shepherd), we must immediately stress that meanings change when their traditional support is changed and they are grafted onto new wood. Thus serious differences appear. Even at the purely sociological level differences loom large: Christianity was for everyone, distinct in that from the mysteries and truly international; its "mystery" was an open secret, having been "revealed" to all; and Christian initiation was not susceptible to being repeated as was the case with most mysteries. Mysteries might have helped the expansion of Christianity, but they did not cause it. A profound rerouting took place when heroes and spirits of old were interpreted as saints and the lesser gods as angels or demons, and myths began to lose their luster to historical events. In a real sense religion had passed under new management.

Gnosis and Gnosticism

Mystery religions were going their quiet and confident way when the most formidable threat to Christianity rose in the mid-second century in the form of the Gnostic movement, perceived by some as the Gnostic landslide. With roots in previous traditions, the movement underwent a pre-Christian phase and continued to enjoy a non-Christian career. As a fully constituted system of life and thought, it belongs mainly to the second century and in its Christian form is of special interest to us.

In the Gnostic lore, syncretism came to a new blossoming and brought the previous syncretist elements it incorporated to a new pitch. Such all-out syncretism was judged to be excessive by the emerging mainstream church, bent to tolerate but a limited amount of syncretist features. It was felt to be execrable to Marcion, for whom any form of syncretism had to be radically excised, even the syncretism that aligned the Christian message with the Hebrew Bible. Christian Gnostics for their part did not reject the Old Testament out of hand; they subverted it.

Gnostic Sources

Until recently, the "Gnostic religion" was chiefly known through the usually hostile reports of the church fathers who fought them, the so-called *heresiologists.* In the eighteenth century Egypt yielded some Gnostic writings from the third century written in Coptic (Codex Askewianus, Codex Brucianus) and a few more texts (including the Berlin Papyrus 8502) were brought to light in the nineteenth century. Altogether this amounted to a rather modest collection of authentic writings compared with the "library" uncovered by the momentous event of December 1945: Thirteen codices or books (not scrolls) were discovered at Nag Hammadi (Upper Egypt), hidden in a jar, close to ancient monastic settlements; they contained fifty-two tractates, of which forty were previously unknown, most of them bearing the Gnostic stamp. They appear with more or less fantastic titles such as *The Gospel of Truth, The Apocryphon of John, The Hypostasis of the Archons, The Thunder Perfect Mind,* and *Trimorphic Protennoia.* The so-called Coptic Gnostic Library, better called the Nag Hammadi Library (or Nag Hammadi Codices), buried around the turn of the fourth century, is made up of texts translated mainly from Greek originals produced in the second and third centuries. This sensational find ranks, next to the discovery of the Dead Sea Scrolls, among the most extensive manuscript finds of our times. It has altered the state of research on the second and third centuries and prompted a reconsideration of the nature of the Gnostic phenomenon.

Origins of Gnosticism

The origins of the Christian Gnostic movement still constitute the object of a lively debate among scholars. In addition to the view that Gnosticism was simply a Christian heresy, and the theories of an Iranian or purely Greek origin, some favor is now accorded to theories claiming a prevailingly Jewish origin. Thus it is asserted that in the late first and early second centuries Jewish fringe groups in Egypt or in Syria-Palestine or in Samaria, with qualified apocalyptic tendencies, began to claim a superior form of "knowledge" *(gnosis)* able to explain the miserable state of the world and to correct the unacceptable shortcomings of the biblical writings as to the nature of God and the human self.

Besides the many literary difficulties and doctrinal misconceptions found in Genesis, grave stumbling blocks were encountered in the Bible: How could an all-powerful God produce a deficient cosmos and such a failed creature as the human body, plagued by illness, suffering, and death? How can one speak of a God leaving his dwelling on high to become an artisan, plant a garden, walk around it, make a man and a woman? How can one speak of that maker/creator as a god of wrath and vengeance, jealous, exclusive, and caring only for his own people? That god could not be the true God but only a caricature. The Bible had to be corrected and completed; borrowings from Greece, Egypt, Chaldea, and Iran might help construct a more adequate view of reality. At least the creator/demiurge of the Bible and of Plato had to be demoted and a disjunction introduced between him and the true, unknown God.

Main Gnostic Tenets

At the risk of oversimplifying and flattening a highly variegated subculture with many disparate groups and very different views, we can describe the basic outlook of influential (mainly Valentinian) Gnostics in the following manner.

The superior knowledge postulated by the Gnostics and mediated to them through messengers (Jesus and his secret teaching, apostles, etc.) found expression in diverse versions of a myth depicting the phases of a theogony and cosmogony focusing on the true genesis of the human Self and on a powerful explanation of the origin of Evil. It posits a primordial deity, the Father, transcendent, unknowable directly, and "unknown," from whom a number of emanations (aeons) proceeded, the last of which is usually called Sophia/Wisdom. For her disorderly passion to know the Father directly, without intermediary, she became guilty and sinned; her passions had to be expelled from the divine world (Pleroma or Kingdom of Light), condemned to wander below the Pleroma and thus, so to speak, to inhabit two worlds. Out of her abortive passions the creator-God (demiurge) was made, the Old Testament God who formed bodies and souls, unaware that he was thereby hijacking the world and holding captive (in some or in all creatures) fragments of the divine or sparks of the spirit surreptitiously inoculated in them by the Unknown God or by Sophia, that is, holding captive their selves like gold in the mud.

Gnostics who, thanks to a revealer, are "in the know" as to the origin of their true Self yearn to break out of the fetters of matter and the rule of the demiurge. But this is readily achieved: by knowing their origin they already know that they are released from their cosmic prison and assured of their final return home away from the despicable created order. Rites, faith, observance of the law, all are left behind because they only add to the intolerable alienation that is the lot of humans; asceticism (world renunciation), though, is a fitting rebuttal of the claims of the created world.

Echoes of the Jewish scriptures, candidly or maliciously distorted, are unmistakable here. The Jewish God is firmly rejected and found lacking for his blindness and meanness. Only here and there in the Old Testament is the voice of the superior Unknown God perceptible under ciphers that the "knowers" alone can interpret. So Gnosticism has all the marks of a rebellion against the Jewish God, who is now superseded by the true God. Indebted to the Bible, Gnosticism otherwise grew as a "parasitical" phenomenon. It amalgamates around a biblical core most religious ingredients of the epoch: astrology, magic, Oriental mysticism, bits of Greek philosophy, but above all Jewish fringe elements, the whole proclaiming a split (dualism) between God and the creator, spirit and matter, mind and body. The latter part of the dichotomies ought ever to be denigrated by those who know that they are destined to higher ends than the ends proposed by the ruler of this world, the creator-God.

Gnostic "Schools"

For people unreconciled with the rule of this world and inclined to "curse the creator," the lure of Gnosticism was (and remains) enticing. From around the mid-second century, prestigious teachers knew how to channel the religious protest, augment it, and anchor it in a graphic world view. They were active mostly in Alexandria, Rome, and Antioch, and headed creative and colorful groupings. Among them Valentinus was perhaps the most influential, and his impact was still felt in the eighth century; but Basilides, Heracleon, Theodotos, and their like exerted significant influence as well and kept manufacturing systems. Their power of invention was boundless, if we give credence to the heresiologists. In the ancient sense they constituted "schools" *(haireseis)* or alternative groupings, soon to be labeled sectarian or heretical by their church opponents. In fact, various groups of Gnostics were given various names by heresiologists eager to exclude them and to deny them the name of Christians.

Gnostics were skilled in biblical criticism and had a passion for speculation, philosophical and mystical. They are said to have been the first speculative theologians of the Christian tradition. Their speculative ability received free rein in the interpretation of scripture. Scriptural passages were read through the eyes of a "secret revelation" and secret tradition of the kind "These are the secret sayings which the living Jesus spoke and which Didymus Judas Thomas wrote down" *(Gospel of Thomas)* or "You asked that I send you a secret book which was revealed to me and Peter by the Lord" *(Apocryphon of James).* With the help of an elaborate allegorical method of interpretation, developed by Hellenistic authors interpreting the myths of the gods and by Jewish predecessors, and by means of a precabalistic decoding of names and numbers, Gnostics were able to tease out of the text meanings consonant with their views. For that reason unsympathetic critics were prone to describe their procedure as allegory run amok.

Manichaeism

The third century gave birth to the consummate form of Gnostic syncretism: the religion of Mani (216–277), emerging from Persia-controlled Mesopotamia to become a truly world religion, in fact "the only premeditated universal religion in the history of thought."[4] After spending his early life among the Jewish-Christian Elkesaites (a fact now better established thanks to recent finds), Mani received a revelation that made him into the prophet summarizing all previous prophets, especially Zoroaster, Buddha, and Jesus. His mission took him to India and the Near East; his religion spread all over the inhabited world, becoming state religion in Central Asia in the ninth century and surviving in China until the seventeenth century. Manichaeism

---

4. P. Brown, *Religion and Society in the Age of Augustine*. London: Faber & Faber, 1972, p. 188.

became a serious competitor of Christianity in the fourth century, claiming to be superior to Christianity or a superior form of Christianity. The core of its system is a dualist *gnosis* affirming the all-determining influence of two co-eternal principles, Good (Light) and Evil (Darkness) over a space of "three times" (times of separation of the two principles, of their mixing in combat, and of their final separation), engaged in a cosmic war that echoed in human history in that particles of light turned out to be imprisoned in bodies, the whole resulting in a total condemnation of the material world and the promotion of moral encratism (extreme asceticism) among the perfect (or true members, elect) of the community. Augustine spent close to ten years in the sect and we shall see later (chapter 5) how he wrested himself from it.

Christian Search for Identity and Difference

The second-century dealings with the "knowledge falsely so-called"[5] propelled to the front stage Christian writers called today "heresiologists." They were writers perceptive enough to discern what was at stake in the clash with the Gnostics and determined to take up the fight. Those grave Christian writers found quite unpalatable the mixture of Gnostic syncretism and early Christian ideas encountered in Christian Gnostic teachers. They saw there the intrusion into the Christian world of alien ways of thinking, "fabricating monstrous myths"[6] and covering them with a varnish of respectability. Had the Gnostics professed their speculations in the quiet of study rooms, they could have been ignored, but by their public display "they brought dishonor on the church,"[7] hurled calumnies on it, and had to be denounced. For reasons analogous to those put forward by heresiologists, even philosophers such as Plotinus thought they had to speak out against Gnosticism and its denigration of the visible world.

In addition, because Gnostics brought up, for the first time in the Christian tradition, speculative questions of cosmology, anthropology,

---

5. The original title of Irenaeus's *Against Heresies* is *Exposé and Overthrow of What Is Falsely Called Knowledge.* See also ACW, vol. 55. Trans. D. J. Unger. New York: Paulist Press, 1992, pp. 1–3.

6. HE 4.7.4.

7. AH 1.25.3.

Christology, and trinitarian doctrine, leading members of the church feared a theoretical free-for-all and felt forced to take a stand and articulate the position of the "great church." The church could not afford being dissolved into the surrounding melting-pot and, it was thought, run the risk of being identified with self-proclaimed prophets whose conduct was not always commendable. The task was one of authentication of true prophets and carriers of revelation and of elaboration of a normative self-definition of the Christian movement.

Pistis or Gnosis?

To the manifold Gnostic challenge a no less manifold response was offered by church writers who considered themselves in touch with the public tradition of the apostles. They decided to save the tradition that, in the hands of Gnostics, threatened to fall into arbitrariness, esotericism, and elitism. In order to do that, they had to clarify the question of the relationship of faith *(pistis)* to knowledge *(gnosis)*.

Among the Greek Apologists it is Justin who may have offered the first elaborate refutation of Gnosticism in his lost work, *Syntagma*. It may be possible to reconstruct, on the basis of Irenaeus's report and of Justin's extant works, the list of opponents he attacked and the core of his critical argument: that Gnostics calumniated the creator, disparaged the Old Testament, and gave Christians a bad name.

The Heresiologists

Writing toward the end of the second century and provoked chiefly by Valentinus's teachings and influence (Ptolemaeus and Marcus, also at the center of his attack, both offered variations on Valentinian Gnosis), Irenaeus, bishop of Lyons (130–202), picked up Justin's arguments and developed them further in his highly influential *Against Heresies,* but also in his *Proof of the Apostolic Preaching.* Strongly and repeatedly, Irenaeus emphasizes that God and the creator are one and the same being, and rejects the subversive Gnostic dualism, thus rehabilitating the God of the Old Testament along with the entire creation, spiritual and material. Contrary to Justin, he suspects that philosophy had a fateful influence on the Gnostics' undisciplined discourse that "pours contempt on the church."[8] Their appeal to a secret tradition upsets him most not only because it introduces arbitrariness into matters of faith and salvation but also because it tends to restrict the salvific message to a chosen group of "knowers" who disparage the simple faith of ordinary people. Irenaeus is adamant in his rejection of *gnosis* in favor of *pistis,* or rather he firmly holds that "true gnosis is the doctrine of the apostles"[9] and is identical with the "rule of faith." The rule is a kind of creedlike summary of church teachings affirming the basic facts of Jesus' fate as related by the generation of the apostles, and it stands at the basis of ecclesiastical orthodoxy. Thus Irenaeus opts for a concept of Christianity that underscores the apostolic tradition transmitted by the unbroken succession of legitimate bishops and contained in a limited list of inspired books; his concept of Christianity further stresses the structure of authority in the church, affirms the equality of all before God, and exhibits a conservative preference, all points being seen as conditions for Christianity's saving its identity in the Greco-Roman maelstrom and keeping its substance unadulterated by syncretist excesses.

Along with solid arguments, invective also belongs to Irenaeus's style. Indeed, in ancient polemics civility and tact were not particularly the rule. Debates were an occasion for rhetorical display often less enjoyed by hearers and readers than by writers. Still more than in Irenaeus is invective evident in the *Refutation of All Heresies,* generally attributed to Hippolytus of Rome (170–235/250) and written in the first half of the third century. Here philosophy is bluntly suspected of being at the source and origin of all distortions. Heretics are seen as plagiarizers of the Greeks; to denounce this shameful recourse is already to have refuted their claims and to reveal them in the end as failing to recognize the true author of the cosmos. Like most ancient polemists, Hippolytus exhibits an amazing liking for the bitter tone, a propensity brought to its extreme in the next century by Epiphanius. Controversies of the time, it is true, reveal a capacity to hate, shared by all sides, that today gives us pause, for we cannot see how they could fail to betray or induce negative attitudes no longer commendable. Yet it has to be kept in mind that polemical attacks, then still more than now, contained more bark than bite.

The North African Tertullian (160–225), in turn, resolutely privileged faith over knowledge (nothing is needed besides faith, he claimed)

---

8. AH 1.15.3.
9. Ibid., 4.33.8.

and thought that philosophical speculations had perverted scripture and the "rule of truth." This at least he could write. In fact, he was able to make a sophisticated use of both philosophy and knowledge in his highly creative writings, such as *Apology, On Prescription Against Heretics, Against Valentinus,* and *Against Marcion,* written around the turn of the third century. What Tertullian could least tolerate was the light consideration given to the authentic tradition (written and oral) of the church and to the constant faith of the community.

The Alexandrians Clement and Origen were less inclined to deny to the Gnostics all Christian substance. In calling Christianity "true philosophy" and "the truly best *hairesis*"[10] and sketching a portrait of the true believer whom he called the "Christian Gnostic," Clement (150–215) annexed to the mainstream church all he found acceptable in *gnosis.* In doing so, he tended to subordinate mere faith to higher knowledge but in such a way that he would raise but little suspicion of heterodoxy. His views are expounded in a trilogy, *Protreptikos* (or *Exhortation to the Greeks), Paidagogos (Tutor),* and *Stromateis (Miscellanies),* the sum of what well-educated Christians are expected to think and do.

Less sympathetic to Greek philosophy than Clement, Origen (185–254) was, however, able to incorporate into his system still more philosophic elements, first of all Platonic ones, than Clement had done. He valued dialectics and speculation very highly. Through his method of exegesis he thought he could draw from scripture alone a specific *gnosis:* rejecting the Gnostic understanding of a fall within the godhead itself, his *gnosis* is made up of treasures hidden in the Bible, pertaining to the descent and ascent of souls and of Christ in a kind of eternal history that was to be of great appeal to the mystical tradition. The most significant theologian of the third century, Origen left behind a rich legacy, astonishing for its range and depth, contained in commentaries on most biblical books and in more speculative works such as *On First Principles* and *Contra Celsum.* Some of his doctrinal positions were hotly debated in the fourth and fifth centuries, as we shall see (chapter 9).

Such were the main opponents of the Gnostic "hydra." With the later rejection of Manichaeism by Augustine, it can be said that the church publicly broke with syncretist *gnosis,* which, however, gone

---

10. Str. 7.15.

underground, was to reemerge here and there with a vengeance in the history of the West.

The Dwindling of Tolerance

The rejection of *gnosis* and the encounter with mystery religions had a double implication for Christianity. First, the option for *pistis* led to a stabilization of the Christian movement. Orthodoxy was born. In the course of the debates with the Gnostics and with Marcion, the need was felt for more reliability and accountability concerning Christian sources. Not just any book could henceforth be received as authoritative by the self-appointment of a prophet; the canon of New Testament books had to be defined. Belief in arbitrary myths and obscure mysteries was no longer receivable; the rule of faith, found in inspired books and in the apostolic tradition, set the norm of what was certain and essential to the believers. Authority in the church had to be identified and strengthened. Bishops were to constitute the backbone of the organization, looking to Rome for the spiritual center of authority. The option against full-fledged *gnosis* was thus an option for an institutional model of the church, with a certain preference for conservatism and uniformity, and with a clear authoritarian structure based on the criteria of antiquity (apostolicity) and consent (majority). Many a colorful and creative element thus vanished from visibility, but such was the price to be paid for the church's surviving as a distinct entity.

Second, the option against *gnosis* amounted to a resolute rejection of all-out syncretism, but this happened in such a way that many syncretist elements could be subsumed, especially in the area of practice (liturgy, ritual) and thanks to the high rank accorded to knowledge in the theological appropriation of the saving doctrine. Here both similarities and differences in relation to the Greco-Roman culture were manifested. Pagan thought was familiar with ideas of a suffering and dying son of God; it also knew of approximations to incarnation and resurrection. Those aspects constituted valuable points of contact, making possible a favorable response to the church's proclamation. Nevertheless the pagan world was hardly prepared to consider the crucifixion of its founder as a criminal by civil authorities a recommendation for a doctrine promising bliss and happiness.

When all was said and done, the rejection of unbridled syncretism and of unrestrained *gnosis* never boiled down to a final elimination or even to a totally effective rejection. Both would accompany the development of Christianity in the centuries to come, with *gnosis* remaining a permanent shadow alluring highly creative thinkers from the wings of the main stage.

READINGS

R. Beck	"Mithraism since Franz Cumont." ANRW II.17.4 (1984): 2002–2115.
W. Burkert	*Ancient Mystery Cults.* Cambridge, Mass.: Harvard University Press, 1987.
R. Cameron and A. J. Dewey	*The Cologne Mani Codex "Concerning the Origin of His Body."* Missoula, Mont.: Scholars Press, 1979.
M. Desjardins	*Sin in Valentianism.* Atlanta, Ga: Scholars Press, 1990.
H. Jonas	*The Gnostic Religion.* Boston: Beacon Press, 1963.
B. Layton	*The Gnostic Scriptures.* Garden City, N.Y.: Doubleday, 1987.
A. Le Boulluec	*La notion d'hérésie dans la littérature grecque des 2ième et 3ième siècles,* 2 vols. Paris: Etudes augustiniennes, 1985.
S. N. C. Lieu	*Manichaeism in the Later Roman Empire and Mediaeval China.* Tübingen: Mohr, 1992.
S. R. C. Lilla	*Clement of Alexandria: A Study in Christian Platonism and Gnosticism.* Oxford: Oxford University Press, 1971.
E. Pagels	*The Gnostic Gospels.* New York: Vintage Books, 1979.
B. A. Pearson	*Gnosticism, Judaism and Egyptian Christianity.* Minneapolis, Minn.: Fortress Press, 1990.
J. Robinson, ed.	*The Nag Hammadi Library in English.* San Francisco: Harper & Row, 1988.
K. Rudolph	*Gnosis: The Nature and History of Gnosticism.* Edinburgh: T. & T. Clark, 1984.

F.-M.-M. Sagnard	*La gnose valentinienne et le témoignage de saint Irénée.* Paris: J. Vrin, 1947.
M. Tardieu	*Leçon inaugurale.* Paris: Collège de France, Chaire d'histoire des syncrétismes de la fin de l'antiquité, 1991.
R. Turcan	*Les cultes orientaux dans le monde romain.* Paris: Les Belles Lettres, 1989.
G. Vallée	*A Study in Anti-Gnostic Polemics: Irenaeus, Hippolytus and Epiphanius.* Waterloo, Ont.: Wilfrid Laurier University Press, 1981.

5

The Painful Partitions (150–430)

The formation of an orthodox or mainstream position in the church was prompted by historical necessities that began to press in the second century. A unified structure could hardly develop out of the earliest traditions: Paul had "left behind too many loose ends relating to church organization, belief and worship."[1] By 100 C.E. there was a wide variety of gospels and collections of Jesus' sayings, forms of Eucharist, and even versions of the Lord's Prayer. In the middle of the second century, on the same streets of Rome one could have run into Marcion, Valentinus, and Justin, all three then active as Christian teachers. Far from being a monolithic entity, second-century Christianity saw the proliferation of traditions, writings, beliefs, and hopes, which, although centered on the unique figure of Jesus, nevertheless threatened to take the edge off the movement and compromise its identity.

Thus, not given at the start in a well-formed shape, orthodoxy developed out of a variety of Christianities and by means of a series of exclusions aimed at securing the contours of the movement. It was not sufficient to deal with the challenges coming from "outside" in the form of Judaism and Hellenism. Conflicts "inside," since dissenters made their mark first within the church, soon revealed a latent crisis of foundations and norms that had to be addressed if the movement were to survive.

From Paul to Origen the conviction widely prevails that heresies and dissent were necessary and useful for the construction of orthodoxy. Unable to let everything in, the church felt the pressure to take a stand and close some doors. To understand that process it is clear that ideally heresy and orthodoxy should be studied together and simultaneously. For to identify dissent and heresy meant by the same token to

---

1. W. H. C. Frend, in R. Williams, ed., *The Making of Orthodoxy.* New York: Cambridge University Press, 1989, p. 36.

uncover and express a norm: The right doctrine was constituted by means of exclusions that gradually defined the final notions of heresy and orthodoxy. All the same, in dealing with that process, the anachronism of retrojecting the labels *orthodoxy* and *heresy* back into the earliest Christian stages should be firmly resisted.

The strategies devised to meet the first serious internal challengers (Marcion, the Gnostics) identified as dissenters and heretics were decisive in that they kept being applied to all those diverging from the majority and were even applied to others from outside. At best, dissenters were recognized as holding to a merely partial truth; at worst, they were denounced as victims and instruments of Satan. Heresiologists also had a practical concern: The harsh treatment meted out to heretics was mainly due to their being perceived as obstacles to the conversion of Jews and pagans. Confident of speaking on behalf of the church, heresiologists made use of the polemical techniques and rhetorical arsenal of the time to disqualify their opponents and deny that they could count as Christians. Thus the tactic against heretics was first to denounce them as alien to the authentic Christian tradition, as reducible to pagans and philosophers. Then, less charitably and more aggressively, they were accused of being fraudulent imitators, liars, presumptuous in their boundless curiosity, deceitful sophists, traitors renewing Satan's apostasy. That is why, as typically seen in Epiphanius, invective, abusive language, and slander were felt justified. Heretics must be ejected by all means, their teachings eradicated and their writings destroyed. In that, the orthodox party was successful: Only scant heretical writings have survived, mostly embedded in the hostile arguments of the winners, the heresiologists, making an impartial study of orthodoxy and heresy hardly possible.

Not all teachers and bishops espoused the mean attitude and verbal assaults of the most aggressive heresiologists, but they shared the same major concern, that of ascertaining what was held to be the one original truth of Christianity. The emerging "orthodox" group was willing to see the church for a while sacrifice some universality in favor of some uniformity, prune itself and even amputate itself of some cumbrous members if it was felt that to do otherwise and to let everything in would lead to a loss of its essential contours. Diversity itself gradually was perceived as an embarrassing commodity.

The necessities of controlling dissidence and of defending, isolating, and refuting brought about the development of norms and the explicitation of doctrine. Exclusion and self-assertion went hand in hand, as did gains and losses. A brief overview of the rejected groups with the corresponding reaction of the growing mainstream church will document this double impulse of painful door-closing and anxious securing of a self-definition.

The developments outlined in this chapter were considerably aided by imperial occurrences that will be dealt with in chapter 6. If Gnostic and Manichaean world views reappear in the present chapter, they are this time viewed not as syncretistic movements but rather as "Christian heresies."

The Marcionites

Marcionite churches flourished from the first half of the second century until well into the fifth century in the East, when they were mostly absorbed into Manichaean groups. Their success was cause for worry, less perhaps because of their rigorism in ethics and their docetism (the belief that Christ only *seemed* to have a human body) in Christology than for their radical breach with Judaism. Marcion of Pontus (ca. 85–160) had no use for the Old Testament, which, he thought, dealt with an inferior God, the clumsy creator-God, God of the Jews, called the "just God" who judges. Rather, he proclaimed a greater God, Father of Jesus, called the "benign God" or good God who saved, until recently an Unknown and Alien God. Any syncretist alliance with Judaism was ruled out, even when encountered in "apostolic" writings corrupted by people inclined to keep Christianity Jewish. Along with this, the permanent validity of Torah was denied, the Old Testament robbed of its authority, the law discredited in favor of the gospel, and allegory rejected as a poor way of glossing over the contradictions (the "antitheses") between the Old Testament and authentic Christian writings. Finally, Marcion dispelled all association with Jewish nationalistic hopes dangerously exasperated at the time of the Bar Kokhba rebellion. Perhaps more radical than the Gnostics, Marcion rejected any oral tradition and opted for a drastic shrinking of the Christian sources[2] that left only a truncated Paul/Luke as authoritative gospel and

---

2. Tertullian, in Adv. Marc. 1.1.5, talks about "the Pontic mouse who has nibbled away the gospels."

infallible teacher. Thus he created the first collection or canon of New Testament scriptures and introduced the idea of a Christian Bible.

Confronted with the Marcionite position, Justin, Irenaeus, and their like took as their first task rescuing the Old Testament for Christian usage. They did so by asserting that both "testaments" came from the one and same God, the Old Testament being a stage toward a final revelation at the same time that it was an essential instrument to secure the antiquity of the Christian movement. Thereby an impetus was also given to the church's defining more precisely those recent books that could unquestionably be considered authentic documents. Thus began the movement toward the definition of the canon of the New Testament. By 180 we find widespread, though still debated, the idea of a collection of scriptures as a closed corpus universally and forever valid. Christian writings then took their place alongside the LXX version of the Old Testament. New scriptures (the name "New Testament" appeared for good ca. 200) combined with old scriptures to form a new totality: the bipartite Christian Bible. The process of definition had moved into high gear by the end of the third century. Whereas the expression canon of faith (rule of faith) had long been used to refer to standard summaries of Christian faith current in the churches and expressed in baptismal confessions, canon as a technical term to designate normative scriptures came into use only in the fourth century. The New Testament canon found its final form in the West around 400, in the East around 600.

No doubt Marcion helped the church sort out its writings, but his drastic reduction of the writings was firmly refused as partial and as a harmful impoverishment of the Christian sources. Future generations were left with sticky problems, for the process of canonization is difficult to document and was to remain a sensitive issue. No official decisions by the church are recorded in the early centuries. Questions about who took the decisive steps toward defining the canon, what instances initiated them and when all received traditional answers. These included such explanations as the regular usage of writings for liturgical reading, the judgment and awareness of the church, the faith of the church, or that authentic books were self-authenticating. Such answers only highlight the intricacies of the issue.

The Gnostics

Far from following the Marcionites in their dealings with writings, the Gnostics went in the opposite direction. They accepted the Old Testament but subverted it by means of their allegorical interpretation. In addition, they welcomed a great number of gospels and writings as authoritative, and were open to a multiplicity of new reports about the risen Jesus' words and deeds, of unknown acts of prophets and apostles, of recovered epistles; if necessary, appeal to a secret tradition would secure the wanted authority. It must be recalled here that, as witnessed by Papias, even in 130 oral traditions mediated by the elders who had known the apostles were more trusted than written testimonies.

Heresiologists had to work on many fronts when confronted with the mushrooming *gnosis*. From Justin on, "heresies" are said to be recent productions when contrasted with the pure tradition of the apostles, a thesis widely received well into the twentieth century. In addition to depicting opponents as associates of Satan, conspiring to introduce novelties (they are novelty-mongers), heresiologists assign to each opponent a place in a "succession of heretics" *(successio haereticorum)* that presumably goes back to Simon Magus. In that genealogy recent perpetrators borrow from previous ones in a sequence of arbitrary inventions that slowly degrade the true teaching of the apostles. Placed in that succession of evildoers, an opponent's claim to the Christian title is automatically disqualified. Facing the succession of error we find a succession of truth, presumed more ancient since it comes from the apostles, and preserved intact through a genuine succession of bishops. According to this view, early in the second-century, when it became clear that the end of the present age was in fact not in sight, the prophet yielded to the bishop, who became the guardian of the tradition. Thus not everybody was entitled to speak for the church but only the bishops, who stood in the apostolic tradition and in communion with the bishop of Rome, and the teachers, who often happened to be those very bishops or men in agreement with them.

If the task of the church confronted with Marcion had been to reclaim the Old Testament and the Jewish element and to broaden the body of authoritative writings, confronted with the Gnostics the church had to adopt the reverse attitude—to limit the number of authentic writings and also to rescue the interpretation of scripture from gnostic mishandling. For a while allegory was questioned as well as the appeal to a secret tradition to justify an idiosyncratic interpretation. Nothing could be added to or subtracted from the apostolic tradition in which the core of the faith resided; only that was valid which agreed with the rule of faith, that public declaration of the church's faith based on indisputable writings and soon to be fixed in the articles of the creed.

Dissent thus compelled the church to spell out the elements that really counted for its structure and substance. Those elements had to be verifiable through the public tradition coming from the apostles. By 200 "secret" or "apocryphal" ceased to be impressive epithets and began to take on a negative sense, while a definitive impetus was given to the church's definition of its authoritative writings. Much was lost by the exclusion of the Gnostics, their colorful visions and creative minds; but much was gained in terms of disciplined attention to the sources of revelation and reliability of its witnesses. Obviously the problems of a valid interpretation of the received scriptures remained a permanent task for future generations.

The Montanists

Not all believers were ready to see in the apostolic times the final norm of faith. Very early the principle of authority based on apostolic tradition was challenged by a Christianity of the Spirit emphasizing the freedom of Christians. Prophecy and apocalyptic beliefs never totally deserted the early church; rather they were prompt to reemerge in times of crisis and intensified suffering within groups submitted to hard times. When Montanus and his two companions, Priscilla (or Prisca) and Maximilla, began to prophesy in Phrygia (in 156/157 according to Epiphanius, in 172/173 according to Eusebius), the situation was apparently one of exasperation due to persecutions, inner conflicts, and social turbulence (warfare, plague). The "new prophecy," uttered in ecstasy as being the very word of God, claimed not only that God-given changes were at hand but that the New Jerusalem was soon to be established. Hence Christians were to prepare themselves for that event by a life of renunciation, continence, and fasting, and to be ready to confess the name of Christ at the (welcome) risk of martyrdom.

What puzzled the bishops at the time Montanism was spreading beyond Asia Minor to North Africa, Lyons, and Rome was that they felt overrun by a movement that appeared doctrinally orthodox. The Montanists, in fact, represented a movement of restoration and reaction, nourished on the old Jewish-Christian prophetic and apocalyptic traditions that had surrounded the birth of Christianity in the first place but had been superseded. They espoused, as did many other "dissidents," rigorist idealism. So it was difficult to attack a movement merely aiming at reviving the primitive situation with its fervent expectation, but obviously archaizing Montanists were clashing with the established traditions. Further, they proclaimed new prophecies and commandments surpassing and relativising the earlier revelation. This could not be admitted. The church was now becoming aware that prophecies and writings that had taken form after the "apostolic" period were not receivable as normative and "inspired," and that the process of limiting the New Testament collection had to be hastened. Bishops were also certainly aware of the subversive slant of any revival allied to apocalyptic exaltation at a time when they were searching for an accommodation with the empire. The sharp-witted Tertullian, who joined the Montanists around 206/207, had no use for such accommodation; he made no secret of favoring a church of the Spirit and prophets over against a church of the bishops. In rejecting Montanism, which survived until sometime after 500, the church opted against uncontrolled prophetism but at the same time deprived itself of a certain spiritual pliability. Suspicion will always be tied to apocalypticism and often to asceticism itself, at least in its extreme form called "encratism."

The Donatists

Akin to Montanism for its strong regional and rural appeal and its quasi-orthodox doctrine, Donatism strictly belongs to the aftermath of the Great Persecution that raged between 303 and 305 under Diocletian. But its antecedents in North Africa go back to the time of the pillars of Latin Christianity, Tertullian, and, above all, Cyprian (210–258), when the scenario, so to speak, was rehearsed before being fully staged in the fourth century.

The persecution that started under Decius (249–251) saw, in North Africa as elsewhere, a number of clergy waver under duress, surrendering the holy books when requested or offering incense to honor the gods and the emperor, thus becoming "material apostates" and putting themselves outside the church (schismatics). The question arose then: What to do about those who had been baptized by a fallen minister but wished to be in full communion with the church? The bishop of Rome, Stephen, declared around 200 (against the intransigent Novatian) that they should be readmitted by simple imposition of hands without being rebaptized since the sacraments were Christ's, not the minister's, and a fallen clergy could act with validity. The eighty-seven bishops attending a council at Carthage in 256 (consultations among bishops, starting in Asia Minor at the time of Montanism and following procedures modeled on the Roman senate and municipal councils, appeared increasingly necessary) disagreed. Their leader Cyprian, an urban notable made bishop and soon to die a martyr in 258, argued that baptism administered by a fallen minister was invalid; he further propounded his ideas in *On the Unity of the Church*. In fact, unity was somehow restored and the two diverging positions were tacitly allowed to stand without being formally reconciled.

Some fifty years later the situation came to a head. During the Great Persecution, again summoned to surrender *(tradere)* the Christian scriptures, many among the clergy, including bishops, complied and fell. They became *lapsi* (lapsed, renegades or backsliders) and *traditores* (surrenderers)—in other words, collaborators. Others refused to comply and became confessors, even martyrs. When the persecution having ended, the situation throughout the empire had to be assessed; in North Africa (and in Egypt with the Melitians) it led to a schism. Old scores were settled and the fronts hardened. Adding a new element to the old controversy, the consecration of Bishop Caecilian of Carthage (312) by an alleged *traditor* was contested. The Numidian clergy supported the mob of Carthage and elected a counter-bishop soon to be succeeded by Donatus (hence Donatism). If we are to believe Jerome, within a generation, his party became the religion of "nearly all Africa," aided for a good part by the social and economic conditions of Numidia. With utter intransigence it espoused a concept of ritual purity and separation from the world, turning its back on the more moderate view of the "catholic" church interested in being at peace with state and world.

In the meantime (Donatus does not seem to have been fully willing to register this fact), the empire had ceased to be the symbol of a world ruled by demonic powers and, in the person of Constantine, had laid the foundations for an alliance with the church. Advised by the bishops of Rome and Gaul, the emperor offered his support to Caecilian and thereby to the Roman position already expressed around 250.

For the first time, the "secular arm" was made available to defend the orthodox position, and it was willingly used. Unity was reestablished for a while in 348 and again in 411 (at a conference in Carthage attended by 570 bishops), but at a high price: The Donatist clergy was banned and exiled, and the Donatist church proscribed and expropriated. Nevertheless it somehow managed to survive until the Arab invasions of the seventh and eighth centuries. Archeological evidence seems to indicate the persistence of Donatism in Southern Numidia over that period, steadfast in the view that the empire was ruled by demonic powers with Constantine himself subsidizing "apostates" and backing them with the force of law and arms.

When Augustine entered the fray around 393 and above all between 400 and 421 with his anti-Donatist writings, he could echo the transition from a situation when Donatists were branded as mere schismatics (such was the accusation levied against Donatus in 313/314) and deviationists to one where they were accused of heresy. The latter stage was reached officially in 405, with formal condemnation in 412, making it possible to invoke the anti-heretical legislation of 392 against them, including the loss of rights and protection of the law. Thus the controversy that had looked like a lengthy family litigation ended in the total dispossession of the opponents and their coercion into compliance, political pressure being allowed to bear on an ecclesiastical debate, and Augustine ending up justifying the persecution of dissenters in the name of "fatherly correction."

The arguments of the orthodox party, summed up and elaborated by Augustine, put forward a view of the nature of the church that was to characterize the prevailing form of Christianity until the Reformation of the sixteenth century. First, the church is not a sect exclusively made up of righteous elect and pure members and constituting an alternative to the surrounding society (like the small society in the Ark of Noah— saved within, damned without). Rather, never without spot or wrinkle, it includes both "wheat and tares" that will mix until the end. Holy in spite of its unholy members and ministers, coextensive with society, it is confident that it is able to absorb, transform, and perfect society without losing its identity. In other words, the church is "catholic," extended throughout the world well beyond North Africa, and able to include all who are in communion with the apostolic sees. Second, sacraments, especially baptism, are valid even when performed by a *traditor*. They are, as was emphasized at the time, acts of Christ, of grace, of the church, and hence have an objective validity irrespective of the worthiness or unworthiness of the minister who dispenses them and who is a mere channel of grace.

What is being excluded here, ultimately, is the African tradition of Tertullian and Cyprian. Theirs was a church of the persecution made up of confessors and martyrs, suspicious of pagan culture and pure from *traditores* and sinners. This tradition was excluded in favor of a church in which the "two cities" mingle, a conception that made integration into the Roman Empire and society possible. In fact, the majority in the church consistently favored indulgence and opposed rigorism. Perhaps a compromise with "civilization" was struck, but it proved necessary for the catholicity of the Christian movement. It is "in and through Africa that it (Christianity) became the religion for the world."[3] The independence of national churches vis-à-vis Rome suffered in the process, a price that the Coptic church of Egypt after 451 would not be ready to pay when it rejected a form of orthodoxy forced on it by the eastern emperor.

The Arians

The optimist Christians of the late third century who had hoped that the evidence of scripture and the authority of the bishops, once asserted, would be enough to eliminate or solve all possible internal conflicts were in for a surprise. Obviously scripture was not always clear; bishops/teachers were not always in agreement. Concerning God and Christ, many loose ends stood gaping not only in the New Testament writings but also among second- and third-century writers. It was particularly the conflicting legacies of Tertullian and Origen that constituted the most pressing appeal to clarify the issues. With increasing urgency the need was felt to take a stand on the question of how the uncompromising monotheism of the Judeo-Christian tradition could be reconciled with the worship of Jesus Christ as divine. To that question, no "orthodox" answer was given at the start. The traditional doctrine of God had to be reconstructed and a new solution invented. Great minds went to work in the fourth century,

---

3. Th. Mommsen quoted in P. Brown, *Religion and Society in the Age of Augustine*. London: Faber & Faber, 1972, p. 338.

step by step groping toward the light by "the method of trial and error"[4] and fashioning a position that was to become the orthodox one.

Prior to 318, nearly all positions had been tried concerning the status of the Son, all attached to prestigious names—especially those of Tertullian and Origen—all appealing to scripture, tradition, and predecessors. That was the time when even conceptions of a "qualified divinity" of the Son were found adequate to account for the suffering of God. Some thought that no distinctions ought to be found in the Godhead (monarchianism) or that the Son was a mere man adopted by the Father (adoptionism); others that he was inferior to the Father (subordinationism); still others that he was fully God. Many more variations on the theme circulated. A doctrinal storm was gathering.

The storm broke out in 318 when Arius, a respected Libyan presbyter in Alexandria, began to teach what many thought acceptable in view of the sufferings of Jesus: that the Logos/Son was a creature, made from "nonexistence" and had not always existed. Hence he was not quite equal to the Father. Immediately, perhaps precipitately (Arius's alliance with the schismatic Melitians of Upper Egypt may have brought panic among Alexandrian clerics), he was excommunicated by his bishop, Alexander, with the result that now two fronts built up and the stage was ripe for an open controversy. Between 318 and 381 more than twenty conferences or councils were summoned to sort out the true position of the church. The controversy went through episodes of such violence, unfortunately not only verbal violence, that Emperor Constantine, badly concerned with the peace and unity of the estate, called a general council at Nicaea in 325, which he himself attended and which was presided over by his representative and messenger, Ossius, bishop of Cordova. Anxious to safeguard the reality of the redemption wrought in Jesus Christ, the council proclaimed two main theses, incorporated in the so-called Nicene creed: that Christ had a real body (against those who still thought he only "seemed" to have one, the "docetists"); and that the Son was perfectly equal to the Father ("of one substance" with the Father: *homoousios*). Imperial approval was given to the findings of the council, with penalties meted out to those who disagreed with its decrees and lasting vilification tacked to the name of Arius.

---

4. R. P. C. Hanson, *The Search for the Christian Doctrine of God: The Arian Controversy 318–381*. Edinburgh: T. & T. Clark, 1988, pp. xx, 873.

For all its epoch-making importance, the agreement reached at Nicaea proved to be no more than apparent. The Greek terms used then to settle the dispute (above all *ousia:* substance or person; *hypostasis:* person or substance) were susceptible to a variety of meanings. Imperial politics, dissension between East and West, cabal, all those nontheological factors complicated the stormy debates of 330 to 361. Around 360 there were many who feared that the whole world was tipping over to the Arians. Doubts were raised as to the ability of Greek conceptuality to interpret the biblical tradition: Does it not rather promote, even create, heresies? After Athanasius, the shrewd but ruthless bishop of Alexandria, had entered the debate in 339/340, new alignments of views gradually emerged. Further refinements of doctrine appeared on the stage; they resulted in the reaffirmation and reworking of the Nicene creed at the general or ecumenical council of Constantinople in 381. The council brought to fruition the elaborations of Athanasius's views offered by the Cappadocian fathers (see chapters 8 and 9). It was able to be clearer on the status of the Son and on the humanity of Christ (that he had a human soul as well as a human body) while adding a statement on the divinity of the Spirit, thus rounding up a full-blown doctrine of the Trinity. Emperor Theodosius I, by confirming the conclusions of the council, "rendered the pro-Nicene version of the Christian faith the official religion of the Roman Empire."[5] In a sense, orthodoxy was established by coercion: Because the emperor wanted all bishops to sign, nearly all did. Once more Theodosius demonstrated the active role played by emperors since Constantine in the development of doctrine, acting as the de facto head of the church (the leadership of the Roman bishop was only timidly emerging in the fourth century), controlling the course of the council and ruthlessly enforcing its implementation. It must be said in his defense, however, that Theodosius was also reflecting the wide consensus that was finally appearing in the church and that needed expression.

It is difficult today to understand that huge segments of the empire got excited about such subtle linguistic nuances. Yet the debates paid off richly. The discussions that were to follow on the council of 381 and that finally culminated in the decisions of the councils of Ephesus 431 and Chalcedon 451 contributed to a superb "fine-tuning" of

5. Hanson, *The Search for the Christian Doctrine of God*, p. 821.

the doctrine of God and especially to the clarification of questions of Christology. Those decisions became normative and ruled out a further series of not insignificant options (especially Nestorians and Mono-physites); those issues will be addressed again in chapter 8.

The condemnation of the Arians and their like in the fourth century meant a certain escalation in the motives for exclusion from the main-stream of the church—the exclusion of apparently sincere Christians who, for intellectual reasons, were tampering with the unqualified divinity of the Son and were inclined to divide the Trinity. A wind of conceptual intransigence was blowing among the orthodox ranks. Variations in termi-nology, concepts, and ideas were reason enough for depositions of bishops, for condemnations and excommunications. The post-Nicene debates exposed an amazing readiness to ostracize fellow Christians because of one word, even one letter in one word (e.g., *homoousios/homoiousios*: of the same or of like substance, though a sin-gle letter obviously made a big difference). Variance in opinion had become "thought crime."[6] Certainly much was at stake in those debates and people saw the danger of undermining faith and salvation through sloppy language. In particular, they smelled practical idolatry in the Arian willingness to worship a Son-creature. But from the fifth century another danger loomed: the temptation of credal fetishism, which attached salva-tion to the anxious keeping of the articles of a creed.

The Manichees

The Arian controversy of the fourth century saw each side brand its opponents with the label "Manichaean." As noted previously (chap-ter 4), Manichaeism posited two co-eternal principles, God/Light and Evil/Darkness, out of whose mixture, through a complicated process of downward weakening of the divine substance ("devolution"), our world emanated. While Arius was felt to come too close to admitting two opposite principles, the created and the uncreated, he could accuse his accusers, because of their way of conceiving the origin of the Son from the Father, of espousing the Manichaean emanation thesis that the Son is "from the substance" of the Father. The term of opprobrium was

6. P. Brown in P. Veyne, ed., *A History of Private Life,* vol. 1. Cambridge, Mass.: Harvard University Press, 1987, p. 276.

generously flung as a disqualifying epithet until well into the late medieval period. It sometimes looks as though everybody had been fighting a secret personal temptation he tried to exorcise, projecting intimate fears unto others.

The Manichaean church seems to have flourished among the cultivated classes of Egypt, Syria, and North Africa, but its presumed "Persian" origin was not to endear this kind of secret society to Roman emperors sporadically at war with Persia. Already in 302 (297 according to some) a rescript of Diocletian banned that "poisonous snake"[7] for putting forward vile novelties that contradicted the established religion. Manichees were excepted from the edict of toleration of 372; they suffered many more repressive measures, proscription and persecution. In 386 in Trier the Christian Priscillian was condemned on the wrong charge of Manichaeism and executed, the first "heretic" to undergo that fate. The arrival of the Vandals in North Africa (429) forced hordes of Manichees to seek refuge in Rome, where they met with the hostility of both church and empire.

The factors that made the religion of Mani (216–277) attractive to educated people in the West can be gathered from the career of Augustine (354–430), associated with it for some nine years. The radical dualism of the two principles offered a simple solution to the problem of Evil and suffering while the same doctrine with its essential determinism proved to be a soothing device for the conscience plagued by guilt and now finding in the overwhelming power of Evil a welcome alibi. Moreover, to follow the Manichees meant that one could dispense with the crudities of the Old Testament "fables," a source of continuous embarrassment for the educated. Finally and paradoxically, the "scientific" facade of Manichaeism, its confident speculations in physics, cosmology, and psychology as well as its clever use of astrology, the whole cast in the appealing mold of graphic poetry, were enough to impress the searching minds. All the same, Augustine's doubts and misgivings soon accumulated and were exacerbated by his encounter with Ambrose's "more scientific" theology, indebted to the Alexandrians, and above all by his discovery of the "Platonists" (especially Plotinus). He broke with the Manichees and between 388 and 404 got down to refute them in a series of writings (the anti-Manichaean writings)

---

7. In J. Stevenson, *A New Eusebius*. London: SPCK, 1987, p. 267.

dealing with God as creator of all, the origins of the world, sin and free will. Typically, Augustine the anti-Manichee proclaimed that everything is good though threatened.

As early as around 280 the church denounced Manichaeism as being a "Christian heresy." Was it merely rejecting a caricature? Some of the objections raised against Gnosticism in the second century applied to Manichaeism and were reaffirmed. Uninhibited syncretism, arbitrary mythical speculations, denigration of matter and the body because of their evil origin, rejection of the Old Testament tradition (but not of apocalypticism)—these were for the church non-negotiable items that had to be firmly opposed. The church was looking for a solution to the problem of Evil and suffering that would stay away from the unacceptable consequences of extreme dualism and fatalism. Masses were not to be discouraged in their hope for salvation and their efforts to make spiritual progress.

Manichaeism always kept the stigma of being perceived as a foreign body not only in the empire but also in the church in spite of its Christian varnish. Thus its rejection meant the ejection of yet one more form of alienation. It also meant the reaffirmation of the biblical tradition complete with its Judaic and Greek legacy at the expense of the foreign "Oriental" importation and "compound of all errors"[8] that Manichaeism, doubtless unjustly, was perceived to be.

This new exclusion overlooked the civilizing influence of the Manichees as documented in Central Asia and China where they flourished along with Buddhism and Nestorian Christianity until the fourteenth and sixteenth centuries. It also overlooked the resilience of its appeal, similar to that of Gnosticism, throughout the centuries; Manichaeism kept resurging in Europe (e.g., in the twelfth-century Bogomils and Cathars). Finally, it overlooked the remarkable ascetical ideals and practices of the Manichees, and their possible contacts with nascent Christian monasticism, especially in Egypt. However, in proclaiming the evil origin of the body, the Manichees trespassed the fine line beyond which the body is seen not only as a burden but even as a disgrace. That was indeed too much for the church's religious sensibility.

---

8. Leo the Great, *Sermon* 16.16, in J. Stevenson, *Creeds, Councils and Controversies.* London: SPCK, 1989, p. 325.

The Pelagians

The Donatist and Arian controversies had demonstrated that even synods could contradict one another. This was to be further exemplified in the course of the Pelagian debates. Additional norms of Christian teaching, beyond scripture, creed, bishops, and councils, had to be carved. At this juncture the role of the bishop of Rome and imperial pressures came into play.

Sometime around 402–405 a distinguished personality in Rome took open exception to Augustine's prayer to God, "Grant what you command, and command what you will."[9] This view seemed to sound the death knell of human free will. The author of the protest was a certain Pelagius (ca. 350–425) who had come from Britain to Rome around 380. A rival of Jerome, this pious layman had become the spiritual advisor of a prestigious Roman family and the leader of a reform-minded and ascetical group. Driven out of Rome along with many others by the Goths of Alaric (410), he moved on to Palestine, where he again encountered Jerome, who did not intend to leave him in peace. He eventually accused Pelagius of Manichaean leanings. Asceticism, especially in its extreme, "encratic" form, was regularly suspected of being under the influence of some Mani-like virus. Athanasius had gone out of his way to dispel the doubt and to insist that the austere monk Antony had always shunned the company of Manichees, but perhaps some ascetics had not done so.

But it was Pelagius's way of understanding the freedom of human actions in relation to God's help that was to be at the center of a controversy that raged from 402/405 to 431 and saw again the involvement of Augustine. This was to be the clash of two religious giants whose legacies generated two notable poles of Western religion: Augustinianism and Pelagianism.

At issue was indeed a typically Western problem. It must be recalled that since 395 the empire was split into western and eastern parts and that incomprehension kept mounting between Rome and Constantinople in all respects, including the religious outlooks. It was not so much the lofty mysteries of the Godhead, so attractive to the East, as that concrete area of interaction between God's grace and human freedom that was Pelagius's concern and that of his supporters.

---

9. Conf. X.29 (also X.31 and 37).

He saw in Augustine's statement the danger of utter passivity, discouraging all efforts at practical reform as well as our strivings for perfection. Without denying the reality of divine grace, Pelagius saw in free will a divine gift, already a grace—a "natural grace"—allowing one to act freely toward one's salvation. Before baptism, he argued, infants are not under the rule of Adam's transgression and after baptism free will makes one capable of living without sin. Thus perfection is in the reach of all since God's grace is given to all at creation and in the law. Origen had already propounded a similar version of inclusive optimism. As a champion of reform, Pelagius wanted to put an end to the ravages of debilitating determinism. All must work toward perfection and (anticipating Kant) if they must, they can; God's help will certainly crown their efforts. Pelagius was not a monk, but he wanted every baptized person to be like a monk because everyone had the potential to reach the state of Christian perfection and to meet the high standards of the ascetic movement.

To Augustine such a view meant the collapse of Christian faith. For a while he hesitated before intervening, perhaps in regard for Pelagius's powerful protectors among Roman aristocratic families recently attracted to Christianity, or out of deference to trustworthy common friends, such as Paulinus of Nola, who preferred to leave Pelagius in peace. But when, close to home, Pelagius's companions (e.g., Celestius) turned to radicalism, he thought he had to speak out, spurred on to do so by Jerome. In his anti-Pelagian writings (412–430) Augustine insists that our freedom is bound by sin and has first to be set free by grace in order to be able to produce good deeds. God has sovereign power over our wills and all good; even our very desire for perfection, though proceeding from our wills, comes from above. Conversely, everything that does not originate in faith is sin. Augustine's anti-Manichaean battles had led him to emphasize freedom over fatalism. Now, reflecting on his own experience of conversion in which God had all the initiative, he inclines toward a certain determinism, which brings him full circle back to a kind of semi-Manichaeism in his concern to vindicate grace. That evolution was already reflected in the conflicting parts of *On Free Will,* written between 388 and 397. The logic of his new position would lead him in the last years of his life to his dreadful statements on predestination with its predetermined quota of saved (the council of Orange in 529 would substantially tone down such views) and to his theology of original sin and its transmission that was to be a typical feature of Western thought.

If in the course of the controversy Augustine developed views that made him into the "doctor of grace" universally acclaimed, it would be wrong to depict Pelagius as the enemy of grace. The mysterious interaction of free human action and God's help was an open question at the time and was ever not going to receive a definitive, satisfying explanation. Human thought encounters here a dilemma: Our ethical convictions require our freedom, but our religious convictions require our dependence on God. Perhaps Pelagius minimized grace in applying the term grace to the gift of freedom, or he overemphasized free will, untainted by original sin, as preparing the way for grace. Perhaps Augustine minimized free will in insisting on a doctrine of original sin (his second achievement in this debate along with his doctrine of grace), or he overemphasized grace as necessary even for preparing free will to move toward the good. In all this Augustine might have been the "innovator," seeing life after conversion as "one long temptation"[10] that reveals the enduring weaknesses of a wounded human nature, while Pelagius held to a tradition for which the ideal of a blessed life was a possibility in this world because baptism opened the door to the kingdom, not to a "church of convalescents."[11]

The Pelagian controversy was certainly compounded by the contemporary controversy on Origen's orthodoxy (see chapters 8 and 9) stirred up by the same Jerome, and in Augustine's case by the resilience of the Donatist schism in North Africa. As a result, Augustine's heart hardened toward the end of his career. He saw in Pelagius one of those pseudo-monks denying the grace of God under the cover of defending the freedom of the will. In his efforts to debunk Pelagius he felt justified in lobbying his patrons at the court of Ravenna in order both to crush Donatism and to have Pelagius condemned by the church that the same Pelagius had wanted to reform. Pope Zosimus would apparently have liked to wait; a synod in Diospolis had just acquitted Pelagius. But the pressure was too strong. In 417–418 Pelagius was excommunicated and banished from the Italian peninsula by imperial rescript. Nineteen Italian bishops who refused to subscribe to the condemnation were

---

10. Conf. X.28.
11. Brown, *Religion and Society*, p. 205.

deposed. The council of Ephesus (431) gave faint attention to the problem but ratified for the East the decisions taken in the West where North Africa so to speak had hijacked the church. Pelagius was condemned for taking a position on an open question; unlike Origen, he was never to be rehabilitated. The debate he had initiated was never totally closed; picked up by Julian of Eclanum after Pelagius's death, it would remain endemic in the West and be vigorously revived in the sixteenth and seventeenth centuries.

With the defeat of Pelagius, an optimistic view of the human condition with its ideal of perfectibility takes its leave from mainstream Christianity and pursues its career outside. Augustinianism was the realistic position. It had a better grasp of the human predicament with its congenital failings and its craving for grace, and it could offer a coherent explanation of that predicament in spite of a certain obsession with sin, concupiscence, and hereditary guilt. Questions kept nagging because the "synergy" between God's grace and human freedom remains unfathomable, although it should be possible to say clearly how the act of faith, though given by God, can also be one's own act. One cannot help wishing that the debate in the fifth century had been allowed to go on without the massive ecclesiastical and civil intervention that took place. But soon after the second ecumenical council (Constantinople 381) a hardening of orthodoxy had clearly gained an undeniable momentum.

Dissent and Development of Norms

It could not be expected that champions of orthodoxy active at the time of the first ecumenical councils, such as Athanasius, would take a relaxed attitude and repeat the thoughtful remarks of Paul and Origen as to the necessity and utility of heresies.[12] The fact remains, however, that without dissent, and vocal dissent, the church would not have been compelled to define itself in the way it did. It is in debating controversial issues that the authority of bishops, the determination of the normative writings, the uncompromising elements of the faith, and the nature of the church were progressively affirmed. In the process, while at the start a bishop's pronouncement could settle a debated matter, other

---

12. 1 Cor 11:19; C. Cels. 3.13.

forums had soon to be called into play: synods, councils, expert theologians, and, not least, the religious sense of the believing community.

Every time a matter was resolved, the result was the exclusion of dissenters who were thought willfully to stray away from a mainstream assumed to embody the tradition flowing from the apostles. To part from dissenters always implied a double movement. First, it meant giving up possible options seen as inadequate interpretations of Christianity; second, it was accompanied by the affirmation and formulation of the faith of the church in a way that left no doubt as to what it considered right doctrine. Interestingly, though, ancient "heresies" were never reduced to total silence, for the first heresies represented various types of interpretation of Christianity, permanent and recurrent at all times; each epoch has its Pelagians, its Arians, its Gnostics, its Marcionites. The day Christianity will be entirely deprived of them, it will cease to be alive.

Formalization of Norms in Christianity and Judaism

Did some pervasive historical pressure befall intellectual and religious movements in the third century and push them to try to eliminate a great deal of the diversity that had characterized them hitherto? It is striking to observe that Judaism and Christianity, for instance, at roughly the same time, were engaged in the business of denying authenticity to some of their subgroups blamed for mistaken views concerning what it meant to be either Christian or Jewish; they both then took steps toward the codification of their beliefs.

In the aftermath of the Second Jewish Rebellion (132–135), left without the center of religious life that the Temple had represented, the Jewish community restructured itself around the synagogue in the local community, and prayer and ritual in private homes. In both places study and practice of Torah became the center of Jewish religion. The process of transfer of the religious center from the Temple to homes and local communities was completed around 200, the date of the compilation of the Mishnah, the great achievement of victorious Rabbinic Judaism and the basis for the normative Judaism of the centuries to come.

The wrestling for Christian norms began in the second half of the second century. The first heresiologists had formulated the main creed-like statements by 200. What came afterward brought a deepening and hardening to the substantial delimitations carried out at that time. An orthodox position had been defined, which had to be defended, invented further, and specified over against alternative options judged unacceptable.

The shaping of orthodoxy, however, is not adequately accounted for by exclusive reference to ideological preferences, clerical preroga- tives, or, at the limit, political pressures. Impulses came as well from the practice of Christian life. In particular, the way toward lasting doc- trinal positions was already marked out by forms of prayer and ritual commonly in use, whose implicit contents called for more precise theo- logical explication.

Religious and Liturgical Practices

One point raised against Pelagius in 417 by Pope Innocent I was that his views were contrary to the use of prayer and the practice of infant bap- tism. The ritual of baptism, from the start, was accompanied by represen- tations of the sacred action taking place and by confessions of faith. Similar contents inhered in the Eucharist and in religious practices and beliefs generally. Christian devotion developed on those foundations, embodying practical theological views that came to be expressed in doc- trinal assertions. For instance, Mary's title "Mother of God" *(theotokos)* was employed by people long before it was officially accepted (431) and theologically explicated; Augustine took recourse to people's long-stand- ing belief in original sin to justify a position absent from most previous theological discourses. In the end, theology was forced to come to terms with people's devotional preferences and liturgical customs.

That the prayer of all in the church preceded formal theological def- initions and that rite preceded doctrine were encapsulated in the axiom *"lex orandi, lex credendi"* (the rule of prayer lays down the rule of faith). It was tacitly assumed that the orthodox consensus had to take its orientation from the religious sense of believers past and present. Creed and theology followed on the faith of the church universal. When Vincent of Lérins in 434 found the astute words for what is meant by an orthodox consensus (*"quod ubique, semper et ab omnibus creditum est"*: that which has been believed everywhere, always and by all), he was expressing, doubtless with some historical, geographical, and sociological short-circuiting, what had been the driving force behind the process of consolidation that led to the Christian form of orthodoxy.

No doubt similar developments could be found outside the Christian movement, even in the formation of secular orthodoxies. To a large extent praxis comes before theory. Christian liturgical practice, up to 70 sharing with Jewish worship, carried along devotional doctrines from the primitive tradition that called for explication. It embodied symbolic expressions of theological discourse. This can be seen in literary remains dealing with liturgical usage. From the *Didache* (arguably a late first century manual of Syrian origin, close to Jewish traditions, e.g., in its doctrine of the Two Ways and in the formulation of liturgical prayers) through Justin's *Apology* to Hippolytus's *Apostolic Tradition,* one can observe a remarkable continuity in the implied dogmatic substance. Evidently the Christian community expressed its emerging distinctiveness first through its worship. Such a cultic term as *Kyrios* (Lord), for instance, was used of Jesus Christ in worship before it became a creedal statement. The same could be said of the preexistence of the Logos, of the divinity of the Spirit, and so forth. Early theologians were well aware that the doctrine of the Trinity was adumbrated in the baptismal formula long before it was formally defined.

The separate courses of Rome and Byzantium after 395 (the date of the division of the empire into western and eastern parts) and especially after 476 (the end of the western empire) did not alter the principle of the interrelatedness of worship and dogma. The East, including Egypt, may have been more inclined to speculation on divine matters and metaphysical elaboration; the West, including North Africa, may have been more interested in matters of ethics and issues related to salvation. When it came to worship, liturgical practices embodied doctrines that were strikingly common throughout the Christian world and which constituted the subterranean feeder of orthodoxy.

READINGS

W. Bauer — *Orthodoxy and Heresy in Earliest Christianity.* Philadelphia: Fortress Press, 1971.

G. Dix — *The Shape of the Liturgy.* London: Dacre, 1949.

G. Dix — *The Treatise on the Apostolic Tradition of St. Hippolytus of Rome.* London: SPCK, 1937. Rev. 1991.

W. H. C. Frend — *The Donatist Church.* Oxford: Clarendon Press, 1971.

W. H. C. Frend — *Saints and Sinners in the Early Church: Differing and Conflicting Traditions in the First Six Centuries.* Wilmington, Del.: M. Glazier, 1985.

R. P. C. Hanson — *The Search for the Christian Doctrine of God: The Arian Controversy 318–381.* Edinburgh: T. & T. Clark, 1988.

A. von Harnack — *Marcion: The Gospel of the Alien God.* Durham, N.C.: Labyrinth Press, 1988.

C. Kannengiesser — *Arius and Athanasius: Two Alexandrian Theologians.* Brookfield, Vt.: Ashgate, 1991.

S. N. C. Lieu — *Manichaeism in Mesopotamia and the Roman East.* Leiden: Brill, 1994.

G. May — "Marcion in Contemporary Views: Results and Open Questions." *Second Century* 6 (1987–1988): 129–151.

H.-Ch. Puech — *Le manichéism: Son fondateur, sa doctrine.* Paris: Civilisations du Sud, 1949.

B. R. Rees — *Pelagius, a Reluctant Heretic.* Wolfeboro, N.H.: Boydell Press, 1988.

T. A. Robinson — *The Bauer Thesis Examined: The Geography of Heresy in the Early Christian Church.* Lewiston, N.Y.: E. Mellen Press, 1988.

W. Rordorf and A. Tuilier, eds. — *La doctrine des douze apôtres (Didachè).* Paris: Cerf, 1978.

A. Solignac   "Pélage et Pélagianisme." *Dictionnaire de spiritualité* 12 (1986): 2889–2942.

Chr. Trevett   *Montanism: Gender, Authority and the New Prophecy.* New York: Cambridge University Press, 1996.

R. Williams, ed.   *The Making of Orthodoxy.* New York: Cambridge University Press, 1989.

6

Inversion of the Empire (200–500)

Christianity was born in an empire that was thought to be the object of the manifested care of the gods. Certain circles went so far as to believe that it was overseen by one distant god (e.g., Jupiter) governing through the ministrations of traditional gods in charge, like imperial governors, of specific sectors of his great realm. It was in response to the evidence of the gods' favor that cultic institutions developed in Roman society. Traditional public worship aimed to keep the *pax deorum,* the peace of the gods. If the gods were pleased or placated by the exact performance of religious rites, the maintenance of the good fortune of the empire as well as the harmonious balance of the universe was expected to be secured.

Roman religion was made up of a complex of local traditions and inherited or borrowed elements. Oriental cults had been widely received throughout the empire, adopted as such or transposed and placed under "new management." Permeating civic life, those religious cults showed an amazing vitality up to 350 and even well after being outlawed, a phenomenon often underestimated by Christian writers ancient and modern.

Religious Toleration

By its very nature, then, Roman rule was more than a purely secular rule. One was required to participate in certain public ceremonies aimed at securing the gods' protection for the emperor and the realm. Beyond the recognition of a particular alliance of gods with the fate of the empire and the consequent practice of certain rites, Roman religion did not require much and was not particularly interested in binding doctrines. But then observances had to be kept. The authorities of the state saw to the maintenance and regulation of religious practice. As a principle, and this will be cause of embarrassment for Christians, those who did not profess the Roman religion were expected to take part in Roman religious ceremonies. Governing Romans were deeply convinced that their religion was, in the words of Cicero, "the foundation of our state";[1] they saw it as a body of civic laws relating to sacred matters and devised to preserve the *pax deorum* by means of the appropriate ceremonial, irrespective of one's personal faith or inner feelings or rational justification. That is why external compliance was deemed sufficient to express one's religious care for the welfare of all.

Beyond that, toleration was the rule. If the Jews, respected but little loved in Roman society, were excepted from even the minimal prescription of outward compliance, it was due to the fact that theirs was a cult of ancestral origin. They were expected, though, to pray for the well-being of the emperor. Needless to say, Jews, for their part, never experienced the Roman Empire as a regime of generous toleration nor paganism as compatible with their religion. It is more accurate to say that all they got was "hostile and contemptuous tolerance."[2]

Persecutions

Given that situation and the fact that Christianity started as a Jewish sect, historians have long been searching for the precise reason why it was illegal to be a Christian. No legal enactment to that effect is known. Strangely enough, the sporadic persecutions between 110 and 211 were carried out "because of the name";[3] it is even the only known case of a cult's devotees being executed for the mere profession of adherence to a name. The "name" must have contained something explosive. In fact, the name Christian evoked an inherent disloyalty to the state. Porphyry denounced the Christians for having "turned away from those recognized as gods" by all "and [having] rather chosen what is impious and atheistic among men."[4] Christians declared themselves

1. Cicero, *On the Nature of the Gods* iii., 5–9. Translated by H. C. P. McGregor. New York: Penguin Books, 1972.

2. A. H. Armstrong in E. Ferguson, ed., *Church and State in the Early Church.* New York: Garland, 1993, p. 357.

3. See Athenagoras in J. Stevenson, *A New Eusebius.* London: SPCK, 1987, pp. 66–67.

4. Porphyry as quoted in Praep. ev. 1.2.1–4.

to be "atheists of all those gods";[5] exclusively clinging to their "super-stition,"[6] announcing the impending ruin of the empire and belittling the gods. They appeared as "enemies of the Roman order,"[7] despisers of the sacred rites and apostates of the traditional Roman religion, the essence of Roman citizenship. They were dangerous not so much for the crude "abominations"[8] (ritual murder, cannibalism, incest, magic) they were suspected of fostering, but first of all because they belonged to an antisocial organization that made a virtue of the neglect of the gods, of the ceremonies, and of the commonwealth kept healthy by those ceremonies. To be accused of being Christian made people trea-sonable and liable to the death penalty.

Thus when Pliny the Younger toured Bithynia and Pontus around 112 as the emperor's personal legate, accusers denounced Christians before him as malefactors. The name had been associated with riots, subversion of public order, neglect of the temples, and noncompliance with traditional religious ceremonies. The danger Christians represented justified, in the eyes of Pliny and the mob, the application of capital pun-ishment. Some were executed. Christians called the victims of this oper-ation "martyrs" (witnesses), and they were reminded of the career of the Maccabees, their source of inspiration. Pliny's hesitation concerned only the fate of those who recanted their allegiance to the group. Investi-gating this category, he discovered that they were guilty of none of the abominations ascribed to them and wanted to hear from the emperor what to do. Trajan's rescript confirmed the Roman tradition. Those who attacked established religion ought to be punished, yet there was no need to search the area for Christians nor were anonymous accusations to be received. For the rest, neither Trajan nor Pliny showed any interest in finding out what really motivated Christian behavior.

Until 250 harassments and persecutions took place here and there, mainly due to the zeal of governors and the violence of the mobs hold-ing Christians responsible for sundry disasters. It is only in 250, at a time when the Roman frontier was threatened by Persians as well as bar-barians, and population was shrinking due to social maladies, that an

---

5. Apol. 1.6.

6. See Tacitus in Stevenson, *A New Eusebius,* pp. 2–3.

7. R. MacMullen, *Enemies of the Roman Order.* Cambridge, Mass.: Harvard University Press, 1967.

8. Tacitus in Stevenson, *A New Eusebius,* p. 2.

emperor, Decius, and with him the government seized the initiative of persecution. To cement the unity of the realm, he decreed that all inhabitants should openly sacrifice to the gods, failing which they would become outlaws. Scores of Christians apostatized. This caused a major setback for the church, which had recently been experiencing a steady expansion. The persecution was general under Decius (in 250–251) and almost general under Valerian (in 257–259). Bishops were singled out as privileged targets in order to demoralize the community.

There followed a period of complete tolerance from 260 to 302, a crucial time for the growth of Christianity. Then established Roman religion made a final attempt at silencing Christianity—this was the Great Persecution (303–313), begun under Diocletian with all the appearances of a pagan revival. It was sparked in part by the fear of seeing Christian presence in the army and the civil service reach alarming proportions, and by the desperate efforts of conservative intellectuals bent on inflaming the emperor against those people who were contemptuous of the gods and underminers of the social order. To Christians the renewed persecution came as a brutal shock. "They found themselves officially outcasts in the society with which they had so strenuously identified themselves. It was a terrifying and, on the whole, demoralizing experience."[9]

Even where local authorities showed merely lukewarm enthusiasm in carrying them out, persecutions were a savage business, especially the Great Persecution. They involved destruction of churches and scriptures, confiscation of property, prohibition of worship, cancellation of legal and civil rights, arrest of clergy, orders to sacrifice to the gods on pain of death, torture and execution. Manichees were most severely treated, doubtless because their doctrine came from a Persia at war with the empire. Perhaps the number of martyrs, on scrutiny, "was not large," yet it would be wrong to underestimate "the great suffering caused to the Christians by the atmosphere of hostility, liable to turn at any moment into active persecution, in which the church grew up and ultimately triumphed."[10]

It is easy, in hindsight, to attribute much of what happened dur-

9. P. Brown, *The World of Late Antiquity, AD 150–750*. London: Thames & Hudson, 1971, p. 86.
10. G. E. M. de Ste. Croix in Ferguson, ed., *Church and State in the Early Church*, p. 214.

ing the persecutions to a "tragic misunderstanding"[11] Christians, it is sometimes said, could have complied with many imperial demands without really compromising their faith. Apart from the "name," the mood of governors, and imperial decisions, several grounds have been suggested for the persecution of Christians: the will to secure unity in the empire through elimination of centrifugal sects; the violent intolerance of mobs unable to cope with differences; the impatience of people who "felt offended at being snubbed"[12] by the kind of club the Christians constituted; the unpopularity of Christians (according to Celsus) held to belong to an illegal association and to be apostates from Judaism; the provocative behavior of "voluntary martyrs," those who smashed images and "blasphemed" the gods, provoking an acute emotional antagonism by endangering the political stability of the empire. When all is said, however, the religious motive was predominant. Romans were willing to extend their protection to all kinds of peaceful and undisturbing cults, but not to "the devotees of a new-fangled sect which threatened almost every element of Roman religion, and indeed of all the traditional cults conducted by the inhabitants of the Roman world."[13]

Irritable as they were in religious matters, Christians were an irritant to the Roman conformist society, which feared divine displeasure at the neglect of traditional rites. They remained such an irritant even after the mid-third century when the enormities of which Christians had been suspected were shown to be based on prejudice rather than knowledge. Many Christians ("masses" according to both Cyprian and Eusebius) were prompt to apostatize in order to save their skins, or paid lip service by placing a pinch of incense on the altar or swearing in order to clear themselves of suspicion; but those who stood firm were those who really counted. Their actual behavior might have been embellished by hagiographers who drafted the various *"passiones."* What remained, though, was the memory of their unflinching courage; it had signaled the failure of persecutions and was to influence the future course of events.

---

11. L. Koep quoted in R. Turcan, "Le culte impérial au IIIe siècle." ANRW II. 16.2: p. 1075.

12. R. MacMullen, *Christianizing the Roman Empire AD 100–400*. New Haven: Yale University Press, 1984, p. 19.

13. de Ste. Croix in Ferguson, ed., *Church and State,* pp. 40–41.

Growth of the Movement

A quick look at the evolution of the Christian community between 150 and 300 conveys the clear impression of a minority moving up: from a negligible "superstition" to the doors of the imperial palace, close to the center of power. Missionary fervor, unique to Christianity, accounted for much of that ascent. Sporadic harassments could not stop the progress. Persecutions may not have entirely constituted the "publicity feat" that Tertullian saw in them.[14] It is no less certain that the death of a limited number of believers[15] did not succeed in depleting their ranks. Rather, the striking example of the martyrs constituted a pressing invitation to the masses to look into the profound motivation of the Christians.

As already emphasized, population estimates are an extremely risky exercise. Nevertheless a few general figures, undeniably highly debatable, may help visualize the growth of the movement. Against the background of fluctuating imperial demographics (60–70 million in 110 C.E. for the entire Roman empire, ca. 95 million in 192, then decline to ca. 50 million around 260, 55–60 million around 300, 45 million around 410) we first find in 110 a small minority of around 50,000 Christians (the empire counted then some 4 to 5 million Jews), recruited from among people of low standing in cities. Although they could still be described around 179 as a small prickly lot, Christians by 200 had been able to attract a growing number of adherents from the lower middle class, and several respectable artisans in cities, even winning over such powerful minds as Clement of Alexandria, Origen, and Tertullian. In the course of the third century, while it is still more hazardous to give figures (1 million Christians by 260?), it appears that Christianity was making great headway among all classes of Roman society and was spreading geographically. The "third race"[16] was in the process of becoming a "nation." A sharp expansion took place between 260 and 302, a period of peace decisive for the "triumph of Christianity." Christianity was effectively tolerated and began to reach the countryside.

---

14. "The blood of the martyrs is seed…. The oftener we are mown down by you, the more in number we grow": *Apology* 50 in ANF, vol. 3.

15. "…hundreds rather than thousands" says W. H. C. Frend, *Martyrdom and Persecution in the Early Church.* Oxford: Blackwell, 1967, p. 413.

16. Tertullian, *Ad nationes* 1.8, in ANF, vol. 3.

By the turn of the fourth century the Christian community with around 5 million (close to one-tenth of the population) almost equaled the Jewish group, in number if not in standing and influence. At the time of the Great Persecution, Christians were encountered in all major cities, especially in the highly Christianized eastern provinces. They had gained in self-confidence and openness to Roman civilization, culture, and ideals. Many of them saw those Roman achievements as divinely ordered, an evolution that made Constantine's conversion (312) understandable. It comes as no surprise that, due to the momentous event of the emperor's conversion and to the contemporary irresistible impulse of the movement, among other favorable circumstances, Christianity was soon to experience its greatest expansion—from about 5 million around 300 to about 30 million around 410 (representing two-thirds of the population). It was now the religion of the majority, however timid the commitment of those claiming to be within the Christian pale might have been. At the end of that development Jews trailed with 6 to 7 million in the empire, having become a minority even in their own land. Paganism went underground, branched out, or, if the silence of our sources can be relied on, disappeared.

After 312

If we give credence to Eusebius (265–340), the first church historian, and to his enthusiastic celebration of Constantine, the emperor's conversion, on attributing to Christ his victory on the battlefield, was an unequivocally advantageous event for Christianity. The nature and sincerity of the conversion of the ever ruthless Constantine, the quality of his understanding of Christianity and of his notion of the church, his persistent flirtation with Sun worship, mixing up Sun cult and Christian monotheism—those are some of the problems that have been scrutinized and argued by a great number of scholarly studies. Perfect clarity has never been reached, except to say that Constantine, doubtless raised as a monotheist, had been sympathetic to Christianity long before 312, and that he then became convinced of the truth of Christianity and clear about his personal mission to convert the Roman empire to that religion. His conversion, at the time he was establishing his control over the western provinces, and his patronizing of the church clearly altered the fate of the Christian movement. Henceforth the destinies of church and state were linked.

Galerius's decree of toleration in 311 had already put an end to the Great Persecution, though it still lingered in the East for a while. Two years later, through the so-called Edict of Milan, Constantine and his co-emperor in the East, Licinius, granted universal religious freedom, giving legal equality to all cults and restoring to Christians their confiscated property. But soon, with Constantine's favor, the situation of the church changed radically. Before long, bishops were given judicial functions in their own cities, gradually taking over other secular activities; some joined the bureaucrats at the emperor's court, an ideal position from which to influence the course of events. Constantine himself liked to be seen not only as the representative on earth of the Christian God, but also as "bishop extraordinary"[17] (an enigmatic expression that can also mean "bishop of those outside the church" or "bishop for external affairs"). He liked to be seen as the patron of a church he intended to shower with favors and raise to a privileged position. His summoning of the council of Nicaea in 325 was an important step toward consolidating the place of Christianity and establishing orthodoxy within the church, two elements essential to his personal prestige. In Christianity thus promoted by Constantine the empire had found a new religious cement. To the old ritualistic religion, a new formal clause was added: If the displeasure of God and the resulting threat to the maintenance of the empire were to be avoided, not only neglect of ceremonies but also infringements on doctrinal conformity had to be ruled out.

Toward Establishment

Thus the fourth-century empire saw a dramatic shift of religious allegiance and a heavy swing toward Christianity. Christianity first became a licit religion, then favored, and finally recognized as the official religion of the Roman Empire. Except for a brief spell under Julian "the Apostate" (361–363) and his attempt to restore polytheism under the name of Hellenism, and in spite of retarding factors due to the Arian tendencies of emperors between 337 and 378 and to difficult dealings with the Donatists, the impulse given by Constantine prevailed and

---

17. Eusebius, *Life of Constantine* IV. 24, in NPNF 2nd Series, vol. 1.

Christianity experienced an almost steady progress through the century. Victories and other happy events that used to be traced to the protection of the ancient gods were now attributed to the Christian God's assistance and served as sanction of the true faith. Imperial propaganda invited people to receive baptism. The cross was brandished on all possible public occasions. In all this it was seldom easy to discern between religious and political motives.

After defeating Licinius and founding Constantinople—the "New Rome"—in 324 on the site of ancient Byzantium, and now sole master of the empire, Constantine went on to conquer hearts in the eastern provinces. That move meant the grafting of a highly Christianized region, especially Asia Minor, onto an empire that, otherwise, remained generally and covertly "pagan" in many ways. Constantine was in for a shock. He discovered that the East was torn apart by theological bickering that had flourished even through the years of persecution. Immediately he felt that something had to be done to appease God's anger at such discord in his church and to soothe his own anxiety concerning the unity of his domain. So he called the bishops together at Nicaea and put the imperial purse at their disposal to allow them to attend the council.

Two policies of Constantine were continued by Constantius II (337–361). Along with purges of pagans in the administration, sacrifices and oracles were prohibited, and an increasing number of Christians were appointed consuls and praetorian prefects. The established Roman religion was indeed under siege, a fact that was to be graphically underscored by the removal of the Altar of Victory from the Senate in 382.

Ultimately, the so-called triumph of Christianity took place in three stages: the rapid growth from 260 to 302, Constantine's conversion in 312, and the reign of Theodosius I (378–395). With the latter, Christianity became legally enforced. Paganism and heresy suffered repression; deviationists were submitted to coercion; exclusiveness and intolerance triumphed. Understanding himself as chosen by God, Theodosius reigned at the head of a Christian state, with the bishops administering an established church. Not all Christians were happy with this new prosperity. The birth of monasticism coincided with the time when church and state were becoming integrated. In that situation monks rose to lodge a silent protest against this process, unable to reconcile themselves with the fact that, in the words of Jerome, "after it came to Christian rulers (the church) became greater in power and riches but inferior in virtues."[18] (See chapter 7.)

Pro-Christian Legislation

Imperial legislation, most of which is preserved in the Theodosian Code published in 438 and later in the Code of Justinian, was to reflect this new situation. It openly favored Christians with preferential treatment, often at the expense of others. Admittedly, allowance must be made for differences between East and West. Reviving Diocletian's experiment, the empire was divided in 364 and became definitively split in 395; relations between church and state took on different styles in Rome and in Constantinople (see below). But religious imperial legislation affected both parts equally. The certain parity that Constantine had observed between paganism and Christianity was definitely abandoned by Gratian (ca. 379), who, under the influence of Ambrose, bishop of Milan, tipped the balance in favor of Christianity. The process of Christianization had then reached a point of no return. In 380 Theodosius enjoined his subjects to profess the Catholic religion in its orthodox form embodied in Damasus of Rome and Peter of Alexandria. The findings of the second ecumenical council (Constantinople 381) were given the force of imperial law.

After sacrifices had been generally stopped, paganism itself, in the wake of the shock created by Julian's attempt to restore it, was prohibited in 391/392. The prohibition affected the oracle of Delphi, the games at Olympia, the mysteries at Eleusis. It also affected the conservative Rome. In Alexandria the temple of Sarapis was demolished, the peak of antipagan vandalism. Similar destruction took place in Apamea, Gaza, and other places. Antiheretical legislation reached its culminating point in 392 and from then on citizenship and orthodoxy fell together. Non-Christians became outlaws around 407 and in 428 Theodosius II declared heresy to be a crime. All pagan rites were prohibited in 451. Justinian (527–565) topped up the development by imitating Theodosius and giving to the canons of the first four ecumenical

---

18. Jerome, *Vita Malchi,* in PL 23:53.

councils force of imperial law. Religious freedom, so liberally proclaimed in 313,[19] became a thing of the past.

Jews were struck by various civil penalties although Theodosius's
policy toward the Jews was generally more equitable than the behavior
of many bishops. Ambrose, for example, stopped the emperor from
forcing the local bishop to reconstruct the synagogue of Callinicum on
the Euphrates burned by the Christian mob, also responsible for the
destruction of a Gnostic sanctuary. The Jews enjoyed only limited toleration, their legal status gradually worsened, but their religious worship was never prohibited.

The fall of the western empire in 476 did not alter the situation
thus created in the whole empire. For its part, western Europe was to
inherit a heavily mortgaged state of justice along with various penalties
affecting things non-Christian, now liable to curtailment of all sorts.
After such developments it would be the permanent task of the post-
Constantinian church to reaffirm in a credible manner its actual links
with the church of martyrdom and persecution, links that oppressed dis-
sident groups were well placed to claim. It also became clear that to
destroy temples did not always mean to eradicate the gods; fertility rites
continued as well as the popular concern with the peace of the gods.

Christianity and the Barbarian Kingdoms

The Germanic invaders who, in the later fourth and fifth centuries, had settled within the imperial frontiers of the western provinces
gradually were led to create their own kingdoms on Roman soil. These
were often seen as so many parts of the empire. With the collapse of the
western empire, which in many respects had rather the appearance of a
soft-landing fall, Christianity was presented with new opportunities; it
was now called on to play a creative role in the shaping of the new Germanic societies, otherwise generally committed to maintain *romanitas*.
Since the empire had become Christian before fading out, it can be said
that Christianity was both heir and bequest of the moribund empire.

Roman aristocracy had at last rallied to Christianity in the 430s; in

---

19. "No one whosoever should be denied the liberty to follow either the religion
of the Christians or any other religion which he personally feels best suited to himself,"
proclaimed the "Edict of Milan" in 313. See Stevenson, *A New Eusebius,* p. 284.

the end social and legal pressure allied with authentic conversions to bring about a religiously unanimous society. In that society were found increasing numbers of aristocratic Christians conversant with late Roman learning and thought. Thanks to them a continued interest in secular thought and letters among Christians was to be assured in spite of a persisting suspicion of antagonism between Christianity and classical secular culture (not a few considered teaching grammar a pagan affair!). Frequently made bishops, those aristocrats saw their inherited culture as an integral part of their Christianity and often turned their households into centers of education. To the "barbarian heretic" (from the reign of Constantius II, 337–361, most barbarians who had converted, mainly the Goths and their fellow tribes, had joined Arian Christianity, owing to the mission of a convert Goth, Ulfilas, ordained bishop by Eusebius of Nicomedia) this is what they now had to offer: classical learning and Christian faith in its orthodox dress. A new beginning seemed to dawn with the conversion of Clovis and the Franks (496) to Catholic Christianity. The missionary activity of monks intensified in the 500s, with monastic communities now playing a significant role as centers of learning along with episcopal households. By then and for good, Christianity ceased to be limited to the cities around the Mediterranean and turned to the "outer barbarians" across the Roman frontier (see further chapter 10).

Church and Empire

The establishment of Christianity as official religion, completed under Theodosius I, took different forms in the two halves of the empire. Since Constantine had become ruler of the West before he converted, there he followed patterns of behavior set by his pagan predecessors. He remained "supreme pontiff," as did his immediate successors, continuing public support of the ancient cults and staffing the priestly colleges. But in the eastern provinces where Christianity was more solidly implanted and to which he came after his conversion, traditional cults were eagerly discouraged. There Constantine and, after him, Constantius and Theodosius followed the consistent policy of substituting Christianity for the ousted cults. In both East and West financial aid was made available to Christian charitable activities and for the construction of churches all over the empire but especially in Palestine. Henceforth heretics and dissenters were roughly dealt with.

In the centuries after Constantine, more Christians were persecuted as heretics than had been persecuted as Christians by the pagans.[20]

Emperors and Divine Providence

The historian Eusebius hailed the reign of Constantine as the culmination of human history foretold by ancient prophets. Philo had already praised Augustus as the godly monarch who had brought peace to the world; similarly, Eusebius acclaimed Constantine himself as the inspired instrument of God's designs, almost as a god among humans. On this point, a century later, Augustine initially concurred. Starting with Constantine, emperors had recognized their role in the growth of Christianity and given their sanction to its universal mission; they had understood that the state is there to serve God's plan and the church; they were willing to listen to bishops, who now had stepped into the role of philosophers of old.

However, Augustine was gradually led to distance himself from Eusebius's lofty views. The sack of Rome by Alaric and his Visigoths in 410 shook the euphoria of Christian times that had characterized Theodosius's reign and bewildered all subjects of the empire. Had not recent events demonstrated what calamities can result from the neglect of the ancient gods? Augustine wrote his *City of God* precisely to refute the idea that the crumbling of the empire was due to the termination of the worship of ancestral gods, and to reassure those Christians baffled by a Providence that allowed a Christian empire to suffer such reverses of fortune. Emperors, Christian or not, could not make up for the fragility of all human governments. Augustine went further by noting that far from being the cause of the present misfortunes, Christianity alone could safeguard the best traditions of Hellenism and save the empire from total annihilation. This was the level at which emperors could help.

Both Eusebius and Augustine were taking leave from a view of the totally irrelevant role of emperors in the life of the church that went back to Tertullian and had been taken over by Donatus when he asked: "What has the emperor to do with the church?" According to that bygone view, a

---

20. Stated by G. Arnold in 1688 as quoted by P. Brown, *Religion and Society in the Age of Augustine.* London: Faber & Faber, 1972, p. 243.

"Christian emperor" was a contradiction in terms; governments, pagan or Christian, were good only to make martyrs. After Eusebius and Augustine, only a few people entertained an entirely defeatist alternative—the apocalyptic belief in an imminent end that rendered any reflection on fleeting human institutions futile.

Empire and Theology

Because he saw a Christian empire as the fulfillment of ancient prophecies, Eusebius was ready to develop a somewhat uncritical "political theology." He considered the imperial institution a "sacred monarchy," following the Hellenistic theories of kingship in which an earthly monarchy was a copy of the divine kingship, and the monarch the viceroy of God. According to Eusebius, empire and church, both universal in intention, are like two copies or images of the divine rule and both tend toward identification. Byzantium was to illustrate that absence of distinction between church and state; at a minimum, political institutions were expected to help achieve the right—that is, Christian—order in the world.

After the shattering of the "Theodosian euphoria" and "mirage,"[21] which he had shared for a time, Augustine rejected the prophetic interpretation of Roman history. He came to see as a delusion the very idea of a Christian empire functioning as God's instrument for realizing his salvific plan. The sacral pretensions of the empire and of all political institutions were accordingly deflated and their function restricted to a negative one: merely that of minimizing disorder, of keeping sin and the wicked in check. Human society and the church itself were ever to remain a mixture of "two cities." No political society could claim to be an image of the heavenly Jerusalem. Indeed, the Roman Empire was neither sacred nor diabolical; religiously it was a neutral entity, home of a fundamental ambivalence. The value of human institutions was measured by the piety or impiety of their members and leaders. Augustine refused to forget that present-day emperors were and remained the successors of the persecutors. It is a painful paradox that, in spite of his critical view of the state, Augustine was willing in the end to endorse the government's coercive measures against the Donatists.

---

21. R. A. Markus, *Saeculum: History and Society in the Theology of St. Augustine*. New York: Cambridge University Press, 1988, pp. 29, 52.

Augustine's position grew out of the Roman republican tradition, which, contrary to the Hellenistic theories, was not inclined to develop a notion of the emperor as God's viceroy. For him political authority had its own autonomy,[22] although its exercise remained a matter of personal concern. The way it was exercised alone was able to legitimize power.

Throne and Altar in the West

The relationship between state and church in the West evolved out of the memory of emperors as potential persecutors. From the time of Constantine, throne and altar were integrated realities, yet they remained two distinct powers. It was held that the state ought to be brought to serve the church, in that the state was not different from any other finite reality, subordinated to transcendent goals. A radical difference was maintained between the Christ-founded church and the God-ordained empire, a difference based in a theology of two orders (natural and supernatural) and soon to result, with Pope Gelasius in 494, in the theory of two powers. In secular matters bishops should obey the sovereign, in spiritual matters even emperors must submit to the judgment of bishops. The powerful bishop of Milan, Ambrose, was adamant that the emperor is in the church, not above it. That is why the sovereign, not exactly conceived of as God's viceroy as in the East, could be judged and corrected by the prophet/pope when his behavior threatened the interests of the church. In a real sense the church was in the position to inflect the state and tended to absorb the state, a view that was to be bequeathed to medieval Europe. The forged document called the "donation of Constantine" went so far as to claim that rulers themselves received their authority through Peter, who thus combined in his person all temporal and spiritual power.

Rise of Bishops and Popes

As Christianity gradually took root in cities, a "new style of urban leadership"[23] emerged. The traditional "notables," with their acquired

---

22. Ibid.

23. P. Brown, *Power and Persuasion in Late Antiquity*. Madison, Wis.: University of Wisconsin Press, 1992, p. 77.

power, superior education, and religious conformism, woke up in the fourth century to see their role challenged by the bishops, who, respected by the imperial powers, not only represented the interests of "a newly formed urban grouping,"[24] the local Christian congregation, but particularly took to heart the care of the poor for whom the state did so little. Step by step the bishops became the "major urban patrons"[25] and outflanked the traditional leadership of the notables who, concerned to bring honor to themselves, were willing to pay for public games but saw no advantage in providing welfare for the poor and destitute, slaves, and women. Ambrose, Augustine, and Theodoret exemplified the new form of authority that often went far beyond the merely religious sphere. Bishops received the powers of civil magistrates from Constantine, generally administrated justice within their community, and ran their own courts. They were in a position to coordinate the secular and religious aspects of their people's lives.

At the level of the empire it was not self-evident at the start that the bishop of Rome would obtain unquestioned primacy among patriarchs and bishops; indeed, the rise of the papacy did not follow a straight line. The pope kept a noticeable distance from the first ecumenical councils, which all met in the eastern part of the empire; he had a limited impact on them. Nevertheless, it was always recognized that Rome had been the see of Peter and had seen the martyrdom of both Peter and Paul, in addition to being the original center of the empire. That was reason enough to show regard for the Roman see. By 180 Rome enjoyed some kind of primacy and the writings of Irenaeus clearly indicate a deference to Rome when orientation in doctrine and practice was sought. Cyprian, around 250, equally looked to Rome, although he felt justified in picking and choosing among the directives that were reaching North Africa. When an eastern synod in 271 wanted to depose the bishop of Antioch Paul of Samosata, who was suspected of heresy, Emperor Aurelian rejected the demand, indicating that the cause was to be handled by the bishop of Rome with his Italian synod. In the West, nascent papal ideology was increasingly to curtail the religious status of the emperor. Over against the Byzantine theory of Constantine's "transfer of the empire" to Constantinople, which Byzantine

---

24. Ibid.
25. Ibid., p. 101.

circles thought should make the latter the head of Christendom, religious Rome endured and received wide consideration. It seems that representatives of the Roman church signed the acts of the council of Nicaea (325) before all other bishops. Even the council of Constantinople (381) declared that the "new Rome" should have primacy of honor only after the bishop of Rome, very much to the chagrin of Alexandria. In the following year a council at Rome justified this high position of Rome, saying that it rested not on the statements of synods but on Christ's words ("Tu es Petrus") and on the Roman martyrdom of Peter and Paul. Finally, the Roman primacy was formally recognized under Valentinian III in 448 and fully expounded and exercised by Leo the Great around the time of the council of Chalcedon in 451. In time the papacy gave up links with Constantinople and threw its lot with the West, taking over much of the former pomp and pageantry of Roman emperorship along with spiritual authority. With such an evolution, alienation between Rome and Constantinople was almost fated to grow.

Patriarch and Emperor in the East

Due to the exalted notion attached to the person of the emperor, which Eusebius had promoted in the East, the Byzantine empire (330 on) did not quite follow the path of the western half concerning the relationship between church and state. If, in the fragmented West further weakened by the imperial collapse of 476, the tendency was that the state should serve the church, the opposite tendency was observed in the prosperous East, where it was expected that the church be answerable to and serve the state. Here the state embodied the formidable legacy of Theodosius the Great and was more markedly Christian. God was seen as the Emperor of Heaven, and the emperor as God on earth; at least he was God's image and his rule reflected the superior kingship of God. So the person of the emperor was quite at the center of life both civic and religious, the very copy of the Father and his viceroy, guiding his people to their ultimate end. Constantine himself, though an eminent Christian emperor, could not be deified at his death, but he came as close as possible to being declared a god. He was made a saint, equal to the apostles as the thirteenth of them.

A theory of "two powers" was never welcome in Byzantium. There was *one power,* concentrated in the person of the monarch, who had priestly character and cared for both the temporal and the spiritual well-being of his subjects. When in 404 Arcadius deposed John Chrysostom from the see of Constantinople, nothing was perceived as abnormal in an emperor deposing a patriarch. The reverse would have been inconceivable. Never did a patriarch of Constantinople excommunicate an emperor. Typically, Emperor Anastasius in 514 retorted to the pope's urge: "You may thwart me, Reverend Sir; you may insult me: but you may not command me."[26] In the battle over images (726–787), the emperors' overriding of the ecclesiastical authorities was questioned only by the monkish party; the patriarch himself had to be satisfied with being the tool in the hands of the emperor, who tended to combine both secular and spiritual power in his own person.

Eusebius's lofty view of the imperial office became full reality in the person of Justinian (527–565): one empire, one church, both led by one emperor. The temptation of "Byzantinism" (inaptly termed "Caesaropapism") was obvious: to dominate the church, to render it subservient to the state and to its sacred ruler. The two institutions did more than exist in harmony. They were coterminous and in many ways they were one and the same. The emperor's interference in church matters and his practical jurisdiction, though sometimes criticized, were not really perceived as irregular. They were grounded in the fact that boundaries between kingship and priesthood were conflated in the person of the emperor, as the borderline between empire and kingdom of God also was. The artistic conventions of the day reveal the sacred character of the imperial office: Byzantine mosaics regularly associate the majesty of the monarch with the kingly attributes of Christ himself, in whose divine power he shares and from whom he directly receives his authority.

A Landmark: The Closing of the Academy

In 529, significantly the very year Benedict of Nursia founded a monastery at Monte Cassino, another momentous event took place, equally filled with religious and intellectual meaning—the closing of the Platonist Academy in Athens by Justinian. The symbolism of the gesture was pregnant. It meant either that the ancient learning was superseded by Christianity, or that it was absorbed by it. In the disap-

---

26. Quoted in Brown, *The World of Late Antiquity*, p. 148.

pearance of the Academy the last elements of paganism in the form of Hellenism were ousted and the last champion of religious tolerance was hunted down. Pagans were forbidden to teach. Not merely pagan rites, but pagan beliefs as well were banned. Paganism then had to be silent or go underground or branch out. Somehow it survived until modern times. Platonists sought refuge in northern Mesopotamia before, it is thought, meeting in the eighth century the Arab scholars of Baghdad, who thus became the guardians of Greek philosophy through the Middle Ages. A Platonist Academy reappeared in Florence in 1430.

READINGS

| N. H. Baynes | *Constantine the Great and the Christian Church.* London: Oxford University Press, 1972. |

P. Brown — *Power and Persuasion in Late Antiquity.* Madison, Wis.: University of Wisconsin Press, 1992.

P. Chuvin — *Chronique des derniers païens.* Paris: Fayard, 1991. (Abridged English Translation, *A Chronicle of the Last Pagans.* Cambridge, Mass.: Harvard University Press, 1990.)

F. Dvornik — *Early Christian and Byzantine Political Philosophy,* 2 vols. Washington: Dumbarton Oaks, 1966.

E. Ferguson, ed. — *Church and State in the Early Church.* New York: Garland, 1993.

W. H. C. Frend — *Martyrdom and Persecution in the Early Church.* Oxford: Blackwell, 1967.

R. M. Grant — *Eusebius as Church Historian.* Oxford: Clarendon Press, 1980.

J. N. Hillgarth, ed. — *Christianity and Paganism 350–700: The Conversion of Western Europe.* Philadelphia: University of Pennsylvania Press, 1986.

A. H. M. Jones — *The Later Roman Empire 284–602: A Social, Economic and Administrative Survey,* 2 vols. Norman: University of Oklahoma Press, 1964.

N. Q. King — *The Emperor Theodosius and the Establishment of Christianity.* London: SCM Press, 1961.

R. A. Markus — *Saeculum: History and Society in the Theology of Saint Augustine.* New York: Cambridge University Press, 1988.

H. Musurillo — *The Acts of the Christian Martyrs.* Oxford: Clarendon Press, 1972.

J. Neusner and
E. S. Frerichs, eds.
"To See Ourselves as Others See Us": Christians, Jews and "Others" in Late Antiquity. Chico, Calif.: Scholars Press, 1985.

S. Runciman
The Byzantine Theocracy. New York: Cambridge University Press, 1977.

R. Stark
The Rise of Christianity: A Sociologist Reconsiders History. Princeton: Princeton University Press, 1996.

R. Turcan
"Le culte impérial au IIIe siècle." ANRW II.16.2 (1978): 996–1084.

7

The Practice of Christian Life (100–600)

Living in the expectation of the imminent end of this world, the earliest Christian community had little inclination to develop a comprehensive moral code that would go beyond the factual teachings of the Sermon on the Mount and articulate theoretically the command of love of God and neighbor. Discipline and life-style of the community just took over contemporary standards of morality found in Judaism and popular philosophy, but gave them a fresh impulse and wider currency. That process might surprise today, for Christian morality and secular culture no longer overlap to the same extent. The injunction to be kind to each other, then known to the elites, is today far from being self-evident to the masses and rather often goes against people's everyday maxims.

Jewish-Christian Beginnings

Perhaps ethical teachings were not regarded by the earliest Christians as the center of the gospel. At any event, they became increasingly important. As the eschatological tension receded, an ethic of transition had to give way to one of indefinite duration more receptive to ideas long practiced by Jews imbued with Old Testament prophecy and Jewish wisdom and living in a Greco-Roman society. The writings of around 100 that can be called "Jewish-Christian" showed some emphasis on moral codes derived from the Hellenistic synagogue, such as doctrine of the "two ways" (one of life, one of death), lists of virtues and vices, almsgiving and charitable activities, and a view of the substance of the Old Testament law as identical with the moral law of nature. Gradually moving to the center of Christian practice, those elements were destined to act as a ferment in pagan society.

Roman and Christian Mores

As Christianity moved into the Roman world, it was of necessity confronted with Roman mores. Over against the Gnostic options for extreme asceticism or lax immoralism, and the Gnostic and Marcionite rejection of the Old Testament law, Christianity held to its Jewish legacy, combining it with the conventional notions current in Greco-Roman moral teachings.

At their best, Roman mores were penetrated by Stoic, Cynic, and Middle Platonist views. Those philosophical circles, a minority elite, were noted for their high standards of morality. They were in tension with the situation fostered by traditional cults, which displayed little interest in shaping the behavior of their adherents or in giving divine sanction to morality. It is significant that the concept of "conversion" belonged then to the philosophical, not to the religious, context. One converted to philosophy, that is, to a life devoted to the search for and the doing of good.

The philosophical ethic was encapsulated in Greek natural-law thinking and the sages' ideal of self-sufficiency. While the social sense of responsibility and community was clearly not its strength, it did provide individuals with directions for a reasonable and decent, frugal and disciplined way of life.

When Justin and Clement stated that Christianity was compatible with much of Greco-Roman life and culture, they first of all had in mind the life recommended by contemporary moralists. To that life-style Tertullian himself insisted that Christians were not a menace; on the contrary, they gladly shared with Romans all legitimate social activities and moral ideals. As Origen thought, in the end a philosophy was ranked according to its "power to change men from evil."[1]

Some Roman activities, however, were not easily compatible with Christian rules. They had to be rejected—occupations that had to do with idolatry and magic, with killing and bloodshed, with sexual immorality. Without globally repudiating social participation, Christians were invited to discern what amounted to abuses in society.

---

1. C. Cels. 1.64; 8.76.

A New Ethos

Once those abuses had been censored, Christians were not concerned with changing the social system they lived in; rather conservative as to the social order, they were concerned with mitigating its harshness and with furthering its moral transformation. To be sure, "Christianity altered profoundly the moral texture of the Roman world,"[2] but almost without innovation. Indeed, Christianity did not try to develop "its own particular way of doing everything."[3] By correlating Christian insights with classical ideals, Christianity offered as it were a new ethos rather than propounding a new ethic. It invested a commonly praised life-style with strong convictions and a prophetic mark; that way of living was now proclaimed to be God's revealed will. Apologists claimed (and in this they were not contradicted) that Christians needed only their simplest parables and directives in order to live according to the best maxims of ancient moralists. The call to imitate Jesus of Nazareth would encompass those maxims and then indefinitely more. It welcomed and redirected moral precepts preached by pagan philosophers, such as the equality of all before nature and God (in principle, for slavery was left out of consideration), the love of neighbor and the Golden Rule, the contempt for wealth and power, the advocacy of temperance and chastity. Yet it went further than philosophers in its concern for the poor and the weak—a care quite alien to the pagan world—and in its exacting prescriptions in the realm of sexual ethics. Altogether a change in the moral sensibilities of the masses gradually took place and the "rapid democratization of the philosophers' upper-class counter-culture by the leaders of the Christian church"[4] can be counted as a real revolution in the ancient world.

Many questions of moral conduct remained open questions for Christians in those centuries. A variety of solutions were advanced and practiced, for example, as regards the problem of reconciling riches with Christian life, the justice or lack thereof of owning property, the

---

2. P. Brown in P. Veyne, ed., *A History of Private Life*, vol. 1. Cambridge, Mass.: Harvard University Press, 1987, p. 260.

3. R. MacMullen, *Christianizing the Roman Empire*. New Haven: Yale University Press, 1984, p. 74.

4. P. Brown in Veyne, ed., *A History of Private Life*, p. 251.

legitimacy of holding public office. The variety of solutions increased over time, as did the stress on the responsibility of the rich and the powerful to abolish social injustice and abuses.

Public Life

Christian writers of the second and third centuries were virtually unanimous in their recommendation to obey civil authorities, even to pray for them. If they were reluctant to see Christians hold office in civil government, the reason was not a suspicion of government per se but rather because the exercise of a civil office was regularly linked with the risk of spilling blood. For the same reason, military service and participation in war were rejected until the fourth century, often leading to accusations of disloyalty.

Slavery was not condemned, yet moral entreaties, from Paul on, succeeded in softening its practice. Shaken in the second century but again blossoming in the third through fifth centuries, slavery at last receded only in the ninth century when serfdom appeared.

The Christian attitude toward public cults was intransigent and brought them persecution and harassment. Theater, games of all sorts, and baths (not only mixed baths) were discouraged although people generally ignored the church's disapproval in those matters and were regularly criticized by preachers.

Christian leaders and writers had little to say about civic virtues beyond "obey authorities" and "pay your taxes." Christians who happened to take up imperial service were enjoined, in a prevailingly negative manner, not to oppress widows and orphans, not to pervert justice, not to indulge in extortion. However, the prevailing sentiment seemed to be that, having entered public service and having thus committed oneself to a less than noble activity, indeed to a sinful life, one might as well go all the way and sin mightily. It remains that Christianity was generally outspoken in its criticism of misuse of power, its fight against social injustice, and its struggle to break down social barriers.

As time passed, involvement in political life could no longer be forbidden. It became ever more evident that "the nature and exercise of worldly power are not matters so secular as to be of no concern to the people of God";[5] that "politics cannot be exempt from moral judgments, and indeed has to be treated as a branch of ethics";[6] that "religion itself is abused if its function becomes that of providing an ultimate legitimization for whatever be the current order."[7]

Private Life

Major transformations to moral life introduced by Christianity affected the private sphere. Made into a sacrament, marriage was held in high esteem, although some expressed such esteem only grudgingly. Celibacy and virginity were higher. The church encountered serious difficulties in its efforts to change accepted moral standards in sexual matters. It kept condemning absolutely homosexuality, adultery, incest (marriage of close kin), and abortion, but had to temporize concerning divorce. For its part, imperial legislation through the mid-sixth century grew more rigorous. Family structures remained untouched by Christianity. But if women, children, and slaves were enjoined subordination, kindness toward them was so forcefully preached that some changes ensued. Exposure of children, common in Roman society, gave occasion for extra care and charitable activities. Prostitution was condemned as well as fornication, but prostitutes were helped and often rescued.

For followers of Jesus the poor, property, and riches raised an obvious dilemma. Romans considered wealth a morally indifferent matter whose loss had to be borne with equanimity; they showed no special concern for the "poor," feeling responsibility only to the family and the city. For Christians riches were a positive handicap to salvation, especially when accompanied by greed. Detachment toward riches was commended and it was a good thing to "give them all to the poor" (Mk 10:17–30), who enjoyed God's particular favor. Yet a change of attitude toward riches gradually took place, toning down the rigorist criticism of property encountered in many quarters. Clement of Alexandria cautioned against too literal an interpretation of the gospel's saying, for wealth is also a source of obligation and can be put to good use in works of mercy. Thus

---

5. H. Chadwick in J. H. Burns, ed., *The Cambridge History of Medieval Thought c. 350–c. 1450.* New York: Cambridge University Press, 1988, pp. 19–20.
6. Ibid.
7. Ibid.

an "effective compensation"[8] had to balance the possession of riches. Around 250, the Roman community was, on a regular basis, taking care of some 1,500 persons in distress, showing that such compensation was in fact taking place. Reflecting on that situation, Emperor Julian had to concede that Christians were putting pagans to shame. Hence Christian moralists will ever be disturbed at the sight of a "nonprofit organization" such as the church succumbing to the temptations of property and riches. Nevertheless, while sailing far from the high seas of the primitive community's ideals, Christianity contributed to lifting the opprobrium from poverty and to promoting the model of a real sharing of goods. Concretely, the insistence on almsgiving, the substitute "for the ancient competitive and conspicuous works of public munificence,"[9] was intended to foster an effective redistribution of wealth.

Moral Failure of the Church?

Throughout the period we are considering, Christians remained the object of the preachers' criticisms as to the laxity of their sexual morals, their addiction to games, their oppression of the poor. Violence in society did not seem to diminish nor the general level of morals to rise. In opposition to an idealized view of Christian beginnings and to the utopian image of blessed first centuries, the question has been raised as to the failure of the church, especially in the period following the second and third centuries. After Christianity became the religion of the majority in the empire, moral perfection was clearly not achieved. Rather, general patterns of conduct seem to have remained static, even to have sunk in some respects, although moral exhortation took place with far more vigor and reached a much wider audience. Certainly, Christianity did not change human nature. The standards preached from the pulpit were perhaps too high and the rigor of penance was too exacting. Codes initially devised for a small, closed society became obsolete or inexpedient when extended to the masses. If one adds that city life seems to have deteriorated after the third century, one can understand that the masses grew impervious to disheartening demands.

---

8. M. Hengel, *Property and Riches in the Early Church*. Philadelphia: Fortress Press, 1974, pp. 60–73.

9. R. A. Markus, *The End of Ancient Christianity*. New York: Cambridge University Press, 1990, p. 127.

In those circumstances, much of the high quality of moral achievement had to emigrate from the general society and find a more adequate abode in monastic houses. The masses were only too happy to delegate to monks the practice of virtue and the fulfillment of evangelical demands. In time, a double standard of morality, one for the masses and one for the ascetic "athletes," threatened to obtain.

Church Life

The reasons one found to become a Christian in the second and third centuries, when it was a question of joining a minority group, varied from the reasons appealed to from the fourth century on, when Christianity became the religion of the majority. However, an option for the good life was regularly implied in conversion. The synagogue itself had been described by Philo as a school for training in a life according to God's law—so also the church in many respects. It resembled philosophical groupings that promoted upright life. But an additional element made the church distinctive—the converts turned also to a new kind of worship. The church was a cultic gathering, characterized by its intense relationship to Jesus Christ as Son of God and Savior.

Church Rituals

Most early Christian rites can best be understood as echoes of Jewish rituals from which they evolved, although scholars disagree on the extent of such dependence or tend to emphasize how little we know of first-century synagogue liturgy.[10] Aside from New Testament accounts, we can glimpse the origins and evolution of early Christian worship from ancient church orders such as the *Didache* (ca. 90), Hippolytus's *Apostolic Tradition* (ca. 200), the *Didascalia* (ca. 230), the *Apostolic Church Order* (ca. 300), and the *Apostolic Constitutions* (ca. 380), most of them recovered in the nineteenth century, and from occasional references in early writers. They all show important borrowings from the synagogue while incorporating a growing number of elements from pagan culture, the whole invested now with novel intentions.

---

10. P. F. Bradshaw, *The Search for the Origins of Christian Worship*. New York: Oxford University Press, 1992, pp. 17–24.

If we disregard significant differences of time and place, we can say that initiation into the church basically took place in two stages. After an extensive period of moral training, testing, and instruction, an adult candidate (infants were baptized from the late second century only) was baptized during the Easter festival. Baptism was a ceremonial bath (also called "enlightenment": *photismos*) symbolizing the participation in the death and resurrection of Christ. Its ritual included the renunciation of demonic powers, a cleansing by water accompanied by a profession of faith in the triune God (or in Jesus Christ), and anointing as signs both of cleansing and of identification with Christ the "Anointed" through reception of his Spirit. (Public baths knew that double use of oil, for its cleansing virtue and for its good scent.) The anointing that was linked to the conferral of the Spirit gradually developed into "confirmation." Because emphasis was increasingly put on cleansing and the remission of all sins by baptism, candidates tended to put off baptism until the end of life, as did Constantine himself. That delaying was critically debated in the fourth century.

Having been baptized, a candidate could now join the community for the Lord's Supper (*eucharistia*: thanksgiving), a ritual more and more elaborate, made up of readings from scripture with interpretation, prayers, reconciliation, corporate decisions, collection for the needy. The Eucharist itself consisted of a sacramental meal using the bread and wine common at the Jewish Passover, but conceived as a memorial of thanksgiving for the saving sacrifice of Jesus Christ, and the appropriation of divine life signified by the symbolic reception of the Body and Blood of Christ. Sometimes common meals *(agape)* were arranged by richer members of the group and served as one of the many charitable activities on behalf of the more vulnerable members of society.

Liturgical Cycle

The Easter festival was the term of the initiation process and constituted the high point of the liturgical year (*leitourgia:* public worship), commemorating the passion, death, and resurrection of the Savior; it was reenacted in the worship of each Sunday, the Lord's Day. Gradually a cycle of festivities developed around Easter: Lent with its fasting, Ascension, and Pentecost. It is only from the fourth century that a second cycle evolved around Christmas, with Advent and Epiphany,

superimposed on pagan midwinter festivals (such as the Mithraic festival of the "unconquered sun god"). In that manner the entire civil year
was sacralized and its parts related to the history of salvation.

The determinaion of the date of Easter around the spring equinox
gave rise to controversy from the second century. The Jews celebrated
Passover on the fourteenth day of the month Nisan; the gospels reflect
that custom. So the date of Easter first fell with the fourteenth day
(*quartodecima dies*) of the moon ending the paschal fast, whatever day
of the week it could be, and in that manner Easter kept the character of
Passover. Churches in Asia Minor were holding to this tradition, but the
other churches, especially in Alexandria and Rome, preferred to end
the paschal fast on the Lord's Day, the Sunday following the first full
moon of the spring equinox. Those divergences resulted in the Paschal
or Quartodeciman controversy at the end of which the latter view
achieved dominance, thereby rendering it more difficult for pagans to
mistake Christians for Jews.

Church Prayer

The church inherited from Judaism a unique treasure in the
Psalms. In the temple liturgy the singing of psalms was accompanied
by musical instruments and dancing; but not so in the synagogue,
whose practice the church took over. So psalms and hymnic passages
of scripture were chanted unaccompanied (psalmody). Instruments
were viewed as associated with pagan temples and their "immorality"
and were firmly opposed by the church in the third and fourth centuries.
Only in the Middle Ages were they to be condoned. New Testament
hymns (e.g., the "Magnificat") and others as well (e.g., the "Odes of
Solomon") were added to the Old Testament repertoire to constitute the
church's incipient hymnology. Prayers were improvised or fixed (e.g.,
the "Gloria in Excelsis"), recited or chanted. The fourth century saw a
great blossoming in the composition of hymns (above all with Ephrem
in the East and Ambrose in the West), in the development of sacred
music, and in monastic innovations as to the formalization of prayer.
The attempt to overhaul and reorder the prayer of the church was made
by Gregory the Great (540–604), from whom, incidentally the name
"Gregorian chant" derived.

Church Organization

The structure of the earliest Christian community developed out of its liturgy and its concern to safeguard the teachings of the apostles. First modeled on the Jewish synagogue, the local congregation, made up of believers baptized by traveling apostles, was governed by a body of elders *(presbyteroi);* the elders were the first converts, put in charge of preserving the oral apostolic tradition. That body was made up of a leader at the head of teachers and readers entrusted with scripture exposition and instruction. In Gentile contexts, Paul inclined to a more charismatic church order, but especially after the death of the Twelve a fresh organization was needed and the institution of elders appeared in those places as well. From among the elders emerged the bishop as presider at the Lord's Supper and holder of the power of ordination.

By the beginning of the second century, the main ecclesiastical ministries existed, although the terminology remained fluid: elders, bishops *(episcopoi* or supervisors, sometimes synonymous with elders), deacons or servants. Bishops and deacons first had a liturgical function: to preside and help at the Lord's Supper. Soon deacons received larger functions in the service of the community. Gradually the bishop became the chief officer of the local congregation and was called "priest," while the elders were seen to share in the bishop's ministry and to conduct the liturgy with a teaching/preaching function; later they were also to be called priests. The bishop appointed or ordained deacons and elders by the laying on of hands, signifying the bestowing of a spiritual power in a hierarchical society.

Early in the second century, Ignatius of Antioch witnessed an important evolution: the development of monarchical (or, better, monepiscopal) structure whereby there was now only one bishop for a given local church. Around mid-century, prompted by the Gnostic crisis and concerned with internal unity, bishops generally took over the teaching function from the elders, thus conferring greater authority on their own office. By the end of the century Irenaeus had it that the bishops of great cities derived their authority, through an unbroken chain of succession, from the apostles themselves and were the real warrants of the original doctrine. Continuity as well as legitimization was secured by the "apostolic office." That office also included the authority for forgiveness, reconciliation, and readmission of penitents, for bishops were the lords of penance.

A lasting pattern of church organization appeared with Cyprian in 251. First, and in great part due to him, the distinction between clergy (bishops and priests) and laity became strongly emphasized, whereby exclusive authority was given to the office of the bishop (all at once priest, prophet, and teacher), the laity being reduced to a passive role. Second, Cyprian reflected the view that it is the bishops that made up the unity of the church through their mutual recognition and thanks to the ordination of each bishop by at least three neighboring bishops.

A further development resulted from the council of Nicaea in 325. Urban centers with a bishop were grouped into provinces headed by a metropolitan bishop, usually in the capital of the civil province, all linked to the main sees (called patriarchates from the sixth century on) in Jerusalem, Antioch, Alexandria, Rome, and Constantinople, with Rome gaining a clear ascendancy in the fifth century. Thus the church's outward structure reflected the civil administrative geography, often using the very same terminology for its organization (e.g., dioceses, vicars).

The elevated status of the bishops became an accomplished fact in the fourth century. They wielded considerable power within and without the church. Henceforth most teachers and theologians were to be bishops, with monks as increasingly worthy competitors; in fact, "free-floating intelligences" of the kind illustriously represented by Justin and Origen were now to be met only among monks. To express and foster dedication to their task, celibacy became a requirement. In the Latin West it was imposed on bishops first, then also on priests; in the East most bishops were to be celibate, being chosen from among monks.

In general, church ministers were qualified and responsible persons. But as could be expected, not all lived up to their ideals of compassionate leadership, morality, and goodwill. The apostles had already experienced conflicts between themselves and they had anticipated worse bickering in the future. Obviously conflicts among leaders have serious implications; at no time could the general state of the church's morality remain totally unaffected by the virtue and demeanor of its ministers. Such conflicts did take place; the centuries immediately following the peace of the church are among the most tumultuous in the entire history of Christianity. Feuding, fighting, and quarreling over theological or at times hardly theological issues plagued the ranks of church leaders at the same time that a certain relaxation caused by the "triumph" of Christianity spread over the masses.

Two important phenomena, however, ran parallel to the growing organization of the official church with its accompanying frictions, and must be dealt with for the image of concord they projected: the rise of the cult of saints among the masses and the monks' quest for perfection. Significantly, both followed on the end of persecutions, the establishment of Christianity as the religion of the empire, and the emergence of a hierarchy and power structures encapsulated in the rise of the bishops in the third century. It is thanks to those two movements that Christianity really became a mass religion.

The Cult of the Saints in the Western Mediterranean

When persecutions ceased, martyrs as well ceased to be made, at least such that would suffer at the hands of pagan perpetrators. But the bones and graves of the martyrs from the first century on remained. They early became relics and were kept in shrines, a step that deeply shocked the pagan repulsion for corpses. Multitudes gathered around martyrs' shrines and saints' graves: the poor, the sick, women, pilgrims, people from all walks of life, and, not least, bishops and teachers. Recent studies[11] have offered fresh perspectives on the cult of saints and contributed to overcoming the deep-seated contempt for this expression of "popular" piety taken by many intellectuals to be a simple replica of pagan hero worship at the service of the masses' consumption.

The fourth century abounds in discoveries of relics found in remarkable numbers. Reports on their transfer and installation are plenty. Bishops, especially in the western Mediterranean and in Gaul, were far from being disconcerted by that vogue. Because they shared ordinary people's devotion, they knew how to channel their high and awestruck emotions at the sight of those venerable remains, and to give them a theologically acceptable interpretation.

When Ambrose, a provincial governor made bishop of Milan by popular acclamation, ordered in 385 the recently discovered relics of Gervasius and Protasius to be moved into his new basilica, he knew that he had everything to gain by showing himself as a friend of the martyrs,

---

11. Particularly P. Brown in many of his works.

themselves friends of God.[12] Not only was he linking the cult of those saints to the church liturgy[13] and, more significantly, to the bygone church of the martyrs; his demonstrated proximity to the saints also held all the ingredients for increasing his personal status and enhancing his authority. Because healings and benefactions would then take place under the bishop's auspices, his leadership would be confirmed and expanded. In return, now enjoying enough prestige to really impact on society, the bishop could enjoin the rich to discharge their duty toward the poor and mobilize all in the imitation of the saints.

The cult of saints throve and shrines multiplied all around the Mediterranean from the late fourth century. It provided believers with the comforting presence of "invisible companions"[14] who, readily accessible as equal human beings, were able to dispense protection and inspiration. Martyrs' and saints' anniversaries became regular features of the church year. Growing in number, they were occasions for special celebrations, pious and some less pious, often incorporating ancient ideas in a new setting. After some time an entire cycle of festivities had developed, marking each day of the year with the name of a saint so that in the end a Christian calendar of saints emerged parallel to the official cycle of the church liturgy and was soon inserted into it as "sanctoral." Later each believer received a Christian name, linking one's identity to a saint in hope of effective mercy and perseverance. Collections of relics throughout the Middle Ages conferred on their owners (bishops, princes, notables) prestige and honor; their worth rendered their acquisition expensive and even justified less commendable actions called "sacred thefts" *(sacra furta)*.

The rise of the cult of saints is the main novel development that inflected Christian piety from the late fourth century. Paintings on the walls of the catacombs and in shrines depicted the human features of the saints as benevolent "patrons" bent on granting protection to their "clients." The cult of saints and, in its wake, hagiographical literature made everybody familiar with those intimate friends who were also, in the other world, the friends of God. Such ideal relationships retained but little

12. P. Brown, *The Making of Late Antiquity.* Cambridge, Mass.: Harvard University Press, 1978, p. 57.
13. P. Brown, *The Cult of the Saints: Its Rise and Function in Latin Christianity.* Chicago: Chicago University Press, 1981, p. 37.
14. Ibid., p. 50.

of the ancient fear and somber mood that had surrounded death. They made for poise and confidence at the frontiers of earth and heaven.

Ascetics in Syria

While western Mediterranean people gathered around martyr shrines to enjoy the blessings of the benevolent presence of invisible but intimate friends, in the East they mainly turned to holy men—ascetics and monks whom they regarded, so to speak, as symbolic martyrs, as the martyrs' substitutes or honorary martyrs. The great Antony himself was said to have used that kind of language when he was reported to have been "daily martyred by his conscience."[15] In those regions holy men rose and, awesome though they looked, assumed the role of ideal Christians.

Holy men were the ones who "minted the ideal of the saint" in society.[16] They first appeared in Syria in the fourth and fifth centuries, then in Asia Minor and Palestine. "Syria was the great province for ascetic stars,"[17] some being the spiritual offspring of the second-century encratite groups.

The Syrian style of asceticism is vividly described by Theodoret of Cyrrhus in the fifth century. The holy man lived the "life of an angel" as a hermit on the edge of a village, a wild vagrant dressed in skins and fond of striking histrionic gestures, "holding demons at bay and bending the will of God by his prayers."[18] A life of renunciation, feats of mortification, and the evidence of contact with the supernatural world attracted masses to those spiritual athletes who, like the martyrs of old, seemed to be so much on speaking terms with God. Some holy men roamed the countryside with hundreds of followers; others were quite literally nailed to one spot: Simeon the Stylite spent over forty years perched on a sixty-odd-foot column where he "held court." Crowds of villagers and pilgrims, notables and merchants ran to the holy man in search of counsel,

---

15. Life, p. 47. See Markus, *The End of Ancient Christianity,* pp. 70–72, on asceticism conceived as "vicarious martyrdom" and "bloodless martyrdom."

16. P. Brown, *Society and the Holy in Late Antiquity.* Berkeley: University of California Press, 1982, p. 109.

17. Ibid.

18. P. Brown paraphrasing Theodoret in *The World of Late Antiquity, AD 150–750.* London: Thames & Hudson, 1971, p. 102.

enlightenment, or comfort; or they called him in to the village if it was there that he was needed. They rushed to the death bed of a holy man to collect his last words of wisdom or "in the hope of snatching his body as a relic."[19]

P. Brown developed in 1971 the thesis that holy men in Syria functioned as new "patrons" in a society that was going through a crisis of leadership.[20] What people "expected of the holy man coincides with what they sought in the rural patron":[21] protection against adversities and exactors, fair arbitration of disputes, necessary favors, and a line to power. They paid court to those grave friends of God, the holy men (to bishops as well for that matter), where traditional leaders and patrons failed and were no longer in a position to help those in distress. Healings and miracles, forceful and wise advice, but also exorcisms and curses demonstrated the holy men's spiritual power in a society seeking to nurse its disruptive experiences and looking for an impartial mediator (or "charismatic ombudsman") and ideal patron. Twice since 1971 P. Brown has qualified his view of the holy man, preferring to see him first as an "accessible exemplar" of Christ-like conduct[22] and then "as a figure who, in many regions, acted as a facilitator in the transition from paganism to Christianity."[23] He could negotiate an honorable surrender of the gods and ease people's transition to Christianity. At any event, holy men had achieved their high level of power and authority through their exemplary asceticism, baffling the old prejudices in that they had no use for wealth or coercion.

The phenomenon spread to Asia Minor after the fifth century and reached ever higher layers of society. One day patriarch and emperor found reconciliation at the feet of Daniel the Stylite. The entire history of Byzantine society was to be affected by the impressive presence of the holy man. Lay piety became accustomed to the reassuring link established between a lay person and a spiritual father. However, as time passed, holy men were increasingly found

---

19. Brown, *Society and the Holy,* p. 113.

20. Ibid., pp. 103–152, esp. 115–130.

21. Ibid., p. 120.

22. P. Brown, "The Saint as Exemplar in Late Antiquity." *Representations* 2 (1983): pp. 1–25.

23. P. Brown, *Authority and the Sacred: Aspects of the Christianization of the Roman World.* New York: Cambridge University Press, 1995, p. 64.

no longer in the lofty isolation of the solitary but in the middle of organized monastic communities.

Monastic Movement Out of Egypt

The origins of organized asceticism cannot be documented with all the desirable clarity, embellished as they often are by later writers and by later ascetics eager to score a point. But certainly in the late third century monastic groups appeared in Egypt. No longer lingering on the edge of a village as in Syria, rural Egyptian (Coptic) ascetics firmly withdrew from society and yielded to the enticing appeal of the desert. Perhaps as eccentric as the Syrian holy men, they showed enough distinctive talent and discipline to launch a lasting experiment.

It is tempting to search for antecedents to Egyptian monasticism and indeed to find proto-monastic features in various groups, near and remote, that might have inspired the early Christian monks. In that respect we often find mention of the ascetic group outside Alexandria referred to as the "therapeutae" by Philo and Eusebius: Essenes and/or the Qumran community; rabbinic societies with teachings similar to those of the desert fathers; Cynic philosophers and their peculiar lifestyle; Pythagorean confraternities; competitive communes fostered by Manichaean missionaries around 280–290; even far echoes of the Buddhist *sangha*. World renouncers have always and everywhere existed. However, the determined search for predecessors of Christian monasticism runs the double risk of retrojecting well-formed Christian data back into a vague pre-Christian past and of missing the nature of the original shift of viewpoint that took place in Egyptian asceticism. External influences can be granted, but in Egypt monasticism emerged as a novel entity and took over the very features that were to give the great monastic orders of later centuries inspiration and shape. "Egypt was the cradle of monasticism. It was in Egypt that the theory and practice of the ascetic life reached its highest pitch of articulateness and sophistication."[24] From there it soon spawned around the Mediterranean.

It makes little difference whether communal (cenobitic) or solitary (eremitic or anchoretic) forms of monastic life came first. The renouncer's attitude and function in church and society always tend to give voice to a

---

24. Brown, *Society and the Holy,* p. 109.

protest against what is perceived as prevailing laxity. In the present case, to a society witnessing the rapid ascent of Christianity and its seeking of a perhaps compromising alliance with the state, to a society in which the majority of Christians, above all urban Christians, were growing tired of virtue, monks (*monachoi*: the lonely ones) offered an alternative society. They offered a form of life modeled on the community of Jesus' time, above all on the Jerusalem community depicted in Acts 4:32–35, renouncing the conventional forms of settled life (marriage, ownership). They proposed the disencumbered life of single-minded dedication to the quest for self-improvement in the presence of God.

Ascetics had already been living in caves on the edge of villages since the middle of the third century,[25] leading the way for the two great figures of Egyptian monasticism. Antony (250–356) took to the desert around 269 after applying to himself Jesus' enjoining to "follow" him. He began to lead the life of a hermit, moving ever further into the Outer Desert. A "dropout" of civilization, he was, after a while, followed by bands of disciples. The first hermits lived alone or by twos or threes in caves or in primitive shelters, supporting themselves on the produce of their handwork. At times Antony acted as "holy man," as peacemaker between rivals in rural communities, even as occasional advisor to the emperor. But it is mainly as the "father of monks" that the son of Coptic farmers stood out and was celebrated in an influential biography *(Life of Antony)* written by Athanasius. He left his mark on the church everywhere in the empire, not least in the West through the impact of his example on Augustine's conversion.

A more communal style of asceticism was initiated by a former soldier, Pachomius (292–346). His action led to the mushrooming of monasteries in the Nile valley, characterized by careful spiritual and material organization, economic self-sufficiency through manual labor, obedience to a "house-leader" and to a rule, more or less routinized prayer. At Pachomius's death a confederation of nine monasteries of men and two of women existed. Thus cells of hermits and colonies of renouncers were formed into settlements that became the great monasteries of later centuries. By 400 many thousands of monks of various groupings had settled in Egypt alone, with the Thebaid the most prolific center. The high degree of organization accounts for the remark-

25. S. Elm, *Virgins of God: The Making of Asceticism in Late Antiquity.* New York: Oxford University Press, 1994, p. 287.

able economic success of later monasteries, often turning a barren landscape into productive cultivated land.

Travelers, translators, and pilgrims made the Egyptian experiments known throughout the empire. Elements of Western monasticism developed around such personalities as Ambrose and Augustine. Alternative patterns of monasticism appeared in Gaul, England, and Ireland. Egypt also sprouted ascetic communities in Palestine whose influence again reached the West through Jerome and Rufinus, who both spent years in that area and entertained extensive correspondence with friends in Italy. But it is in Cappadocia that the Egyptian example, fertilized by the memory of Origen, caused the most noticeable developments in the ascetic life, called "philosophical life" by Basil (330–379). Bishop of Caesarea, Basil organized communities or "brotherhoods" that, each self-governing and having its own constitution, kept in close contact with church life. All surplus products and wealth were handed over as alms to the poor and the sick; moreover, monks took an active part in the liturgy in the bishop's church. Although he wrote no rules (the rules collected in the sixth century under his name are simply based on his occasional pieces concerning the ascetical way of life), Basil's influence on Byzantine monastic life endured through the centuries, especially from 550. Byzantium regularly chose its bishops from among the monks. In the eighth and ninth centuries monks actively (and victoriously) opposed the iconoclastic movement, which attempted to rid Christian piety of all pictorial representations of Christ and the saints. To the end Byzantium never was without its holy men.

Asceticism: Problems and Theories

Thus a wide variety of ascetic experiments rapidly swept the Roman world from the fourth century on. Even ascetic households were not uncommon. To the church at large, the movement raised essential questions and they were addressed quite early, for example, by Jovinian contra Jerome. Some of them concerned the extent to which evangelical counsels (as to poverty, chastity, etc.) were to be taken literally. Others had to do with the religious value of virginity and sexual renunciation; the role of self-mortification in reforming the human person; the spiritual gain of the mastery over one's will, desires, and passions; the link between training the body and training the soul, between controlling bodily energies and redirecting the heart to God. Obviously such questions concerned not only formal ascetic life but the very practice of Christian life in general. Other questions had to do with the relationship of ascetics to episcopal leadership, for the danger of a split was real. What kept the monastic movement within the church can be traced to Basil's efforts in grounding monasticism on firm connections with church life, and to the fortunate fact that both Antony and Pachomius had entertained friendly relations with Athanasius. In return, Athanasius considered the monks his best friends throughout his stormy career.

The ascetic tradition found a mystical complement and inspiration in the legacy of Origen. His spiritual commentaries on scripture, his conception of the human makeup with a Godlike spirit able to rise to the disengaged contemplation of divine realities, and his consummate speculative talent contributed much to the buttressing of ascetic theory. This legacy was picked up by congenial characters such as Evagrius of Pontus (345–399), Gregory of Nyssa (331–395), and Cassian (360–435), who were able to elaborate it for East and West. The tradition was enriched by reflections on techniques of prayer, discipline, self-grooming; on theories of moral progress; on mystical experience; on the mastery of mind over body; on ways of "terrorizing" the devils. Regularly those practices and reflections were supported by the pithy "sayings of the desert fathers" accompanying edifying legends and anecdotes, a vast reservoir of popular wisdom impregnated with spiritual zest.

Community life ended up prevailing over the life of a hermit in the monastic tradition. Various rules were crafted for monasteries, outlining a style of life that aimed to keep alive the gospel ideals and saw in the monastery a Christian society in miniature, the nearest realization of what "church" ultimately intended to be. This is particularly true of the monastic life inspired by Augustine's theology; akin to Basil's style of monasticism, it fosters the creation of a perfect community over above the pursuit of the individual's perfection.[26]

Benedict of Nursia (480–547) in Italy summarized much of the entire monastic evolution in his *Rule,* a marvel of succinct, moderate, and practical directives that combined prayer, study, and manual work. It became, as it were, the charter of Western monasticism, crystallizing the doctrine of the desert fathers as Cassian above all others

---

26. See Markus, *The End of Ancient Christianity,* p. 158.

had perceived it. As for the East, after Justinian's legislation on monastic life in the sixth century, but without the elaborate organization of Western monasticism, the ascetic tradition produced such masters as John Climacus (579–649) with his *Ladder of Divine Ascent,* a masterpiece of spiritual guidance.

Communities of women also came into existence quite early. Ascetic vocations appeared first in upper-class circles, out of Christian households. The asceticism of early female renouncers is not very well known. They did not take to the desert but remained in settled land, often in convents around shrines. They sought spiritual guidance from monks and clergymen, then from bishops and other women, and their formal organization followed on male monasticism with a certain delay, but basically they espoused the same kind of life-style, perhaps without enough concern about the adaptation of male directives to female conditions.

A number of pitfalls threatened Christian asceticism from the start. First, it began in the proximity of encratite circles in Syria and Egypt prone to excessive requirements typical of sectarian groups; in some of those circles it was believed that all baptized should be celibate. This could have been one reason for the postponement of the reception of baptism and for the belief that only unmarried persons had a place in the kingdom. Many Syrian ascetics were "overachievers" and tended to impose on themselves extreme burdens such as wearing iron collars or chains, or eating grass like animals, or fasting like serpents. For such eccentrics, Benedict's moderation came as a healthy corrective. Second, monastic self-denial often came close to Gnostic and Manichaean hatred of bodily and material realities. It is worthy of note that Pachomius's monastery stood only three miles from Nag Hammadi. The compilers of the prevailingly Gnostic Nag Hammadi Library may have included monks of his own community. However, through his allegiance to Bishop Athanasius, Pachomius and his followers were able to forge a lasting alliance of Coptic monasticism with episcopal authorities, the latter not inclined to indulge in the acute dualistic trends of the Manichaean brand. Finally, monastic life could be perceived as elitist, making the practice of the evangelical counsels the preserve of well-trained athletes while the observance of mere precepts was all that was required of the common believers. The church could not allow that form of separatism and double standard to develop unchecked.

Once solidly established, monasticism promoted the self-reliance of its communities as regards economic conditions, but also to a certain extent vis-à-vis church and bishops. Material independence carried with it the right to property, income, and trade, which drew monks in many regions quite close to the economic structures of the surrounding society.

At times in the fourth and fifth centuries monks were recruited, or were only too happy to volunteer, for the wild destruction of pagan monuments and temples, which were seen as so many repositories of satanic forces. But such activities should not be emphasized to the point of making them a characteristic of monasticism in general. The opposite is rather closer to reality: Monasteries became crucial instruments not only in the propagation of Christian mores but also in the survival of the best of pagan culture, in addition to performing eminent social services.

Basilicas and Monasteries

At first the Christians' religious life mostly took place in synagogues and in households or small assemblies of co-believers. As long as specifically appointed buildings were lacking, house churches were used for meetings and prayers. With the turn of the Christians' fortune in the empire, congregations gradually moved to prayer houses especially built for assembly purposes. Initially those places of worship were modeled not on the ancient temples, as could be expected, but rather on imperial public buildings, the assembly halls known as basilicas, better suited to congregational use. They were large rectangular halls with narrower, lower aisles along the longer sides, divided from the main hall by rows of columns, and with an apse at the far end for the presider. A semi-circular niche, the apse was soon to be the ideal area where artists could lavish their best skills. After a period of philistinism toward pagan temples, the urge to preserve them prevailed and they themselves began being used as churches with only few modifications.

Places of burial received growing care as cultic places. In the third century the Roman catacombs displayed some of the first Christian artistic expressions: common symbols given a Christian meaning (the good shepherd, the dove, the anchor) or illustrations of biblical scenes. When Christianity received public recognition in the fourth century, artists began to express the self-confidence of the movement in mighty depictions of divine power and awe-inspiring images of Christ as judge and savior. Cross and crucifixion, initially signs of the ultimate infamy, gradually became endowed with triumphal signification.

From the fourth century on much of the religious life of the Christians took place around shrines, local churches, and monasteries. In the fifth and sixth centuries the church tended to redirect a large amount of its growing wealth toward cultural and artistic achievements. Rich decorations were then produced: marble columns, mosaics, fresco paintings, sculptures, opulent furnishings, ivories, silver reliquaries, textiles and tapestries. Portrayals of Mary and the saints multiplied. Representations of biblical models and symbolic figurations (the lamb, the fish, the ship in addition to common symbols) abounded in places of worship and homes, where they were used didactically to express beliefs and hopes.

Early Christian art first imitated Jewish ways of representing biblical scenes. Since the recent discovery in Dura Europos on the Euphrates of a modest Christian church next to an opulent third-century synagogue, that relationship can now be studied. Increasingly Christian artists borrowed from Greek and Roman methods and styles, while their interests shifted from the representation of formal beauty to the evocation of sacred events and elevated teachings. As time passed, churches and homes were adorned with iconographical representations incorporating both edifying biblical motifs and mythological themes that, once annexed to a Christian context, could evoke, in a way still meaningful for many Christians, the old local cults.

In the West the usefulness of the religious image for teaching the sacred word was readily recognized. At first a mere substitute for the written word, the image found its belated sanction in Gregory the Great in the sixth century: Painting could do for the illiterate what writing did for those who can read. Byzantium in the eighth and ninth centuries showed reluctance in following suit and there were periods when iconoclasts or "image-smashers" prevailed. But in the end images (icons), provided they complied with the canons of traditional ways, were accepted. Their reception occurred less for the proclaimed utility of images, as in the West, than for their inherent holiness as mysterious reflections of the other world. Created to be the "rungs of heaven," icons are also sometimes compared to a membrane between two worlds—in some fashion they share the properties of the objects they represent. Strikingly, a similar function was discharged by the *Passions* of martyrs and the *Lives* of saints: "Through *Lives,* Christian writers could present an image not only of the perfect Christian life but also of the life in imitation of Christ, the life that becomes an icon"—that is, a verbal icon.[27] Widespread was the view that the holy man himself "was a living icon,"[28] like any icon a transparent sign through which the divine could be perceived.

Without ceasing to be oases of withdrawal and renunciation, monasteries were often homes for scholars, architects, and artists. The time in the monastic routine devoted to study and work could be spent studying and copying classical and early Christian works. In the process, exquisite illuminated manuscripts, illustrations, drawings, and paintings were produced. It is largely thanks to the activity of monks in the East and West that the treasuries of classical culture, learning, and art, long identified with pagan religion, were transmitted through the "Christian" centuries.

---

27. A. Cameron, *Christianity and the Rhetoric of Empire: The Development of Christian Discourse.* Berkeley: University of California Press, 1991, p. 143.

28. Brown, *Society and the Holy,* p. 268.

READINGS

C. Avila   *Ownership: Early Christian Thought.* Maryknoll, N.Y.: Orbis Books, 1983.

P. F. Bradshaw   *The Search for the Origins of Christian Worship.* New York: Oxford University Press, 1992.

P. Brown   *Authority and the Sacred.* New York: Cambridge University Press, 1995.

P. Brown   *The Body and Society: Men, Women and Sexual Renunciation in Early Christianity.* New York: Columbia University Press, 1988.

P. Brown   *The Cult of the Saints: Its Rise and Function in Latin Christianity.* Chicago: Chicago University Press, 1981.

P. Brown   *The Making of Late Antiquity.* Cambridge, Mass.: Harvard University Press, 1978.

P. Brown   "The Saint as Exemplar in Late Antiquity." *Representations* 2 (1983): 1–25.

P. Brown   *Society and the Holy in Late Antiquity.* Berkeley: University of California Press, 1982.

J. H. Burns, ed.   *The Cambridge History of Medieval Political Thought c. 350–c. 1450.* New York: Cambridge University Press, 1988.

H. Chadwick   *The Originality of Early Christian Ethics.* Oxford: Somerville College, 1990.

D. J. Chitty   *The Desert A City.* Crestwood, N.Y.: St. Vladimir's Seminary Press, 1966.

S. Elm   *Virgins of God: The Making of Asceticism in Late Antiquity.* New York: Oxford University Press, 1994.

P. C. Finney   "Early Christian Architecture: The Beginnings (A

	Review Article)." *Harvard Theological Review* 81 (1988): 319–339.
J. Gutmann	"Early Synagogue and Jewish Catacomb Art and Its Relation to Christian Art." ANRW II.21.2 (1984): 1313–1342.
S. G. Hall	*Doctrine and Practice in the Early Church*. London: SPCK, 1991.
J. McKinnon	*Music in Early Christian Literature*. New York: Cambridge University Press, 1987.
W. A. Meeks	*The Origins of Christian Morality: The First Two Centuries*. New Haven: Yale University Press, 1993.
J. Riaud	"Les Thérapeutes d'Alexandrie dans la tradition et la recherche critique jusqu'aux découvertes de Qumran." ANRW II.20.2 (1987): 1189–1285.
H. M. Riley	*Christian Initiation*. Washington: Catholic University of America Press, 1974.
P. Rousseau	*Basil of Caesarea*. Berkeley: University of California Press, 1994.
G. F. Snyder	*Ante Pacem: Archeological Evidence of Church Life Before Constantine*. Macon, Ga.: Mercer, 1985.
A. Veilleux	*Pachomian Koinonia*, 3 vols. Kalamazoo, Mich.: Cistercian Publications, 1980–1982.
A. Vööbus	*A History of Asceticism in the Syrian Orient*, 3 vols. Louvain: *Corpus scriptorum christianorum orientalium*, 1958, 1960, 1988.
L. M. White	*Building God's House in the Roman World: Architectural Adaptations Among Pagans, Jews and Christians*. Baltimore, Md.: Johns Hopkins University Press, 1990.
V. L. Wimbush and R. Valantasis, eds	*Asceticism*. New York: Oxford University Press, 1995.

8

Gods, God, and Christ (381–681)

The declarations of the council of Nicaea in 325 barely represented the tip of an iceberg. They were anchored in thick layers of religious experience and centuries of rational speculations on the nature of
supernatural power in paganism, Judaism, and nascent Christianity.
Contemporary "environmental influences" in the realm of worship and
theology combined with ancient trends in the lengthy process of doctrinal elaboration that moved into high gear during the trinitarian and
christological debates of the fourth and fifth centuries.

Ancient Near Eastern Divinities

Thanks to its proximity to local cults in Palestine and to the
impact of successive Egyptian and Babylonian sojourns, Judaism had
inherited a rich harvest of religious images, ideas, and practices that to
a large extent had merged with its own tradition. The writings of the
Hebrew Bible witness to an acute awareness of other gods besides Yahweh, be they perceived as weaker competitors or as empty fabrications.
The Baals and Astartes of Canaan along with the Marduks and Tia-
maths of Babylonia, while forcefully rejected by the prophets, left
unmistakable traces in the Old Testament. All those "foreign" cults
held beliefs about gods, goddesses, and heroes that both attracted and
insulted the believers in the God of Israel. Temples housing great stat-
ues of gods and goddesses, sacrificial practices, initiation rites, prayers,
processions, shrines as places for incubation, dreams and oracles—the
Hebrews knew of all those things. They argued against them at the
same time that they shared many of them. As for the alien gods themselves, they were seen as local or national deities whose ability to pro-
tect their adepts was continuously questioned by the biblical writers;
their failures regularly became occasions for the self-aggrandizement
of Yahweh.

Greco-Roman Pantheons

Closer to our period, Hellenistic Judaism and early Christianity were also in contact with the religious beliefs and institutions of Greece and Rome, and developed their own thinking about God in the course of an encounter with them.

Greco-Roman pantheons presented systems of ranked divinities allotted to the many areas of human life and the cosmos over which they exercised their respective competence. But pantheons were no static entities; they evolved under the pressure of events and the stimulus of human pondering. Hence Greek and Roman mythologies reflected successive stages of human thinking about the gods; they actually functioned as substitutes for theology or even as its embodiment. Further, when hegemony passed from Greece to Rome, the gods themselves also traveled in the baggage of soldiers and traders, immigrants and slaves. They were added to the Roman pantheon or, more often, absorbed into it by receiving Latin names—Zeus became Jupiter; Hera, Juno; Athena, Minerva.

Gods and goddesses presented, for all their elevated status, quite familiar traits. Regarded "as absolute masters, like Hellenistic rulers,"[1] they often wore military uniform or were dressed like urban notables. Only a step above humans, they were respected for the protection they could afford as patrons and feared for the malevolent deeds they could cause.

Relations to the gods largely reflected the sociopolitical relations on which they were based. As toward earthly protectors, relations were free and stamped with admiration. Organized in a hierarchy modeled on human ones, gods held court, handed out rewards and punishments, and presided over boom and doom, good and bad fortune. The pagan process of imaging the divine realities inevitably influenced Christian conceptions of God. In particular, by 300 "the Roman Empire here beneath had had some centuries in which to suggest itself as a model of the Empire above."[2]

---

1. R. MacMullen, *Paganism in the Roman Empire*. New Haven: Yale University Press, 1981, p. 80.

2. Ibid., p. 83.

Pagan Critique of Mythology

From Homer through the "poets" and philosophers up to the third century C.E., an undercurrent appeared that led Greco-Roman paganism to some form of monotheism. Indeed solar monotheism, the syncretistic Helios cult, constituted the last stage of ancient paganism. In that sense an Orphic hymn could claim: "God is one yet has many names." Neglecting the lower subordinate gods of popular beliefs, attention became centered around the main characters of the divine hierarchy, and above all around a "divine monarchy" according to which one supreme God rules surrounded by a host of ministering spirits like "provincial governors of His far-flung empire."[3] This kind of subordination seems to have been sought and advertised by successive emperors during the third century.

Philosophers not only had a great impact on the rise of monotheism, emphasizing that the many gods were in fact aspects of a single god; they also were able to overcome the current anthropomorphism and spell out the essential features of the transcendent God. Critique of superstition and even of polytheism was a common philosophical pastime. That mythology was folly or insult to the beings above became a commonplace among the lettered elite. Cicero's *On the Nature of the Gods* offered a good summary of the state of the religious debate around the turn of the era. It was widely read by Latin writers through the formative centuries of Christian theology. We later find, in the work of writers such as Seneca, a typical "repudiation of mythology,"[4] also echoed by many Christian writers who were thus drawing on pagan critics of paganism, for use against pagans.

Polytheism Interpreted

Philosophical reflection on religious beliefs aimed to clarify what those beliefs ultimately amounted to. It can be said that the Latin Varro (116–27 B.C.E.) summarized the results of centuries of Greek and Roman thinking about religion in his presentation of the current tripartite distinctions. Three groups of "users" are held to have introduced

---

3. P. Brown, *The World of Late Antiquity, AD 150–750*. London: Thames & Hudson, 1971, p. 50.

4. MacMullen, *Paganism*, p. 64.

the gods: philosophers, poets, rulers (or people). Correspondingly there are three classes of gods: physical, mythical, and national; and three kinds of theologies: natural, mythical, and civil or political. Tertullian and Augustine were to criticize those distinctions. Nevertheless they illustrate the kind of clarification philosophers were able to concoct.

Cicero (106–43) for his part made it clear that philosophers in general thought that paganism had its providence, looking after human affairs. The universe itself was object of divine care, each portion of the cosmos being sacralized by such divine attention.

When interpreted allegorically, as the method was practiced by Greek and Roman authors before becoming the trademark of the Alexandrian Philo and Origen, polytheistic beliefs could be reduced to theological views that to some modest extent approximated the Christian doctrine of God. In an attempt to see through current mythological representations, Middle Platonists were able to posit a divine triad, Father-creator-creation, a step likely to have fertilized the reflections of early Christian thinkers. At any rate, that there was one God, king and father of all things, and many gods, sons of God and his coregents, was a common feature of the march toward monotheism.

Equally widespread was the theory called Euhemerism, according to which a large number of the traditional gods were but human heroes of the past. Finally, much of the elevated thinking about God encountered in Plotinus and his followers inspired Christian theologians, Greek and Latin. They could read in Porphyry's *Life of Plotinus* about the latter's experience of and union with the transcendent God "in an unspeakable actuality and not in potency only. So to this god-like man above all, who often raised himself in thought, according to the ways Plato teaches in the *Banquet,* to the First and Transcendent God, that God appeared who has neither shape nor any intelligible form, but is throned above intellect and all the intelligible."[5]

The Unknown God

When he spoke in Athens (Acts 17), Paul showed awareness of the new mood that had seized Greco-Roman religion moving toward

---

5. *Plotinus*, trans. A. H. Armstrong. *Loeb Classical Library*, vol. 1: *Porphyry on the Life of Plotinus.* Cambridge, Mass.: Harvard University Press, 1966, p. 23.

monotheism. He was struck by the abundance of sacred monuments in the city, but especially by the presence of an altar inscribed "To An Unknown God." He used the fact to his own purpose and announced that he was proclaiming that God whose name they did not know. The concept of an Unknown God was to have a great fortune. Marcion, the Gnostics, Hermetic literature, even Neoplatonism, were to talk about that true God beyond the creator-demiurge, totally otherworldly, accessible by revelation only or, perhaps to some extent, by rational contemplation through mental trekking. It was natural for Christian apologists to follow in Paul's footsteps and to find in the idea of an Unknown God a valuable point of contact for their exposition; but they firmly refused to distinguish him from the creator.

The God of the Jews

In fact, Judaism itself was not at all hospitable to the idea of an Unknown God superior to the creator. The creator was not to be conceived as an inferior demiurge. He was the only true God, the God of the fathers, who had demonstrated his creative power by his mighty acts in history.

Further, the creator was not to be equated with the Just God of Marcion as opposed to the Good God. He was both good and just, creator and redeemer. There was no other God. Judaism had from the start been involved in a resounding indictment of all polytheistic idolatry. So the recurrent self-proclamation of Yahweh, "I am the Lord," has to be understood against the backdrop of competing divinities. But then denouncing the foreign gods went hand in hand with the refusal to split the divine. When the figures of Wisdom and the Logos and their presence close to God are mentioned in the Old Testament, they seem to be mere personifications of divine attributes; never are they distinct objects of worship.

The Jewish views of God were mediated to the early Christians by the Hebrew Bible and the lived religion of Palestinian Jews. They also reached Christian thought, as it developed, via Philo's interpretation of his tradition in the Hellenistic context. Well schooled in philosophy, Philo was able (e.g., in his *On the Creation*) to relate Old Testament ideas to Neopythagorean and Middle-Platonist thought. His statements on the role of Logos and Sophia/Wisdom were to have seminal influence on early Christian understanding of the exalted Jesus. He portrayed them as the chief servants of God and his viceregents[6] and thus set them in close relation to God's agency.

Jewish monotheism was the basic presupposition of all Christian reflections on God. Its particular reception within a trinitarian scheme, however, in addition to meeting with Jewish disapproval, was ironically to create internal friction among Christians themselves when the "divine monarchy" happened to be one-sidedly emphasized. It can be said that even the Arians wanted to vindicate the One God when they denied full divinity to the Son, and by insisting on the merely human nature of Jesus Christ, Ebionites of all shades were possibly motivated by the same intention of protecting the unicity of God.

Finally, the Jewish milieu in which Christianity initially grew made large room for good angels and evil demons. In that, both Judaism and Christianity were not that far from the polytheism of the pagans, for whom "demons" were quasi-omnipresent and had ambivalent functions. Theologians would do everything they could to prevent angels and demons from endangering the status of God but popular piety was not always inclined to listen to them.

The God of Jesus Christ

In his proclamation, Jesus insisted on his identity as Son, revealing his particular relation to the Father. In its context this manner of self-identification represented a major change of perspective. It meant that, from the start, Christianity tended to replace the sociopolitical model of "monarchy" for talking of God with the family (or fraternal) model. Relations to God reflected the relations within the family, with the implied attitudes of obedience and love. First, Jesus declared himself and was believed to be the Son of God before being related to God's Wisdom by Paul and to God's Logos by John.

Soon, though, perplexing associations were to give rise to endless speculation and strife. In the Old Testament, heavenly Wisdom was seen sometimes as one with the divine Logos, sometimes as one with God's Spirit. In the New Testament, Christ or the Son was himself also

---

6. L. Hurtado, *One God, One Lord: Early Christian Devotion and Ancient Jewish Monotheism.* Philadelphia: Fortress Press, 1988, p. 46.

identified either with Wisdom or with the Logos. The precise determination of the status of the Son occupied Christians until Nicaea and after. Paul sometimes used a binitarian model to refer to God; the diad "One God, One Lord" (1 Cor 8:5–6) seemed to capture the essential concern of his talk of God. At other times, however (e.g., 1 Cor 13:13), he employed the triad found in Matthew 28:19, "Father, Son, Spirit." How could those diverse trends be reconciled and brought together into a coherent doctrine?

Much had to be clarified here. The first Apologists initiated the clarifications. They and their followers (Clement and Irenaeus, for example) appropriated Greek criticism of the traditional gods, received Euhemerism and its devaluation of the gods to heroes of the past, reclassified pagan deities as demons or angels, and validated the trend toward monotheism at work on the pagan scene. With the help of Plato's thought, amplified and refined by Middle Platonism, they offered the rudiments of trinitarian theology that were going beyond the simple affirmation of a triad, and began to articulate a doctrine.

Contest Over the Divine Around Nicaea

A period of lived faith in the triune God and confession of his active presence was succeeded by a time of reflection and explanation of his being. As just mentioned, scattered elements of a doctrine of God were encountered prior to Nicaea, especially but not exclusively in the writings of the Apologists. The church's preaching and its reception by believers contributed important elaborations. Doctrinal developments, moreover, were never alien to the philosophical, rhetorical, and political statements current among contemporaries. So it was quasi-natural to conceive of God the Father as a "monarch" or of Christ as a ruler. For many, God was simply "an emperor writ large."[7] But for people baptized in the name of Father, Son, and Spirit, it was no less normal and provocative to affirm three distinct beings mutually related like members of one family.

Three major tendencies were observed in the sustained efforts to balance the one and the many within the Godhead. First, under the influence of the Jewish tradition and the general trend toward monotheism,

---

7. Brown, *The World of Late Antiquity*, p. 101.

theologians such as Theophilus in Antioch and Sabellius in Rome strongly affirmed the oneness of God, the "divine monarchy." Various models were then put forward: Son and Spirit were mere aspects of the one God as he revealed himself to us, or the Son was the same as the Father, or he was a "divine" being subordinated to him or a man adopted by him.

Second, on the basis of Paul's assertion of "One God, one Lord," it was tempting to embrace a binitarian scheme and propound a doctrine of two Gods[8] whereby Son and Spirit would be identical, or the demiurge set distinct from God. The inconsistencies implied in the affirmation of two equal gods were generally denounced on mere philosophical grounds. But some Gnostic systems grounded their own binitarian views (Father and demiurge being two distinct entities) on Jewish ideas about the creative agency of the divine Name and of the Angel of the Lord as well as on the figures of Sophia and Logos, a trend that Apologists firmly resisted. Hence the task of clarifying the relation of the Son to the Father became an urgent one.

Third, there was the tendency to tear apart the holy Unity into three separate deities (Denys of Alexandria was perceived to be espousing tri-theism). Triads were known in Greco-Roman theologies (Jupiter-Juno-Minerva) and in Neoplatonism (One-Nous/Mind-Soul). From Athenagoras in the late second century Christian thinkers were inclined to make use of Jewish and pagan speculations to express their belief in a triune God. In relating Father to Son and Spirit, the Son was seen as Logos of the Father, or Mind or Power or Wisdom, and the Spirit was seen as Wisdom. But how precisely was each of the three to be defined? Were they more than personified attributes of the one God? Were the three really distinct? Were they equal?

People were aware of the difficulties involved in having two or three gods. The divine monarchy had to be safeguarded. On the other hand, scripture and the early Christian tradition in its liturgy and confession talked of Father, Son, and Spirit as sharing in the Godhead. That is why a natural solution was found in the many forms of subordinationism, whereby Son and Spirit would be just one notch below the Father. In that regard Arius was only more provocative than the rest in his statements about the Son being a creature. He was following to the

---

8. This, at one point, was Lactantius's inclination; Dial., 58–61, came close to speaking of Christ as a second God.

end a majority tradition that endured until well into the fifth century and saw the Son as a little inferior to the Father.

The Arian crisis forced the church to take a position. As already seen (chapter 5), the councils of Nicaea in 325 and Constantinople in 381 asserted the unqualified divinity of Son and Spirit, equal with the Father in substance, but distinct as "persons." The councils did more than merely proclaim a triad, as was the case in Matthew 28 and in the Apostles' Creed; they articulated a doctrine that henceforth was to be used to test not only the faith of the believers in general but specifically the faith of the bishops. In fact, most people declared heretics from then on were to be fellow bishops. The trinitarian doctrine was thereafter to be expounded for the West by theologians such as Augustine, and for the East by the Cappadocians and Dionysius the Pseudo-Areopagite.

The Christological Question

The condemnation of Arianism initiated a major shift in Christian thinking. Now that Jesus Christ had been definitely declared God and Son, existing prior to his earthly career, fully and truly God from all eternity and to be worshiped as God, account had to be given of his humanity and his human limitations. This question could not be escaped, but people were unable to rely on any unified doctrine that the second- and third-century fathers could have produced. Nicaea had said nothing specific about the "incarnate" nature of the Logos; it even had avoided the term *Logos* in favor of the metaphors of personal relations—Father-Son. It was then natural that in the aftermath of Nicaea the christological question forced itself to the foreground. The discussion could take its start from one item that Nicaea had indeed affirmed: Against the many varieties of docetism, mainly Gnostic and Marcionite, it had declared that Christ had a true body and not only "appeared" to have one. Then Athanasius in his *On the Incarnation of the Word* had laid the basis for future christological developments with his concept of the human mind made in the image of God, his method of dogmatic exegesis, and his concentration on the historical event of salvation wrought in Christ, being reluctant to ground his theology on a religious cosmology of any sort.

It appears that in the firestorm of opposition to Arianism some theologians went astray and overshot the mark in one-sidedly stressing the divinity of Christ. The unfortunate Apollinarius of Laodicea (310–390) is credited with the first christological "heresy." Using the analogy with the human union of body and soul (mind and will), he thought that, in Christ, the Logos had taken the place of the human soul or, more precisely, of the spiritual soul *(Nous)*, with the consequence that Christ could not have been truly and totally human. His view was condemned by the council of 381, stating that Christ was true man, with body and soul; but his approach kept haunting the Alexandrian theologians.

For though at home not far from Antioch, Apollinarius belonged, by affinity, to the Alexandrian tendency in the christological debate, the other tendency being associated with Antioch. The differences between those two approaches should not be over-stressed and hardened; never were there really two opposed "schools." Borders, geographical and ideological, were ceaselessly crossed between the two groups so that the distinction is not totally adequate, could become misleading, and applied only to a limited period. It remains, however, that Alexandria and Antioch exemplified two major ways of defending the dogma of Nicaea and of interpreting the being of Jesus Christ.

Alexandrian and Antiochene Propensities

The Alexandrian approach was mainly indebted to Origen's Logos-theology and to his use of Philo's allegorical method. For this tradition Christ was first of all the Logos and Wisdom of God, of the same substance ("consubstantial") with the Father but not clearly consubstantial with us. His incarnation was described along the scheme of the "Logos made flesh" (Logos-Sarx) according to which the Logos is inseparable from its flesh and the two are fused to form a hybrid of God and man. Such an approach ran the risk, in depicting the union of the divine and the human in Christ, of downplaying his humanity and preferably focusing on his divinity, saying that it was always the Logos who was acting in Christ, only taking on the limitations of the flesh in order to help us. Two correctives were applied to this view, which is known as "high Christology." First, the council of 381 firmly stated that Christ was fully human, discouraging any one-sidedness in the affirmation of his divinity. Second, making use of Origen's and Athanasius's so-called soteriological argument, Gregory of Nazianzus stressed that "what is not assumed cannot be healed,"[9] and that any neglect of the full human nature in Christ endangers humankind's salvation. Thanks to their approach, the Alexandrians had no trouble in saying that Mary was the "mother of God" *(theotokos)* and they acclaimed the declaration to that effect made by the council of Ephesus in 431. Yet the tendency to "privilege" the divine nature perdured even when the affirmation of Christ's personal unity was strongly maintained. It would be unjust to label the Alexandrian approach docetist, of the Gnostic or Manichaean kind, or even quasi-docetist. But it is quite understandable that monophysitism (the view that in the person of Christ there was only one nature, the divine nature), with its typical formulae of "one incarnate nature of God the Logos" and "out of two natures but one nature after incarnation," arose from its ranks. The one-nature Christology remained associated with Apollinarius, who figured as its nemesis, and with Eutyches, the Byzantine monk, as its least acceptable avatar. But understood according to the thought of Cyril of Alexandria (ca. 372–444), it could be and was incorporated into the findings of the council of Chalcedon in 451.

The Antiochene tendency was shared, even championed, by Constantinople. Here the use of allegory and typology was reduced to a minimum in favor of a literal reading of the gospel narratives. Emphasis was put on the humanity of Christ as attested by the New Testament accounts of his limitations (temptations, hunger) and his human progress (Lk 2:40–52). Close to Judaism and to some Stoic teachings, Theophilus of Antioch in the late second century saw Christ first of all as the man depicted in the Synoptic gospels, a second Moses and a moral teacher. In the wake of writers such as the late-third-century Paul of Samosata, it was usual to describe the Logos as of "like substance" (not of the same substance) with the Father and his incarnation on the model of the "Logos made man," or the Logos dwelling in a man, insisting that Christ was a complete human being, with a mortal body and a rational soul like us. Paul talked of the "assumed man" and was inclined to refer to "two sons" (one by nature, one by adoption) to depict Christ's double nature, always operating harmoniously, though.

9. Gregory of Nazianzus, *Epistle* 101:181c, in J. Stevenson, *Creed, Councils and Controversies.* London: SPCK, 1989, p. 90.

Thus the question was raised: How was Christ's unity to be safe-guarded? But another also surfaced: Was he truly divine? Because of its insistence on the human features in Christ, this form of Christology is usually called "low Christology." Theodore of Mopsuestia tried to eliminate the difficulties of this position and insisted on the "perfect conjunction of the two natures." But this did not seem to be adequate. The crisis came to a head in the fate of Nestorius (380–451), who appears to have overly separated Christ's two natures or even, accord-ing to his opponents' unjust accusations rejected by Nestorius himself, his "two persons" or individualities. He was willing to call Mary "*Christotokos*" (mother of Christ) but not mother of God. It would be totally unfair to assimilate the Antiochene position to the Ebionite ten-dency that Christ was a mere man or even to a quasi-Ebionite one. With their preferred formulae for the incarnation—"union of two natures," "two natures after the union"—this two-nature Christology was closer to the thought of Western theologians and especially to that of Pope Leo, and through him to that of Ambrose and Augustine. Like the Alexandrian tendency, the Antiochene one was also incorporated into Chalcedon. Yet Nestorius kept haunting this tradition.

The Council of Ephesus in 431

Clearly the christological question did not wait until the fifth cen-tury to be raised. It occupied the minds of all believers with a bent for reflection. Two extremes were easily rejected: that Christ was "God in human disguise," and that he was merely human. Then the trinitarian controversies themselves included some reflection on the person of Christ. The philosophical concepts of *physis* (nature or life-giving essence), *hypostasis* (individuality or nature), *ousia* (nature, substance, or being), *prosopon* (subject, person, or personality), with their waver-ing, at times interchangeable meanings, plagued and complicated the debate. Many formulae meant different things to different people, though all tried to express the same truth: salvation through the suffer-ing of Christ-God. The debate turned into a highly technical exercise in speculation and notional tightrope walking. The whole was com-pounded by blatant misunderstandings, vicious intimations, manipula-tions, and external pressures. We cannot enter into details here; they are found in more specialized works.

Basically, by receiving some of Cyril's ideas, the council of Ephesus in 431 came up with the ingredients of a doctrine of "hypostatic union," that is, that in Christ was found a true, personal (hypostatic) unity of two natures, though the mode of union remained "ineffable and inexpressible." "One and the same is the eternal Son of the Father and the Son of the Virgin Mary, therefore she may rightly be called Mother of God." Divinity and humanity "must be predicated of the one and the same subject, the Logos" who is of one substance with the Father[10]—in other words, as would be made explicit at Chalcedon, one person (hypostasis) *in* two natures, not "out of two natures." Until 431, Cyril held to the formula "one person out of two natures," which could well be interpreted as if a mixing and mingling of the two natures had taken place in Christ; but he gave up that formulation in 433 and rallied to the notion of "one person in two natures," whereby the integrity of both the divine and the human in Christ is affirmed. To many this may seem a microscopic distinction, but it was a crucial one to the easterners exercised in fine dialectical nuances and to all those interested in the implications of a doctrinal statement for questions relating to human salvation. Nestorius, a monk of Antioch who had become bishop of Constantinople, was deposed, defeated by the machinations of Empress Pulcheria, Theodosius II's sister, and by the formidable Cyril of Alexandria, who did not shun questionable methods (bribes to court officials present at the council, intimidation of his suffragans) in gaining his ends, but whose superior theology was later to be claimed by Chalcedon. It remained influential through the centuries, ironically functioning today, because of its very ambivalence, as a rallying sign between Eastern, Oriental, and Western churches. In 433 the "Formula of Reunion" formally restored the harmony between Antioch and Alexandria; it was agreed to under the emperor's pressure and recognized the legitimacy of certain differences.

The Council of Chalcedon in 451

After years of stormy disputes leading up to an acute crisis, the council of Chalcedon in 451 reaffirmed the decisions of Ephesus and

---

10. A. Grillmeier, *Christ in the Christian Tradition,* vol. 1. Louisville, Ky.: Westminster John Knox, 1975, p. 486.

added important qualifications to its formulation of the hypostatic union. In the process a certain check was administered to Alexandrian theology in that the council received Pope Leo's "position paper" *(Tomus ad Flavianum)*, which happened to express an agreement between Rome and Constantinople. Nevertheless, the influence of the thought of Cyril remained decisive. Leo was received precisely because he was understood to agree with what Cyril had stood for. Confessing the one person of Christ as being "truly God and truly man," the council declared that he was "to be acknowledged in two natures [which exist] without confusion, without change [this was said against Monophysite tendencies of the kind represented by Eutyches, for whom Christ's body came 'from above,' thus viewing Jesus Christ as having a single, divine nature], without division, without separation" (this was said against persisting Nestorians), the two natures being inseparably joined in one single subject, "one *prosopon* and one *hypostasis*, each nature retaining its own properties" yet sharing in the properties of the other.[11] In other words, the council struck a compromise, receiving the moderate elements of both Monophysites and Nestorians while rejecting their extreme forms.

Two circumstances surrounding Chalcedon contributed to making it into a quasi-fateful event. First, in addition to the somewhat unedifying conduct of many bishops at the meeting, political scores were settled. "At the council...the emperor Marcian took advantage of a trend in Greek opinion and of the support of Leo, bishop of Rome, to humble the patriarch of Alexandria (Dioscorus) and so to secure the position of Constantinople as the leading Christian city of the empire."[12] With the intervention of Emperor Marcian, as convinced as his predecessors that he had been divinely appointed and held the control of ecclesiastical affairs, the rivalry between Alexandria and Constantinople turned in favor of the latter, and the bishop of Alexandria was deposed.

Second, no sooner had the council disbanded than many participants felt a mounting frustration at, perhaps, having been tricked or despoiled. "The settlement arrived at in Chalcedon did violence to some of the deepest currents in Greek Christian thought of the time," particularly to the interpretation of the elevated element in Christ emphasized by Alexandria. The unity of eastern Christianity was brutally broken

---

11. In Stevenson, *Creeds, Councils and Controversies*, p. 353.
12. Brown, *The World of Late Antiquity*, p. 144.

and there resulted the lasting division between pro-Chalcedonians and anti-Chalcedonians. "For the next two centuries, the emperors faced the uphill task of restoring the balance, sometimes by palliating, sometimes by by-passing 'the accursed council,' without going back for a moment on the initiative which their 'Ruling City' had won at Chalcedon."[13]

The prolonged debates issued in a babel of language in East and West while efforts were made to keep Constantinople and Rome on good terms. Finally, the relegation of the non-Chalcedonians to the outskirts of Christianity (see below) was further evidence that, unfortunately, the unity of the two Romes was a higher priority than the unity of the two branches of Greek Christianity.[14]

The Sequels of Chalcedon

Before that sad outcome, the century following Chalcedon saw the relentless efforts of parties to have the validity of the council either recognized or rejected. For a while (484–519) there was schism between Rome and Constantinople. For all the profundity they displayed, the debates were above all acrimonious; they opened the gate to a flood of speculations and linguistic subtleties, hair-splitting, intransigence, name-calling, and even riots. Pro-Chalcedonians were suspected to be still too close to Nestorius, anti-Chalcedonians to be crypto-Manichees. It was difficult, in that climate, to find enlightenment among so much extreme accuracy often obscured by temperamental smallness. Gradually Chalcedon ended up producing, if not a split empire, then a divided church. On the one side were found the Chalcedonian or pro-Chalcedonian churches: the Western church and the churches properly called Eastern Orthodox or Eastern Byzantine. They accepted and promoted the statements of the council. On the other side were the non-Chalcedonian or anti-Chalcedonian churches, called Oriental churches and including Monophysite groups (Armenian, Coptic, Nubian, Ethiopian, Syrian) and, after 484, the Nestorian church. They refused to recognize

---

13. Ibid.
14. W. H. C. Frend, *The Rise of the Monophysite Movement*. Philadelphia: Augsburg Fortress, 1984, p. 356.

Chalcedon as the fourth ecumenical council, with the Nestorians, of course, rejecting parts of Ephesus 431 as well.

After successive turns of policy the emperor, in the end, from 519, sided with the Chalcedonian party. Only then did the Monophysite leaders begin to think of setting up rival churches, which they actually did after 541 by establishing a Monophysite hierarchy. Severus of Antioch (465–538) shaped the theology of the movement and provided it with spiritual leadership.[15] Emperors were generally harsh and merciless toward the Monophysites. To be sure, Empress Theodora supported their cause while Justinian was busy fighting the Arian kingdoms of the West, but unwilling to yield to the anti-Chalcedonian voices chorusing around his wife, Justinian resorted to repression to enforce conformity. His rebuilding in grandiose style of the famous basilica Hagia Sophia in Constantinople was to give expression to the (neo-)Chalcedonian orthodoxy of his empire. His action was felt in all corners of his domain—for instance in Egypt, where the imposition of Chalcedon on Pachomian monasticism led to its breakup. Thereafter and until around 634, there were worthy efforts on the part of emperors at mending the rifts between churches, but all were made on the same condition: "without involving the total abandonment of Chalcedon."[16]

Fine-Tuning of the Divine

When seen in perspective, the debates and decisions of the fourth through seventh centuries represent a cumulative set of pivotal elucidations concerned with the triune God and the person of Christ. Ever more nuanced distinctions and refined terminology ended up confusing many and separating some Christian churches from the main church. Fine-tuning of the mystery was bound to lead to divisions. But today the differences do not appear insurmountable; a statement of reconciliation between Oriental churches (recognizing only the first three ecumenical councils) and Eastern churches (recognizing seven councils) is being worked out. It is said that, in order to overcome the fateful pitfalls of the terminological refinements, such a statement "could make use of

---

15. Ibid., pp. 201ff.
16. Ibid., p. 344.

the theology of St. Cyril of Alexandria"[17] and of the Formula of Reunion agreed on in 433 between Alexandria and Antioch, without having to denounce Chalcedon.

The councils of Nicaea and Constantinople in 325 and 381 constituted a firm basis for theological elaborations of the trinitarian doctrine. The great Cappadocians in the East—Basil of Caesarea, Gregory of Nazianzus, Gregory of Nyssa—were able to make use of previous efforts in scriptural interpretation and theological analysis, found above all in Origen and Athanasius, toward constructing a more sophisticated doctrine of God acceptable to East and West. They generally based their thinking on the concrete and historical "trinity of the economy" as encountered in the biblical sources (that is why, in a typically Greek manner, they start with the three persons before dealing with the unity of God) in order to arrive at the contemplation of the "immanent trinity," that is, of God in himself, very much aware that human minds will never be able to comprehend the inner mysteries of the Godhead. For his part, Augustine in the West pursued signs of trinitarian action in the cosmos and in the human psyche, which he used as a device to confirm and clarify the trinitarian faith; characteristic of Western theology, his point of departure is the one God within whose being personal relations develop.

In Christology the main tenets had been spelled out in the first four councils, between 325 and 451. The contributions of Athanasius, Cyril of Alexandria, the Cappadocians, and the Antiochenes had led to essential official statements. For all its divisive character, the Chalcedonian definition remained essential. Because its negative formulations mark the limits of permissible speculation, it is nowadays praised by many as an exemplary conciliar theological statement, while the widespread view that Chalcedon is more of a beginning than an ending point leaves open the path for further christological development.

As has already been said, the christological discussion did continue after Chalcedon, often centering on what might have been the exact meaning of the terms everybody was using, as well as of Cyril's words. Two further councils at Constantinople (553 and 680–681) brought additional refinements to the doctrine of Christ. It is a chronicle rich in both wild episodes and worthy protagonists: First, in the

17. P. Gregorios et al., *Does Chalcedon Divide or Unite?* Geneva: World Council of Churches, 1981, p. 11.

sixth century, the Chalcedonian doctrine of hypostatic union was reaffirmed against Monophysite and Nestorian positions. Second, in the seventh century, urged by discussions on the will and operation of Christ and in a coherent development of the two-nature Christology, the council declared that Christ had "two wills" and "two natural operations," the opposite being seen as diminishing the full humanity of Christ. Was the debate becoming oversubtle? Had it turned into a dispute over words? Had it ever been expected that human categories would be able to bridge the formidable abyss of the being of God and of the God-Man? At any rate, the debate was interrupted by the Arab invasion, which from 634 on amputated the oldest communities, mainly of Monophysite tendency, from the universal church and thereby, by default, gave the final victory to the pro-Chalcedonians. In fact, Monophysites had been "led to the fateful decision...to prefer a permanent second-class status under the Arab Moslems to continued allegiance to the emperors,"[18] who remained eager to restore a Chalcedonian hierarchy by all means and who had made Byzantine rule a synonym of oppression. But "by accepting the 'Ishmaelites' as instruments of God wherewith to punish the Chalcedonians, the Monophysites purchased not their liberty but their grave."[19] Or so it appeared.

What followed after the epoch-making decisions of the councils was a sustained effort at understanding what had been said. An urgent need was felt to clarify central notions such as "person," "nature," and "consciousness" (implied in the double will and double operation of Christ) in order to come to a more adequate doctrine of God and Christ. A still more urgent task appeared to be to draw the soteriological implications from the fundamental fact of the God-Man. But never again was a council to busy itself with the christological question as such. Either it was felt that the possibilities of rational explanation of the mystery had been exhausted, or the conviction grew that more latitude ought to be granted to various ways of understanding the faith. Perhaps many thought that those discussions should never have been entered into by a council of bishops in the first place, whose freedom was often subject to nontheological pressures and conflicts of personalities. The seventh ecumenical council (in Nicaea in 787) dealt with an issue not totally alien to

---

18. Frend, *The Rise of the Monophysite Movement,* p. 347.
19. Ibid., p. 359.

Christology, to be sure: the legitimacy of icons/images. But significantly, no new pronouncement on the person of Christ was attempted.

Judaism's Separate Career

Affected by stifling civil penalties after the empire had changed its religious allegiance, and the object of hostile preaching on the part of Christian leaders, Judaism was hampered in its growth and drastically contained. Henceforth it lost much of its appeal among people who might otherwise have been involved in an open religious quest. Overrun by its former competitor, Judaism became the almost exclusive preserve of Jews, little concerned with making converts but dedicated to the in-depth understanding of its sources and the realization in life of its traditional faith. As Judaism was forced into separatism, its life remained, in a sense, marginal to the rest of the world for centuries to come.

In turning in on itself, Judaism most of the time rejected the Hellenizing elements of earlier generations. Nevertheless, Jews remained a strong and influential community throughout our period, well educated, wealthy, and at home in the culture and society of the later Roman Empire, sometimes drawing the admiration of non-Jews, sometimes their curiosity, sometimes their scorn, but never totally leaving the observers indifferent.

The Silencing of Paganism

The vitality of paganism asserted itself well beyond the third century. Its last two assaults could be seen in the Great Persecution (303–313) and in the efforts of Emperor Julian to restore the traditional cults (361–363). They misfired. The measures taken by emperors from Constantine on to eradicate paganism are summarized in the Theodosian Code: closing of temples, prohibition of sacrifice, suspension of privileges accorded officers of cults. At first temple buildings were to remain untouched, but vandalism took over in many places. A large number of temples were then reordered to Christian worship. Imperial forces came to bear against the unconverted so that paganism, if not terminated, was silenced, presumably along with its gods.

Some pagan intellectuals, such as the philosopher rhetor Libanius, persisted in their faith. Then we should not overlook the "rustics" and the many imperial officials who doggedly held to their pagan beliefs. But in general paganism found refuge outside explicit religion in literary commonplaces, symbolic representations, magic, and old habits; or it emigrated to the secluded villas of urban magnates. Some of its beliefs were clumsily absorbed by Christian piety, such as the obsession with demons, astrological lore, the fear of a revenge of the gods whose interventions were frustrated by the sacraments.

Similar processes took place in the encounter with "barbarian" forms of belief and worship. The nonassumed elements of pagan cults survived as remnants and had to remain private or secret. The official faith of the empire was in one God and one Lord.

As for atheism, it found only narrow quarters in a Christian society. For a long time, monotheist Jews and Christians had been labeled atheists by conventional Romans. Now, by an ironical reversal of fortune, the only real atheists left in the empire were to be found among those who had leveled the accusation in the first place: urban notables, freethinkers of the Epicurean or skeptical type, some poets and philosophers. These also were mostly reduced to silence.

READINGS

A. S. Atiya — *A History of Eastern Christianity.* Millwood, N.Y.: Kraus Repr., 1980.

E. Ferguson, ed. — *Doctrines of God and Christ.* New York: Garland, 1993.

W. H. C. Frend — *The Rise of the Monophysite Movement.* Philadelphia: Augsburg Fortress, 1984.

R. M. Grant — *Gods and the One God: Christian Theology in the Greco-Roman World.* Philadelphia: Westminster Press, 1988.

R. M. Grant — *Jesus After the Gospels: The Christ of the Second Century.* Louisville, Ky.: John Knox Press, 1990.

P. T. R. Gray — *The Defence of Chalcedon in the East (451–533).* Leiden: Brill, 1979.

P. Gregorios et al. — *Does Chalcedon Divide or Unite?* Geneva: World Council of Churches, 1981.

A. Grillmeier — *Christ in the Christian Tradition*, 2 vols. Louisville, Ky.: Westminster John Knox, 1975, 1987.

P. W. van der Horst — "The Altar of the 'Unknown God' in Athens (Acts 17:23) and the Cult of 'Unknown Gods' in the Hellenistic and Roman Periods." ANRW II.18.2 (1989): 1426–1456.

L. Hurtado — *One God, One Lord: Early Christian Devotion and Ancient Jewish Monotheism.* Philadelphia: Fortress Press, 1988.

J. A. McGuckin — *St. Cyril of Alexandria: The Christological Controversy.* Leiden: Brill, 1994.

A. Momigliano, ed. — *The Conflict Between Paganism and Christianity in the Fourth Century.* Oxford: Clarendon Press, 1963.

R. A. Norris, ed.   *The Christological Controversy.* Philadelphia: Fortress Press, 1980.

J.-J. O'Keefe   "A Historic-Systematic Study of the Christology of Nestorius." Dissertation. University of Münster, 1987.

W. G. Rush, ed.   *The trinitarian Controversy.* Philadelphia: Fortress Press, 1980.

F. R. Trombley   *Hellenistic Religion and Christianization c. 370–529,* 2 vols. Leiden: Brill, 1993–1994.

P. Widdicombe   *The Fatherhood of God from Origen to Athanasius.* Oxford: Clarendon Press, 1994.

F. Young   *From Nicaea to Chalcedon. A Guide to the Literature and Its Development.* Philadelphia: Fortress Press, 1983.

9

Heyday of Patristic Literature (Mainly 300–550)

When one skims over the entire Patristic Period for its most distinguished literary representatives, one finds that two authors emerge as unmistakable towers: Origen in the Greek East, Augustine in the Latin West. To study each in his respective context would already yield something essential of the magnificent literary production of the third through fifth centuries, the most prolific of the whole period. Yet in addition to those two towering scholars, the period also produced a remarkable number of imposing personalities. Some of them will be met here, their characters briefly outlined and some of their main works identified. Many of them have already appeared in a flash in the previous narrative. They are here presented in sequence to form, as in a gallery, a series of snapshots of companions-in-arms inviting the reader to get to know them better.

The following portraits are necessarily selective. Careers and works are sketched in such a way that comparison is made possible between various achievements and appreciation is elicited. A striking feature of recent scholarly research has been the rehabilitation of traditional villains (Gnostics, Arius, Origen, Evagrius, Nestorius, Pelagius, Theodoret of Cyrrhus) who, we now hear, were given short shrift by the orthodox party, and the critical depiction of long-held heroes and saints (Irenaeus, Eusebius, Athanasius, Cyril of Alexandria, Epiphanius, John Chrysostom, Jerome), often lionized by hagiographers and indeed receiving the lion's share in the standard treatments, which are mostly interested in the history of winners.

The Origenist controversy of the fourth through sixth centuries will receive special attention in this chapter because of the involvement of so many authors reviewed here and because of the recent reassessment of the part each played in the fateful debates.

General Remarks on the Literature

With the fourth century, Christian literature definitely emerged from its infancy. Henceforth patristic literature appears in a wide variety of genres. Even where, in these pages, all the genres found in individual writers are not mentioned, it will be assumed that most of them tried most literary styles.

The most frequently encountered genres can be reduced to the following. The apologetic literature of the second century made large use of biblical quotations and paraphrases. Thereafter biblical interpretation would be the most common activity of the fathers in the form of exposition, commentary, homily or sermon, or simply interpretation in the service of an argument. Then come the various tractates: apologetic, polemical, theological, or spiritual. Increasingly encountered from the third century on are letters, sometimes a considerable flow of correspondence. Biographies and "lives" multiply. Finally, we can read diverse collections of sayings, especially of famous monks, and of extracts from great commentators, especially *florilegia* or anthologies, and *catenae* or chains of citations that could be used as proof texts.

Much of the literature of the time has been lost, mostly due to the condemnation of authors whose works were then bound to be destroyed; in that case writings may have partially survived in somebody else's work in the form of quotations, or under a pseudonym. In fact, Christian literature of the period knew not only the phenomenon of pseudonymity or false indication of the name of the author, but also that of anonymity or absence of indication of the author, the whole rendering hazardous the task of placing those works in their historical and theological contexts.

The critical assessment of the material produced during that period has attracted the attention of an ever-growing number of scholars in the last two centuries. Authorship, redaction, edition, dating, manuscript tradition, translation are some of the questions to which scholars devote their efforts with a view to presenting the academic community with authentic and reliable texts. I cannot deal here with those highly interesting problems, for I intend only to point, for a first orientation, to the main works of a few writers who made a lasting contribution to Christian history.

When dealing with fourth-and fifth-century writers, the impression might arise that ethical concerns, virtuous life, and questions of justice occupied a back row, especially in the East, in favor of lofty disputes and the subtle paradoxes of the triune God and of the God-Man—speculations that show how far theology had traveled since the gospels and Paul. Yet that impression has to be corrected by the consideration that most participants in those debates were bishops eager to discharge their pastoral duties, preaching regularly to simple people and enjoining all to progress in their religious and spiritual lives. John Chrysostom and Ambrose are among the most insistent on the duties of social and individual ethics. So the literature reviewed here includes that moral component and one should not forget the headway made by asceticism in those times. Still it is true that the bulk of the literature shows an unrepentant inclination to establish Christian faith at a high level of rational thinking.

There were powerful and influential women and mothers throughout the period, but clearly the Patristic Period was unashamedly patriarchal and has reached us through a patriarchal tradition. Some women were written about: martyrs, ascetics, empresses; very few took to writing. Society and history seem to have conspired to push women into invisibility. We slowly discover today that there were indeed Christian women, even women preachers and teachers, leaders, prophets, and ascetics, as early as there were men in the same functions. The history of the early Christian movement is too often written from the perspective of the victors (here men) and lets the vanquished (here women) sink into anonymity. The objective in these pages is not to lift the veil that renders Christian women of the past vastly invisible (recent works mentioned below attempt just that) but to preface the present section with the warning that our sources, and the traditional way of using them, are incontrovertibly limited, one-sided, and monophonic.

A last preliminary remark must be made. After the establishment of Christianity in the fourth century, the church soon acquired wealth, property, and treasures. Office-holding in the church then became attractive to those desiring to make such work a career. Thus it is not surprising that some officials were in it for riches, influence, and power. The literature produced thereafter reflected that situation; it is not uncommon to find biting critique of office-holders, even of colleagues, and of all those who forgot the guidelines of the gospels. It is also understandable that in circumstances perceived as decadent, elevated souls opted for ascetic life and the monastery.

Because of his influence, direct or indirect, on virtually all patristic writers to come, our survey must begin with Origen.

Origen (185–254) and His Legacy

On the basis of the Apologists' works addressed to pagans (Justin's and those of others), of polemical writings debating with Marcion and the Gnostics (especially those by Irenaeus, Tertullian, and Clement), and of the first ventures into theological exposition (by Irenaeus, Tertullian), Origen emerged as a genius of a new kind. Active first in Alexandria, then in Caesarea (Palestine), he pioneered scholarly traditions that marked generations of theologians and gave its shape first to the intellectual landscape of the East, but also, through his legacy, to the West. His works, however, became posthumously a bone of contention and many of them were consequently lost, even most of his quite innocent *Hexapla,* a learned work of textual criticism presenting the text of the Old Testament in six columns for comparison—Hebrew, Greek transliteration of Hebrew, and four Greek versions.

The important parts that have been saved from his copious commentaries and homilies on most books of the Bible show the transition from typological interpretation as encountered in Paul, Justin, Irenaeus, and Origen himself ("typology" looks at the Old Testament writings for prophetic or symbolic anticipations of Christ and of the church) to the allegorical mode characteristic of Alexandria, eager to find, hidden deep under the literal narratives, spiritual meanings concerning the being of God, the cosmic constitution, and human existence. Contrary to Marcion, who globally rejected the Hebrew scriptures, and to some Gnostics who attributed them to unequal deities, Origen viewed them as entirely inspired by the one God, but thought they called for various levels of interpretation and understanding. The exegetical method he developed on the basis of this view was to leave its mark on all biblical studies since.

He also authored a powerful defense of Christianity, *Against Celsus,* written for a lettered public and propounding a form of Platonic Christianity that was the first real attempt to give a rational account of the foundations of faith. He saw in Greek philosophy and ethics providential instruments due to the action of the divine Logos and preparing the way for Christianity. Still more he thought that to become a Christian was to accede to true culture and true learning, or to true philosophy in the sense of a way of life. In *On First Principles,* of which we only have Greek fragments but a complete though tendentious translation by Rufinus, he crafted the first coherent system of speculative theology, containing ideas that were to become questionable in the light of later doctrinal developments. He had a vision of a preexisting chain of rational beings or souls whose descent into bodily existence had been caused by their own free decision and the cooling off of their love, and whose ascent and return to God were carried out through successive existences, at the end of which there would be a final restoration of all spirits. Thus human spirits reintegrate the original unity after exhausting all experiences of history. These ideas were to appeal to such kindred minds as John Scotus, Hegel, and Schelling. Such a vision, expanded in his *Commentary on the Song of Songs* into a graded theory of three sciences—moral instruction, knowledge of the world, contemplation of God—made Origen not only a pioneer in speculative theology but also into a master of the spiritual life conceived as a rising along the spiritual ladder through the stages of self-denial, virtuous life, and union with the Logos, and which found further elaboration in monastic milieux.

Origen's legacy came to fruition mainly among the Alexandrian and the Cappadocian fathers, making Christianity both acceptable and respectable in the eyes of the cultured people. But the first promoter of Origen's ideas was Eusebius of Caesarea (265–339), the father of church history. Eusebius inherited Origen's library in Caesarea, a collection of Jewish, pagan, and Christian literature assembled by Origen and his friends. He also inherited his scholarly approach and vision, according to which the best of Greek learning is confirmed and raised by Christian revelation. In Eusebius's hands, the Roman Empire itself receives a providential status. Thus in his apologetic treatises, *Preparation for the Gospel* and *Proof of the Gospel,* Eusebius, seemingly aiming to imitate Origen, tries to show that Christianity fulfilled pagan and Jewish aspirations. He does not always provide evidence that he really understood Origen's Logos-theology and his allegorical method, but he did succeed in popularizing some of Origen's themes, which made him suspect of the Arian virus anachronistically imputed to Origen. His *Ecclesiastical History* remains his most valuable contribution. In this work firsthand information is couched in the service of an overall thesis: Christianity, the zenith of all human history, has a divine origin and is guided by God's special Providence. The narrative, which Eusebius kept revising, is illustrated by substantial extracts from previous writers, precious documents otherwise unavailable.

Evidently Eusebius spanned a turning point in Christian history. He not only euphorically acclaimed Constantine's conversion and reign, especially in his *Life of Constantine;* he also shone as the first theoretician of Byzantinism. After him most Eastern prelates, with the notable exception of John Chrysostom, agreed on the emperor's elevated status over all, including those very prelates themselves. With the "peace of the church," Christian literature entered a period of remarkable flowering, fed by the imperatives of rapid expansion and the increase of internal tensions and conflicts. Creeds, definitions, and regulations resulted from much-needed councils. Consequently, all literary genres and styles of current culture, and more, were put to use in the marching episodes of Christian conquest. Eusebius's verve witnesses to those gripping times.

Alexandrians

Athanasius (299–373) dominates fourth-century Christian history and thought, providing definitive contours to the Alexandrian brand of theology sometimes labeled "Christian Platonism." His was a turbulent career. Five times exiled during his forty-five years as bishop of Alexandria (from 328), he remained the intrepid defender of Nicaea against the Arians through the reigns of Arianizing emperors. His links with Origen, though real, were mainly mediated through Eusebius's apologetic work; he could not follow Origen's view of a "graduated Trinity" and fought the Arian subordinationism that looked for a footing in Origenism. His *Orations Against the Arians* emphasized that salvation, to be real, required the Logos to be truly God in order to cleanse us from the depth of sin. He developed his soteriological approach in *On the Incarnation,* where the much-debated statement was found: The Son became man, that we might become God. A defender of the monks' orthodoxy, who protected him during his third exile, he authored the influential *Life of Antony,* which, soon translated, spread the monastic ideal in East and West. In fact, at the time of his first exiles in Trier and Rome, Athanasius had forged solid links with Rome and the West. Finally, mention must be made of his *Festal Letters,* which, using the occasion of announcing the date of Easter, contained pastoral exhortations to the communities; one of those letters presents the definitive list of the New Testament books (canon), along with the Old Testament list.

The legend of a meek, compassionate, and upright Athanasius, champion of Nicaean orthodoxy and martyr for the sake of truth, has

been somewhat deflated by recent research. A less favorable portrait
has emerged of a man inclined to intrigue and violence, who misunder-
stood the Antiochene concerns, willfully vilified Arius (who himself
fares better in recent studies), and died a sign of contradiction after a
mixed career. Nonetheless, the study of his writings restores the balance; the coherence and sincerity of his doctrine cannot be impugned.
The uncompromising fighter became more flexible at the end of his
life; and in the end, his positive impact on the shaping of orthodoxy in
East and West can certainly not be lamented.

A more integral disciple of Origen is encountered in the person of
Evagrius of Pontus (345–399), the famous ascetic and cultured man. A
friend of Basil and Gregory of Nazianzus, well trained in Greek learning,
he spent time among the "Origenists" in Palestine, where he was converted to the ascetic life, and arrived in the Egyptian desert in 382. There
he became familiar with early monastic practices and applied his creative
mind to the assiduous study of Origen. Over the years he was able to
translate Origen's notion of three sciences (moral, philosophical, contemplative) into a complete system of spirituality that influenced all traditions of Christian spiritual itineraries. The system can be expressed in a
ternary form (purgation, illumination, union) or in a binary one (*prak-
tikè*/asceticism, *gnostikè*/mysticism), hence two of his major works,
Praktikos and *Gnostikos*. In his speculative musings Evagrius decisively
went beyond Origen's vision of the fall and return of the soul. He refused
to image the incorporeal God, who can be talked about only in apophatic
terms (eshewing precise description or definition). Describing the union
with God in terms of absorption, he made contemplative prayer the goal
of monastic life; yet he was able to use graphic language to depict the
victory over demons leading to *apatheia,* that deep calm of the one in
control of one's emotional life, and to *agape,* the loving state of the one
who contemplates God. Asceticism thus leads to mysticism, both being
dynamically integrated. In Evagrius monasticism had found its lasting
language if not its definitive theology. Cassian and Rufinus made him
known to the Latin West.

The condemnation of Origenism in 553 (see below) affected the
writings of Evagrius; some of them were destroyed but many were preserved in translation (Syriac and Armenian) or survived under someone
else's name. Hence many of his works are available today—among
them, the above-mentioned ones plus the *Kephalaia gnostica,* pub-

lished in 1958 from a Syriac version—and uncover a rich side of the Alexandrian tradition. As early as around 400, Evagrius had been slandered by Theophilus of Alexandria, who started harassing Evagrius's disciples (especially the monks known as the Tall Brothers and their Nitrian colleagues) and fired up anti-Origenist passions. Evagrius's influence endured, though, and the recovery of his works vindicates the memory of a loyal and penetrating genius.

Cyril of Alexandria's (372/376–444) career and personality were and remain highly controversial. Was the "doctor of the Incarnation" a saint, a second Athanasius, a profound theologian? Or rather was he basically endowed with a vicious character, the unscrupulous nephew of the opportunist Theophilus, whom he succeeded in 412, out to secure by all means the place of Alexandria in the contest with Constantinople? There were indeed two extreme sides to his nature, which brought about contradictory assessments of his contribution.

On the one hand, he seemed to revel in rough confrontations—he was said to have worked at despoliating Jews and taking over their synagogue; to have had a hand in the killing of a woman-philosopher, Hypatia; to have fenced with the prefect and helped burn pagan temples. He illustrated and brought to new heights a negative aspect of the Alexandrian tradition: the fanatic intolerance and biting polemic deployed against pagans, Jews, and heretics alike. His bullying opposition to Nestorius from 429 on was particularly dripping with venom; his role at the council of Ephesus in 431 was shameful, managing to have the proceedings start before the arrival of the Antiochenes. But all the same, of his three letters challenging Nestorius, the third one ended up being included in the acts of the council of Ephesus and received canonical status at Chalcedon. In his attacks on Diodore of Tarsus and Theodore of Mopsuestia, whom he suspected of having influenced Nestorius, he did not mind relying on truncated and hostile excerpts and using monophysite arguments to counter his "dyophysite" opponents. Only after the cease-fire of 433, in the Formula of Reunion mainly due to John of Antioch, did he tone down his bad manners and drop the twelve anathemata against Nestorius he had appended to his third letter and that were totally unacceptable to the Antiochenes.

On the other hand, his immense literary output shows clear signs of a resourceful and astute theologian. His anti-Arian treatises, anti-

Nestorian writings, and dialogues on the Trinity, on Christology, on worship in spirit and truth, all reveal a searching mind, clarifying and modifying the work of his predecessors (Athanasius, even Apollinarius), and reaching levels of understanding still inspiring today. He authored the first essays in biblical theology with his homilies and copious commentaries on the Old and New Testaments. In his exegesis, because of the ongoing controversy and under the influence of Jerome and of his uncle's anti-Origenism, he distanced himself from Origen, though holding to the view of two levels of meaning in close correspondence, as best illustrated in the parables. So the allegorical interpretation is used along with typological exegesis to vindicate christological claims. With Christ "recapitulating" Adam, the superiority of Christianity is manifested by a spiritual exegesis of the text and supported by the "patristic argument." Based on the authority of the earlier fathers, the argument aims to document the constant view of the tradition.

Cappadocians

The same reserve on allegory due to the same Origenist controversy is noticeable among the three extremely talented writers of Cappadocia (Asia Minor): Basil and the two Gregorys. Nonetheless, their debt to Origen is unmistakable, and they made great use of his exegetical work. Highly cultured people, children of rich Christian families and destined all three to be at some point influential bishops, they show in their own persons the interplay of classical culture, especially Platonism, and Christianity. They experienced the chill of Julian's prohibition against having Christians teach classical literature and pagan science. They came out of that interlude convinced that, far from belonging to paganism, classical culture is the true fruit of the Logos and hence the ideal vehicle of theology. Athens is indeed very close to Jerusalem. In exploiting that proximity the Cappadocians contributed a great deal to the creation of a Christian literature that went beyond the literary forms of earlier Christian writings; they were able to put the rhetorical tradition to use and began producing essays, poems, letters, orations, of a new vintage.

Faithful defenders of Nicaea, they helped its triumph under Theodosius I (378–395), above all at the council of Constantinople. In the process they opened up the untapped resources of religious language and imagery in order to bring remarkable elaborations to trinitarian theology (especially Basil) and to Christology (especially Gregory of Nazianzus). Here lies their lasting achievement, which they buttressed with the help of an Alexandrian emphasis: Christ's incarnation, still more than his death-resurrection, constitutes the decisive act of salvation. But they did more: They proposed a Christian way of life that remained ideal for its balance, midway between abdication to the world and total renunciation. This they achieved through their efforts at Christianizing philosophy and culture.

Basil of Caesarea (330–379) and his friend Gregory of Nazianzus both studied the classics and Platonism in Athens, among other places, before returning to Cappadocia and entering ecclesiastical careers. Familiar with the monastic establishments of Syria, Palestine, and Egypt, and eventually made a bishop, Basil organized charity and founded brotherhoods not in the desert but "within reach of suffering humanity."[1] He advocated the simple life lived close to the world. The "liturgy of St. Basil" that he developed is still in use today. He shone as a great exegete in his numerous commentaries and homilies and was a powerful theologian as demonstrated in his anti-Arian work *On the Holy Spirit.* The *Rules* that go under his name *(Ascetica)* consist mainly of ascetic works and letters, collected in the sixth century, summarizing his ascetical ideal for use by monks; though not cast in the mold of later codes of monastic life, they did influence the latter. Basil was well aware of the excesses of Syrian monks and opted for Pachomius's ideas of communality and social responsibility, the whole being cast in a Stoic and Platonic framework. His correspondence, which survives in over 300 letters, reflects this spiritual equilibrium.

Made bishop of Constantinople for a short while only, at the time of the second general council (381), Gregory of Nazianzus (330–390) had a declared preference for less stormy surroundings. He was able, nevertheless, to prevail over the Arians of the capital, especially through his five well-known theological *Orations* (there were some forty-five of them in all) in which he reveals himself as a brilliant exponent of trinitarian orthodoxy and of the divinity of the Spirit. His language remains close to the biblical model with the added flavor of mystical and devo-

---

1. F. Young, *From Nicaea to Chalcedon: A Guide to the Literature and Its Development.* Philadelphia: Fortress Press, 1983, p. 108.

tional scent. The compositions of Gregory "the Theologian," as he is known in the East, are worthy of the greatest classical models. He left numerous poetical works and some 250 letters. Together with his friend Basil, he compiled the *Philocalia,* a collection of extracts from Origen, an "Origen reader" of unique value to students of the great master. We owe to Gregory also an autobiography in verse.

The most prolific of the Cappadocians was doubtless Gregory of Nyssa (331–393), brother of Basil and of the ascetic Macrina the Younger. In spite of having received merely informal training, he greatly influenced the council of Constantinople (381) and must be counted among "the greatest philosophical minds of the early church."[2] In his dogmatic and exegetical writings, the doctrine of the Trinity received its final shape and he purged Christology of the last glimmer of docetism still lingering in Alexandria. *Catechetical Oration, That There Are Not Three Gods,* writings against the extreme Arian Eunomius, homilies, commentaries, letters (some thirty survived), all document the ability of this powerful thinker. The *Life of Moses,* on the ascent of the soul to God, and the *Life of Macrina,* on the ideal virtuous life, the truly "philosophical life," show him equally at ease describing mystical experience and propounding a model of ascetic life. In him Christian Platonism—more precisely, Middle and Neoplatonism—found its finest spokesman.

Antiochene-Syrians

Two authors writing in Syriac left their mark on the fourth century and beyond: Aphrahat and above all Ephrem (306–373). The latter lived as a deacon in Nisibis, then in Edessa when Nisibis was ceded to the Persians in 363; he is remembered as hymnist and exegete. Didactic poetry and biblical commentaries in the typological vein embody a vision of the world as a sea of symbols; access to it is given by the incarnate Son, himself "the Lord of the symbols" and the key opening the gate to the true understanding of Bible, nature, and history. Ephrem is credited with the introduction into orthodox Christianity of the early Syriac, non-Greek tradition in close but polemical relation to both

---

2. Ibid., p. 105.

Gnosticism and Jewish-Christianity. His hymns became known, in translation, to all branches of Christianity and he is celebrated as one of the most important poets of the period.

First a student of the philosopher Libanius and baptized at the age of eighteen, John Chrysostom (345–407) then tried the life of a renouncer. Having damaged his health in the process, he came back to Antioch where he worked as deacon, then priest, preaching to wide audiences regularly and with increasing self-assurance. One day he was "kidnapped" to become the bishop of Constantinople (from 397). He was a formidable preacher (*Chrysostom* means "golden mouth"), the greatest of the Christian rhetors, capable of abusing his under-Christianized audience as well as his adversaries. His style and character combined to antagonize almost everybody, including the clergy, who found him severe, irascible, cruel, and imperious. His downfall was the consequence—he died in exile, the victim of his own doing and of the wicked tricks orchestrated by Bishop Theophilus of Alexandria. Because he gave hospitality to the Tall Brothers and their fifty companions, members of Evagrius's community, who were harassed by Theophilus wherever they tried to flee, John was unjustly accused, among other invented "crimes," of Origenism. His writings are characterized by the single-minded concern to uplift the moral level of all, believers, monks, and bishops. He knew of no double standard but thought that the ascetic life could be lived within the daily conditions of the world. However harsh in his criticism, he could also demonstrate compassion. This complex personality appealed to many, which accounts for his works having been carefully transmitted and being still widely read in Greek-speaking churches. His "liturgy" is, along with Basil's, the main source of eucharistic service still used today in the Orthodox church. Commentaries (e.g., on St. John), tractates (on priesthood, on virginity), sermons (e.g., the eight sermons against the Judaizing Christians, not preached against the Jews but addressed to Christians too much inclined to participate in Jewish festivals and attend the synagogue—though they were later used to foster hostility and hatred toward the Jews), baptismal instructions, letters (some 240 have survived): All illustrate the Antiochene approach and style of interpretation, explaining lines and words, and offering a christological reading of the Old Testament.

Theodore of Mopsuestia (350–428) had been, like John Chrysostom, a pupil of Libanius and like him first chose the ascetic life before becoming a bishop. His commentaries, doctrinal works *(On Incarnation),* and catechetical homilies, when not entirely lost, are mainly preserved in Syriac. They typify a historical exegesis close to that of Paul, insisting on the newness of the gospel and keeping away from both the Platonic flight from this world and the Alexandrian allegorism. In spite of his having been disparaged by opponents and posthumously condemned in 553 along with Origen, both victims of Byzantine politics and, in the case of Theodore, of the Alexandrian obsession with the Syrian precursors of Nestorius, his writings remained very influential. Like Origen rehabilitated by recent research and finds, he is honored in the East as "the Interpreter," the best representative of the Antiochene type of interpretation.

A classical villain, the deposed bishop of Constantinople Nestorius (380–451) was born in Syria and educated and ordained in Antioch. He has been considerably vindicated by the recent discovery of his *Book of Heraclides,* which shows him as a quite worthy theologian of the Antiochene style. But devoid of political sense and overzealous in his censoring of heretics and women, he made too many powerful enemies. He had the misfortune of clashing with Empress Pulcheria and above all with Cyril of Alexandria (as John Chrysostom had with Cyril's uncle Theophilus). Even his bad character was no match for Cyril's temper. His account of Christ's unity at the level of the *prosopon* (subject) was certainly consistent though not strict enough for most colleagues. Refused a hearing at Ephesus in 431, he was deposed and exiled to Egypt, ready to live in oblivion provided God was not dishonored. He seems then to have been willing to call Mary the *theotokos* but astutely warned against making the virgin a goddess. He found a more sympathetic hearing at Chalcedon in 451, where Pope Leo's *Tomus* was seen by many to side with him. But, it is said, he did not wish to tarnish truth with his hated name and stayed away from further contest. His followers did not imitate him in that; they, not Nestorius, were the real Nestorians.

Another victim of Cyril was Theodoret of Cyrrhus (399–466), later hailed as the greatest of the Antiochene scholars and the best presenter of the christological disputes. Renowned as historian and hagiographer *(Church History, History of the Monks of Syria),* he also authored apologetic and exegetical works of high quality, as well as over 200 letters. Reluctant to condemn Nestorius, whom he considered misrepresented by Cyril's caricature, and maligned for his lack of ardor, he was first vindicated at Chalcedon. But in 553 his anti-Cyrillic writings were condemned in the hostile excerpts known as the *Three Chapters* (including passages from Theodore of Mopsuestia and Ibas of Edessa). In his dogmatic essays *On Trinity* and *On Incarnation,* he marks his difference from the Alexandrians, interpreting salvation as union with God by participation, not as divinization. Modern research emphasizes his originality, his many-sided talent, and his clear prose; but it considers his historical work most valuable, based as it is on a mass of original documents.

Latins

The literary activity of Tertullian and Cyprian, who stood out in the third century among the first Latin writers, has already been mentioned. In the fourth and fifth centuries, four characters were to eclipse all others. They were active not only in various corners of the Latin West; two of them—Rufinus and Jerome—worked also in the East. All but Augustine were conversant with the work of Origen, if not with Greek Christian thought altogether.

Ambrose of Milan (337–397) is even credited with having mediated the Greek tradition to the West (especially Origen, Athanasius, and Basil), adding to it a further Neoplatonic color. A man of action, the bishop of Milan held his own against the emperor and in the process might have become a bit intolerant; at any rate he determined the future course of church-state coexistence in the West. He gave lasting shape to Western liturgy thanks to his innovations in Milan and his composition of hymns. His sermons, with their nonliteral interpretation of the Old Testament, had great impact, not least on the young Augustine. Among his writings should be mentioned his *Hexaëmeron,* an allegorical treatment of the six days of creation, the *Holy Spirit,* the *Mysteries,* the *Sacraments,* the *Duties of Ministers,* and some ninety letters.

Born in Aquileia and initially a friend of Jerome, Rufinus (345–410) embarked on a course of literary studies that took him to Rome, where, while developing precious contacts with the nobility, he joined an ascetic group that had Jerome as a member. Disenchanted with life among Roman high society, he opted for the ascetic life. This took him to Egypt, where he encountered the living thought of Origen embodied in Evagrius and Didymus the Blind. He then went to Jerusalem, where he founded, with Melania the Elder, a double monastery of men and women ascetics. Soon he fell out with Jerome, who had become a competitor in recruiting noble ascetics (Paula, Marcella) and above all had abruptly joined the anti-Origenist camp with Epiphanius against John of Jerusalem and Rufinus himself. A bitter relationship developed that ended only at the death of Rufinus, who had returned to Italy in 397. Besides scholarly works of his own, Rufinus is mainly remembered for his gigantic work as a translator. We owe him, among other works, a complete though toned-down version of Origen's *On First Principles,* which fed the Origenist controversy; of Eusebius's *History of the Church,* which he updated; of Basil's *Ascetica;* of Evagrius's *Sentences.* Because Rufinus had his coterie of supporters in Jerusalem and in Rome at odds with Jerome's coterie of female friends in Bethlehem and Rome, there resulted colorful intrigues as well as important developments in the ascetic tradition, both offering glimpses into vivid aspects of Christian life.

Similarly, Jerome (347–420) left Dalmatia as a young man for Rome, where he made contact with the imperial house. Having finally chosen the ascetic life, he joined the Syrian monks near Antioch, soon to discover that he was not cut out for the excesses of those extremists. Back in Rome, he became spiritual advisor to noble Roman women and made preparations for establishing houses for ascetic women. He left for Jerusalem in 384 and, with Paula, opened a double monastery in Bethlehem, where he also pursued his scholarly career. A difficult character, grumpy and acidic, after an Origenist period he turned (probably intimidated by Epiphanius) against Origen, as he did against Pelagius; denounced John of Jerusalem for his Origenist leanings; and countered Rufinus's translation of *On First Principles* with his own literal translation, now lost. He demonstrated a remarkable activity in the many letters (about 150 are extant) he wrote, many of them polemical. He was made and remained famous for his translation of the Bible (called the *Vulgate*), which, with its translation of the Old Testament from the Hebrew text, superseded all existing versions and nourished Western Christian thought until today. He also wrote numerous commentaries on biblical books and what could be called the first "patrology," his *Famous Men*. He was an extremely talented writer, yet he delighted in abusive language and often used his intelligence to crush his opponents. It has been said that he basically was a satirist who took his own satires seriously, thus attracting countless enemies. It can be added that to know him well is to know his entire period because he was found everywhere, involved as soon as the possibility of a debate was offered.

It is unique in the history of the Patristic Period, and even of the West altogether, for one single author to have been involved in four major and decisive disputes in the course of which his positive contribution eventually became the lasting position of the church, and to have authored three works that became classics of Western literature. This was the achievement of Augustine (354–430), who did for the West what Origen did for the East: set the tone for all future theological reflection. But he seems to have been, among Westerners, the least aware of the Origenist explorations.

In the course of the four main controversies of his career (see chapter 5), Augustine initiated positions that all future theologians were bound to take into account. Against the Manichees he defended the place and significance of the Old Testament, and discussed the problems of free will, evil, and God. Against the Donatists he developed the doctrine of the church and sacraments. Against the Pelagians he introduced the doctrine of original sin, along with further elucidations of grace and free will. Against the pagans, who occupied his mind from the time of his conversion, he proposed the doctrine of the "two cities," clarified the relationship between faith and reason, and sketched a comprehensive philosophy or theology of history.

Besides his three classic works, the *Confessions, On the Trinity,* and *The City of God,* Augustine wrote a multitude of works that illustrate the greatness of his mind and his command of rhetoric: tractates on specific questions, biblical commentaries, sermons, well over 200 letters, two dozen of which have recently been discovered and published.

Compared with Origen, Augustine exhibits a less optimistic cast of mind and he got grumpier with age. Nevertheless, the traditional saying can be altered and bent to state that the history of Christian theology is a footnote commentary to both Augustine and Origen.

The Origenist Controversy

The presentation of this momentous though fateful controversy had to be delayed until this point, for the main participants it mobilized had first to be introduced. Moreover, the controversy itself was not ended before 553. In it trinitarian and christological debates as well as cosmological and anthropological speculations were dramatically orchestrated, and several of the authors mentioned so far had some involvement. This is to say that an entire epoch finds its reflection in those discussions as in a mirror.

"Origenism" is the name given to a certain theological system attributed to but drifting away from Origen, in doctrinal conflicts of the fourth through sixth centuries. Condemned by various synods and by Emperor Justinian, it contained ideas such as the preexistence of souls, which, because of a pre-cosmic fault, were forcibly united to bodies; the spherical shape of resurrected bodies; the universal salvation of all rational beings; and a tendency to view the Son as not quite equal to the Father. Origen's thought could not, obviously, be reduced to those isolated statements and oversimplifications, the work of certain disciples and above all of bitter foes.

How did the controversy develop? Perhaps we can identify four stages. The first stage coincides with the publication of *On First Principles* and its immediate aftermath. In that work Origen intended to address a Christian audience interested in philosophical questions at a time (219–225) when no "connected body of doctrine"[3] existed and when very few dogmatic agreements had been reached by the church. Using the distinction between *dogmatikos,* what is plainly clear and affirmed as doctrine in the "rule of faith," and *gymnastikos,* what can be said tentatively by mode of research and hypothesis, Origen felt confident that he could safely speculate in the second sense by means of the allegorical approach, and that he could legitimately make forays into unexplored territory. This he did, speculating on the preexistence of the soul, the accidental union of souls with bodies *(ensomatosis),* the imaging of God, the status of the Son, the Trinity, the resurrection of the body, and the restoration of all things—including the final salvation of all rational beings and embracing even the devil. Given his initial distinction, not all of Origen's statements had the same claim to certainty;

---

3. De princ., Pref. 10.

critical discernment in reading his writings and some sense of his historical situation were called for, qualities often lacking at the time of the
controversy.

From the fourth century on, lively and, to some, scandalous discussions broke out among the followers of Origen, the "Origenists,"
marking the second stage of the controversy. Not all had the good
sense of Evagrius in the use of the allegorical method and in discern-
ing what in Origen was an assertion or thesis and what a searching
question or hypothesis. Some, it seems (the Syrian monk Stephen,
perhaps the Tall Brothers of Nitria and their companions, some Palestinian monks), not only tended in their Origenist fervor to apply a
spiritualizing approach to all biblical "anthropomorphisms" and
"material" references, including even such things as the sacraments,
but they even claimed that the allegorical interpretation was the only
valid one, thus rejecting all imaging or representation of God. Even
expressions such as God's love, God's act, Father and Son, had to be
interpreted spiritually. Many thought that this tendency was endangering the humanity of God in his incarnation. Furthermore, an unbridled inclination to mystical speculation appeared that threatened to
dissolve the historical character of Christian revelation, claiming a
direct union with God that did not have to be mediated by historical
events and persons. This was more than Origen would have conceded
or than Evagrius's piety had claimed.

In the meantime, the third stage of the dispute had set in, at the
time the Arian party had piqued powerful opponents among the orthodox. Epiphanius of Salamis (310/320–403) had seen as a young man
how much Egypt was torn apart on the subject of Origen's legacy. Soon
he came to see Origen and his christological views (anachronologically
and not very consistently)[4] as the source of Arianism, and in his
Panarion, written 374–377, charged Origen with heresy. But it is in 393
that the controversy really flared up when the same Epiphanius dared to
broadcast the charge in a sermon in Jerusalem, that is, outside his own
jurisdiction. He then repeated and amplified it in a letter to John of
Jerusalem. Epiphanius also wrote to John Chrysostom prior to 400 urg-
ing him to abstain from studying Origen's writings and to convene a
synod to condemn him. John Chrysostom dragged his feet in that mat-

---

4. See E. Clark, *The Origenist Controversy.* Princeton: Princeton University
Press, 1992, p. 104.

ter and did not see fit to move against Origenism. When begged by the cynical and opportunistic Theophilus of Alexandria, early in 403, to defend the orthodoxy threatened by John Chrysostom's supposed alliance with the Origenists, the old Epiphanius had by then developed the notion that he was the providential "hammer of Origenism";[5] he leaped into action, sailed to Constantinople, made a fool of himself, failed to have Origen's writings condemned by the bishops he could assemble, realized that perhaps he had been enrolled by Theophilus for his own purposes of dethroning and degrading John Chrysostom, and died on the high seas on his way back home.

That stage of the controversy had a second plot. Up to the mid–390s Jerome had been an Origenist of a sort. Doubtless impressed by Epiphanius's denunciations, he suddenly changed sides, making first a half-hearted volte-face and putting out a "lukewarm" attack on Origen.[6] In that he was imitating Theophilus of Alexandria, who had similarly changed his stance and begun persecuting Origenist monks in Egypt. At one point Theophilus himself enlisted Jerome's literary support against Origenist errors. It is at that juncture that the Tall Brothers and some fifty companions, accused of Origenism, had to flee to Palestine and then to Constantinople, where they were given hospitality by John Chrysostom who, in this indirect way, became unwillingly entangled in the controversy. As for Jerome, he shouted his dissociation from Origenism in one breath: "I am no Marcionite, Manichee or Encratite."[7] To a large extent his turnabout served to rescue his own reputation and in the end his ferocious attack on Origen became a means of vilifying his present-day enemies, above all Rufinus, the Origen scholar.

The theological controversy had by then become a political strife and involved the resentment of Alexandria toward the capital Constantinople. Intrigues by Theophilus (anticipating those of his nephew Cyril against Nestorius), gradually losing interest in Origenism and bent on weakening the church of the capital recently (381) given primacy of honor, centered on the person of the bishop of Constantinople, John Chrysostom, himself not very popular because of his rigorous standards and acerbic criticism of clergy and court. The outcome was the

---

5. J. N. D. Kelly, *Golden Mouth: The Story of John Chrysostom.* London: Duckworth, 1995, p. 205.

6. Clark, *The Origenist Controversy,* p. 150.

7. Jerome, *Adversus Jovinianum* 1.3, NPNF, 2nd ser., vol. 6.

deposition of John, secured in 403 at the synod of the Oak (the young Cyril was there with Theophilus) and enforced in 404 by Emperor Arcadius, who exiled him. His successor, Theodosius II, however, considered John a martyr and had his relics brought back to the capital in a fitting display of honor.

The fourth stage of the controversy lingered for the next century, reaching its high point at the second council of Constantinople, in 553. Ten years earlier, writing to Menas, patriarch of Constantinople, Emperor Justinian had given a list of objectionable statements, questionably attributed to Origen (we now know that they were mainly from Evagrius). Those fragments and anathemas were made public at a synod in Constantinople and confirmed at the general council of 553. Origen's works were proscribed and most of them, probably five-sixths of the whole, were lost; Evagrius's speculative treatises (not his ascetic works) left the Greek stage but were preserved in Palestine and Syria, to be partially recovered through recent finds.

This intricate story contained a warning that shrewd analysts were to hearken to. A condemnation had been pronounced with total disregard for the changes that had accrued to the historical situation and to the puzzling variety of charges successively laid at the door of Origen. Origen had written his works at a time prior to conciliar definitions, prior to the formulation of trinitarian and christological dogmas, a time when theological vocabulary was quite imprecise. Three centuries later that situation had significantly changed, but the change was not taken into account in condemning Origen. The distinction between Origen and the Origenists collapsed. Origen's own intentions were neglected and the opponents' interests were allowed to prevail. Justified as the condemnation of Origenist extravagancies was because of intervening doctrinal developments, the condemnation of Origen himself was a total anachronism in addition to being marred by a kind of error on the person. History took care of the due rectification. The East kept revering Origen as its most important theologian while the West, especially since Erasmus in the sixteenth century, has rehabilitated him completely.

The Last Fathers

Before turning to some of the "last" representatives of the Patristic Period, we have to mention the literary activity of various groups at the fringes of, or outside, the empire. They show that Eastern and Oriental patristic literature went on well beyond our period. The works produced are often important in themselves; however, their translations are especially precious for the knowledge they afford of mostly Greek works whose originals are lost but, thanks to the labor of these groups, were translated into their respective languages. Thus we have works in Coptic of the fourth to seventh centuries; in Armenian from the fourth/fifth to fourteenth centuries; in Georgian from the seventh to fourteenth centuries; in Arabic (based on Greek and Syriac works) from the eighth to fourteenth centuries; and in Ethiopic (based on Greek, Syriac, and Latin works) from the seventh to fourteenth centuries. All those works are presently being edited and made available.

Among the last fathers and already mentioned because of his influence at the time of Chalcedon 451, we encounter Pope Leo I (or Leo the Great, 400–461), who wrote many sermons (some forty-six are extant), over 100 letters, and several tractates. But he is best remembered for his *Tomus* (Tome), which, sent to Flavian, bishop of Constantinople, signaled his most important intervention in problems of dogma and politics. In it, using some Eastern sources, he propounded the christological doctrine of "two natures in the one person" of the incarnate Christ, which was received as the orthodox position at the council of Chalcedon, though challenged by important "Oriental" groups for centuries to come. He championed the claim to primacy of the bishop of Rome within the church, seen as the vicar and heir of Peter.

Sometimes called the "founder of the medieval papacy," Pope Gregory I (or Gregory the Great, 540–604) authored the famous *Moral Discourses on Job,* a series of instructions on moral and ascetical questions in the form of a commentary on the book of Job, which is, in fact, a commentary on the entire scripture. In that work he puts to use the best of the exegetical tradition formalized in the three levels of interpretation: literal, allegorical or spiritual, and moral. More than 800 of his letters have survived. His *Dialogues* recount the marvelous lives of holy men and women in Italy. His theological views were generally close to Augustine's. His name has traditionally been connected with the reform of the liturgical practice of the church and the fresh impulse given to sacred music. In 596 he sent forty monks headed by one Augustine to evangelize the Anglo-Saxons of Britain. The first pope to call himself "servant of the servants of God," he was also clear about his own dignity not only as Peter's vicar, but even as "Christ's representative."

The enigmatic figure of the Syrian *(Pseudo-)* Dionysius the Areopagite (ca. 500) had a lasting impact on medieval Western theology with his mystical and spiritual works blending Neoplatonism (especially Proclus), Origen, and the Eastern tradition into a powerful doctrine. Written in Greek, his *Celestial Hierarchy, Ecclesiastical Hierarchy, On the Divine Names,* and *Mystical Theology* significantly nourished medieval theology and mysticism, after being wholeheartedly received by the Monophysites and Severus of Antioch. The best of Dionysius, but also of Origen, Evagrius, and the Cappadocians, was recaptured by one of the most powerful thinkers of the East, Maximus Confessor (580–662), in a synthesis that counts as the great achievement of Byzantine theology.

John of Damascus (675–749), the great opponent of the iconoclast party, well trained in Greek and Arabic culture, closes these centuries of literary production. His *Orthodox Faith* became the standard doctrinal textbook of Eastern Christianity; it intentionally avoids making original statements, extolling the tradition of the Greek fathers, especially Gregory of Nazianzus, to which he adds Leo the Great. His influence was also noticeable in the West from the twelfth century on.

A final writer ought to be mentioned: the learned Photius (820–897), twice patriarch of Constantinople. Although he falls beyond the limits of this survey, he had the good fortune of seeing and reading numerous works of previous centuries now lost to us, and the good instinct of reporting on them and quoting from them in his *Bibliotheca* (Library) or *Description and List of the Volumes Read by Us*, available today in eight volumes. These short notices are full of precious information on works that would otherwise be forgotten, and on the contents of the archives of the see of Constantinople.

Church Mothers

In his history of the desert fathers, referring to the heroic women ascetics who peopled the fringes of the Egyptian desert, Palladius depicted their significant impact by calling them "manly women" and "female fathers."[8] The expression not only baffles our scruples concerning gender propriety; it also uncovers the silent presence of "desert mothers" and "wandering virgins" that traditional treatments of the Patristic Period are quick to forget. The present survey of patristic history and literature is itself extremely male in content. What exactly, then, can be said about the "mothers of the church"? Do excuses based on the paucity of the female record constitute a valid alibi for the thin treatment accorded women in the period under study?

Again, the "Patristic" age was one of unabashed patriarchal dominion, capable of the paradoxical tour de force of combining misogynism with the praise of virginity. All the same, some of the great leaders and writers among the fathers had women associates or confidantes. True, very few women themselves produced writings, but a fair number of them—virgins, widows, mothers, and empresses—were written about.

Much of the literature about women concerns first of all Mary, the mother of Jesus, whose virginity was rhapsodized about, particularly in times when theoretical treatises on virginity abounded. Also quite early, heroines and martyrs found praise and veneration for their faith, but also for their leadership and the challenge they meant to the authorities; such were Blandina and Perpetua, martyred in 177 and 203, respectively. Women ascetics received the widest treatment, mostly because of their association with eminent male leaders. Here mention must be made of the Cappadocian Macrina; of the two Melanias associated with Rufinus; of Jerome's co-workers Marcella, the two Paulas, Eustochium, Poimenia; of John Chrysostom's friend and confidante Olympias. Many of these achieved by their public activity a remarkable emancipation from societal norms.

There were also active prophetesses and women leaders among Montanists and Gnostics, although female roles among the Gnostics should not be idealized—Gnostics often extolled radical forms of antifeminity. Some noble women, aristocrats, even empresses were addressees of spiritual letters and exercised some ruling function. The empowerment of women was not totally lacking in this period, but it was the case of a tiny flock.

As to Christian literature written by women, a few instances are

---

8. Palladius, *The Lausiac History* 41.1. Translated R. T. Meyer. ACW, vol. 34, 1964.

recorded, without really justifying the talk of a lost tradition. The first in date is the *Passion of Perpetua and Felicity,* mainly lifted from Perpetua's diary of 203/204, with editorial additions long attributed to Tertullian. In the mid-fourth century a certain Proba authored a *Cento,* a narrative of sacred history in artificial Vergilian verses to be used as a school text. In 1884 there was found an account of travel to the Holy Land *(Itinerarium)* by the Spaniard Egeria (or Etheria), which contains much information on the liturgical and religious life in Jerusalem around 385. In fact, pilgrimage to the Holy Land had been undertaken by noble women, from Constantine's mother, Helena, early in the fourth century to empress Eudocia, who traveled to Palestine in 438/439 and died there in 460. She herself wrote poetry and even doctrinal works, such as *The Martyrdom of St. Cyprian* (an Antiochene Cyprian), a work made up of Homeric stitchings written in laborious hexameters by a learned and pious person. Although they only occasionally took to writing, the Theodosian empresses were known for their imperiousness, best illustrated by Pulcheria, who personally influenced the proceedings of the council of Ephesus in 431 and exercised organizing and directing functions at Chalcedon in 451, to the point that it was said that she personally triumphed over Nestorius and Eutyches.

On the whole, therefore, though a few women were influential personalities in their times, women in general followed only too well the injunctions laid down by New Testament authors like Paul recommending submission and invisibility. Real empowerment of women can find only fleeting precedents in those centuries and must be wrought on other grounds. However, a globally negative judgment on this topic would be wrong.

> Christianity did...have the effect of bringing women into the public sphere. They could travel to the Holy Land, found monasteries, learn Hebrew, choose not to marry or to become celibate, dedicate themselves to the religious life and form friendships with men outside their own family circle, all things which would scarcely have been possible before. In contrast, we might remember, nearly all Christian slaves and *coloni* remain among the great mass of unknown ancient people, whom nobody wrote about.[9]

---

9. A. Cameron, *The Mediterranean World in Late Antiquity.* New York: Routledge, 1993, p. 148.

READINGS

S. P. Brock	*The Luminous Eye: The Spiritual World Vision of St. Ephrem.* Kalamazoo, Mich.: Cistercian Publications, 1992.
S. P. Brock and S. B. Harvey, eds.	*Holy Women of the Syrian Orient.* Berkeley: University of California Press, 1987.
P. Brown	*Augustine of Hippo: A Biography.* Berkeley: University of California Press, 1967.
E. Clark	*Jerome, Chrysostom and Friends.* New York: E. Mellen Press, 1979.
E. Clark	*The Origenist Controversy: The Cultural Construction of an Early Christian Debate.* Princeton: Princeton University Press, 1992.
G. Clark	*Women in Late Antiquity.* New York: Oxford University Press, 1993.
E. Ferguson, ed.	*Women in Early Christianity.* New York: Garland, 1993.
A. Guillaumont	*Les "Kephalaia gnostica" d'Evagre le Pontique.* Paris: Seuil, 1962.
K. G. Holum	*Theodosian Empresses: Women and Imperial Dominion in Late Antiquity.* Berkeley: University of California Press, 1981.
C. Kannengiesser and W. L. Petersen	*Origen of Alexandria: His World and His Legacy.* Notre Dame, Ind.: University of Notre Dame Press, 1988.
J. N. D. Kelly	*Golden Mouth: The Story of John Chrysostom, Ascetic, Preacher, Bishop.* London: Duckworth, 1995.
J. N. D. Kelly	*Jerome: His Life, Writings and Controversies.* London: Duckworth, 1975.

N. B. McLynn

Ambrose of Milan: Church and Court in a Christian Capital. Berkeley: University of California Press, 1994.

A. Meredith

The Cappadocians. Crestwood, N.Y.: St. Vladimir's Seminary Press, 1995.

R. Murray

Symbols of Church and Kingdom: A Study in Early Syriac Tradition. New York: Cambridge University Press, 1975.

D. J. Sahas

John of Damascus on Islam. Leiden: Brill, 1972.

W. J. Sheils and D. Wood, eds.

Women in the Church. Oxford: Blackwell, 1990.

J. W. Trigg

"Origen and Origenism in the 1990s." *Religious Studies Review* 22 (1996): 301–308.

10

Main Developments Between 500 and 800

The previous chapters regularly tried to place the main patristic writers against their own historical background and the development of the Christian movement. Constant effort was made to maintain a balance between history and literature. In the present chapter, due in part to a certain dearth of the literary record and in part to the relative paucity of comprehensive studies, literature recedes backstage and history becomes the protagonist. Now the historical survey presented here covers, in a few pages, three centuries of no lesser turbulence, so it is inevitable that it be schematic and highly selective. Only general orientations can be mentioned, most of the individual writers being kept in the dark. Nevertheless, short as it is, this survey might inspire further study and serious attempts at doing greater justice to the post-451 period.

The Shaking of the Empire

The division of Theodosius's empire in 395 between Honorius and Arcadius turned out to be an epoch-making event. The two halves they inherited, going back to Diocletian's reorganization of the imperial office with two senior and two junior emperors, were already engaged in a process of growing political and cultural differentiation that became irreversible then. The "fall" of the western empire in 476 put an end to the western half as it had been known. The Byzantine East, for its part, enjoyed times of prosperity, peace, and growth until, increasingly weakened by prolonged wars with Zoroastrian Persia, it lost most of its ancient territories to the Arabs in the course of the seventh century.

Yet in both cases the ancient world did not really disappear. A certain dismantling, slower in the East, did take place, but more continuity with the past prevailed than is usually assumed. New historical research on Late Antiquity and material evidence recently provided by archeology combine to challenge the received view of a "decline and fall" of the empire, held to have been caused by a collapse of army, cities, culture, and economy. Doubtless different, the period was not necessarily inferior, nor did it stand out as a cultural void. The fall of the western Roman Empire is rather viewed today as a "famous nonevent"[1] that left much of the ancient world as it already was. What came thereafter has itself become a historical subject valued in its own right, rich in colorful expressions and innovative aspects, and of great interest to students of both Late Antiquity and the early Middle Ages.

By 500 the Mediterranean remained the center around which a society went about its business, thinking of itself as definitely Christian. Roman paganism had been vanquished; both heretical (Arian) barbarians and pagan barbarians were in the process of being won over to Catholicism. The poor and the sick, the slaves and the prisoners, were entrusted to the good care of church organizations. Gradually, however, the world was tilting away from the Mediterranean. Its center was faltering, being displaced on the one hand toward the north and northwest as a result of Germanic migrations, on the other hand toward Syria and Iraq (southern Mesopotamia), preceding and above all following Arab conquests. The three centuries between 500 and 800 witnessed the self-assertion of frisky new neighbors whose dynamic presence was to alter the situation of Christianity beyond recall.

The "Barbarian" Kingdoms

The so-called barbarian invasions are often imagined as the rumbling and shattering stampede of wild primitives suddenly irrupting from nowhere and rushing into an empire caught off its guard. What happened, in fact, was no doubt less dramatic. Many of those migrants came from territories already Romanized. Their warrior-aristocracies knew the Roman institutions well from having served in the army (old-stock Romans, of course, complained about the "barbarization" of the army) and even in the provincial administrations. Besides, over the centuries Romans had infiltrated those populations and had become familiar to them. Consequently a zone of convergence of the "Roman" and "barbarian" regions had been created. So the misnamed "barbarian

---

1. A. Cameron, *The Mediterranean World in Late Antiquity.* New York: Routledge, 1993, p. 33.

invasions" and the subsequent "fall" of the western empire had less the appearance of an earth-shaking cataclysm than that of "the emergence into ever greater prominence of regions where Romans and non-Romans had long been accustomed to meet as equals to form a social and cultural 'Middle Ground,'"² a ground that kept widening.

There were, nonetheless, movements of populations and migrations of Germanic tribes. Through a complex sequence of events, hard to chronicle, a fragmenting of the western half of the empire took place. Migrations were noticeable as early as the fourth century when, pressed by the Huns, the Visigoths, who had converted to Arianism and were eventually to convert other tribes, crossed the Danube in 376, turned to Greece and Italy, sacked Rome with Alaric in 410, forcing the emperor to move to Ravenna, then moved on and established a kingdom in southern Gaul and Spain where in 587–589 they converted to Catholic Christianity. Similarly, the Vandals crossed Gaul and Spain to establish a kingdom in North Africa that lasted from 429 to 533; they sacked Rome in 455 and took Sicily in 486, but in the end joined the Catholic fold when overcome by Justinian's armies. Led by Theodoric, the Ostrogoths appeared in Italy from 496 to 552, became Catholic in 554 but lost to the Lombards, who ended up taking Ravenna in 751. Thus faded the upholder of the papacy, the surviving "Roman" empire brought back to the West by Justinian, forcing the pope to look for new protectors. There were many more migrations. From 430 on Burgundians were allowed to settle down in the middle Rhône valley, and the Alans in Gaul. Bulgars, Avars, Slavs, and Huns in turn raided or invaded the Balkans and threatened Constantinople between 440 and 580. After the Romans had left Britain in 406, seemingly leaving behind a weakling Christianity, Saxons arrived there to form the Anglo-Saxon kingdoms.

Among those people in movement, a special place was occupied by the Franks. After infiltrating Gaul, they came to prominence around 480 under Clovis and, first among the Germanic peoples and in a move charged with consequence, chose Catholicism instead of Arianism. The Frankish state emerged after a series of victories, absorbed the Visigothic kingdom in 507, and positioned itself at the center of the new European map. Because the eastern empire was forced to busy itself

---

2. P. Brown, *The Rise of Western Christendom.* Cambridge, Mass.: Blackwell, 1996, p. 16.

with its own frontier troubles, the Franks not only were able to assume hegemony in the West but came to view themselves as the true heirs of the Roman Empire and the promoters of Catholicism. Charles Martel and then Charlemagne (768–814) succeeded in making the Franks into the incontestable rulers over the former European core of the German and North Sea periphery;[3] Charlemagne could turn against the Avars of Hungary while having his eye on Scandinavia. Crowned by the pope in Rome in 800 and acclaimed as an "Augustus," and on this occasion showered with gifts by the caliph of Baghdad, Charlemagne henceforth ruled his "Roman Empire" from Aachen.

Those transformations could not occur without shaking the very structures of Western imperial society. Senatorial elite and provincial aristocracy were at first inclined to hold to their privileges, to nurse their prejudices, and to snub the barbarians; so did initially even the bishops taken from their ranks, who found themselves at the service of a beleaguered Roman constituency. For all the accommodation shown to the invaders, Romans intended to make it difficult for barbarians to "go native" and to be really integrated into Roman society. But in the end such reluctance became pointless. No support was coming from Justinian in the East to help Romans hang on to their position, and they were themselves confronted with an uncomfortable decrease in citizen population. In fact Romans and barbarians already had too much in common and were producing "men of power" of mixed Frankish and Roman descent capable of leadership. Among those were the new bishops, now functioning as substitute Roman consuls, but indigenous; everywhere they were taking over the roles of civil authorities and town councils, redistributing wealth and negotiating with provincial governors.

From 500 on Christianity and Roman civilization went hand in hand and spread unhindered along and beyond the former frontiers of the western empire. The populations conquered by the Franks had to be, or to be made, Christians. Church and papacy looked to the Frankish state as their new protector. Imperial patronage of the church, in turn, helped bind disparate territories together. It was not easy to say who controlled whom, but Charlemagne had close relations with 180 episcopal sees and 700 monasteries, and the church seemed to welcome that association. Soon conditions were in place for the cultural

---

3. Brown, *The Rise of Western Christendom*, p. 276.

revolution that the Carolingian renaissance meant. Monastic reform, revival of education, expanded trade, and encouragement of new art forms—those innovations took place spiritedly and prepared the ground for medieval civilization.

Justinian (527–565)

Far-reaching transformations marked the fifth and sixth centuries in the East. Both a landmark and a turning point in Byzantine history, the reign of Justinian started with great hopes of a revived empire. The remaining pagans were made to accept Christianity and a new codified law *(Codex Justinianus)* saw to the ordering of the realm. Wishing to become the restorer of Roman glory, Justinian then launched a campaign of reconquest of the western territories lost to the Arian barbarians. North Africa was quickly recovered from the Vandals in 533–534. But this was the only real success. The long-drawn-out and rude reconquest of Italy, to a large extent experienced as a conquest by the Greeks, ended up disheartening the military effort and undermining the old social order more radically than half a century of Ostrogothic rule.[4]

Many factors combined to hamper the reconquest, in addition to the high cost of reorganizing North Africa and the dragging Italian campaign. The bubonic plague raged in the East from 542 to 570 (even until 750 in some areas) and decimated the population as fiercely perhaps as the fourteenth-century Black Death that was to wipe out one-third of the European population. The Second Council of Constantinople (553–554) made plain the impossibility of uniting the 2,000-odd bishops around the Mediterranean and merely revealed further divisions; between 542 and 578 a Monophysite church, called "Jacobite" after Bishop Jacob Baradaeus, with a full-fledged hierarchy emerged in the East while the Western church still had to contend with the schismatic Arians. The chronic state of belligerency with Persia proved to be an excessively costly affair; peace had to be regularly bought with gifts of gold in the course of the alternating fortunes of Byzantium and Persia. The acute fickleness of the situation was to reach a most graphic stage in 630, when Emperor Heraclius restored to Jerusalem the Holy Rood

---

4. See R. A. Markus, *The End of Ancient Christianity*. New York: Cambridge University Press, 1990, p. 218.

(the True Cross) taken to Ctesiphon just some fifteen years earlier by Persians eager to reward their own Nestorian servants. Finally, it had become increasingly difficult to afford the "subsidies" that kept the neighboring barbarians happy. When Slav and Avar tribes intensified their raids after 550, the situation became totally desperate; soon it was ripe to be cashed in on by the last incursions of the Persians and then by the Arabs.

The Arab Conquests

When they began marching into the Middle East in the seventh century, the Arabs were far from being total newcomers to the late antique world. Over the centuries the Arabian peninsula had entertained trade contacts with the eastern half of the Roman Empire and with Persia via Iraq, regularly sending its caravans to centers such as Gaza and Damascus, al-Hira and Basrah. In turn, Jewish and Christian communities were found not only in Arabian areas bordering on Syria and Iraq, but even deep into Arabia as far as Yemen.

For centuries Romans and Persians relied on Arab federate allies on imperial fringes (Ghassanids and Lakhmids) to prevent nomadic raids into both empires; they even sometimes called on those client-kings to participate in military campaigns. Both imperial powers had always had to reckon with the inherent danger of such alliances; one day the "tribal police" could turn against their masters. That day came after Muhammad (570–632), prophet and political leader, had been able to bring all of Arabia—nomadic and sedentary peoples—under the control of a new Islamic state originating from the sacred enclave of Medina in 622.[5] Soon after his death, the process of political consolidation of the whole of Arabia having been completed, nomadic tribesmen began to raid the Fertile Crescent, first of all with a view to rallying Arab tribes at the fringe of Syria and Iraq. Those raids met with remarkable success thanks to the weakness of the opponents—to the disaffection of the former Byzantine and Persian subject populations glad to welcome new rulers was added the general exhaustion of both Byzantine and Persian empires at the end of prolonged warfare.

---

5. See F. M. Donner, *The Early Islamic Conquests*. Princeton: Princeton University Press, 1981, pp. 267–271.

Consequently, the raids turned into a conquest movement. United Arabs took Syria from the Byzantines between 633 and 648—including Damascus, Antioch, and Jerusalem—and Iraq from the Sasanians between 635 and 642. Alexandria (642), Ephesus (654–655), Carthage (698), and finally the Visigothic kingdom of Spain and south Gaul (711) all fell at a pace and with an ease that historians are still hard pressed to explain.[6] Following on the Islamic conquest, migrations and settlement of Arab tribesmen took place, especially in the Syrian desert and on the fringes of Iraq; a process of Arabization effectively altered all conquered areas. As for Persia itself, the Sasanian dynasty had already collapsed in 655; however, Persian traditions were revived under Islamic garb in the eighth and ninth centuries.

Thus a new empire was born, aggressive and self-confident, propelled by a religious faith that had sparked the entire integration process from the start. From their capital first in Damascus, where the Umayyad caliphs or successors of the prophet resided from 660 to 750, then in Baghdad from 750 to 1258 (the Abbasid caliphate), holding firm to a new scripture (the Koran was finally written down in 660) and with Arabic the sole official language from 699, Muslims confronted East and West with a fresh version of the monotheistic faith shared by Christians and Jews. Being bitterly reproached for having slipped away from their initial message owing to neglect and partisan strife, Jews and Christians were both recalled to the purity of the religion of Abraham. After the war machine had come to a halt at the end of the eighth century, the *pax Islamica* was established and entire regions previously divided between Rome and Persia were now joined together as a result of the conquest. Suddenly, the world woke up to realize that a momentous event had taken place: "The largest empire ever created in ancient times" had just emerged. "Made up of a galaxy of ancient lands, that stretched from Andalousia to Turkestan, the Islamic empire of Caliph Harun al-Rashid (788–809) dwarfed the empire of his contemporary Charlemagne... recently established at the northwestern extremity of Eurasia."[7]

---

6. Ibid., pp. 3–9.
7. Brown, *The Rise of Western Christendom*, p. 8.

Continuities

The new world created by the presence of northern tribes in the West and Muslims mainly in the East, on closer look, was not a totally new world. Germanic tribes preserved what Roman political institutions they could, and trade continued within the Mediterranean as before. Above all, by finally adopting Christianity in its Catholic form, those peoples seized hold of a faith already "ancient" and gave it an extended following. Altogether they offered to the fading empire the possibility of a new beginning. In the long run they saw to it that the demise of the late antique world would not entail the disastrous collapse of the old order but rather would result in the revival of political entities in a new dress, the survival of a newly established religion and the creative transformation of a civilization, a complex fact that made medieval developments look quite consistent with the past.

Until the transfer of government to Baghdad in 762, the Islamic state had introduced very few changes in the day-to-day lives of its peoples. Islam had made its advance without a major break in continuity; the first Islamic rulers took over the main framework of Byzantine administration and employed Greek-speaking officials, or Persian-speaking ones in formerly Persian territories. Generally Muslims saw themselves as perfecting what was best in the late antique world. Then, thanks to the scholars of Baghdad, Islam was able to incorporate a large amount of the Greek and Judeo-Christian legacies. But of course the religious situation had changed. The majority of Christian communities in the East, starting with the Christian groups scattered throughout Arabia, fell under Muslim rule within little more than a century. Among the Christians who did not emigrate from those lands, most converted to Islam. Some held to Christianity and assumed a minority status in their own homes. It must be remembered that those Christian communities were prevailingly non-Chalcedonian (Monophysite and Nestorian) and regarded Islam as a quasi-indifferent alternative, sometimes even as a welcome solution to the religious oppression they had suffered at the hands of the Chalcedonians.[8] In fact, they enjoyed wider freedom of worship under Muslim rule; like the Jews, they were treated as "People of the Book," so that the Christians' position within the Islamic state "was far better than any enjoyed by Jews and pagans in the Christian

---

8. See Cameron, *The Mediterranean World in Late Antiquity,* pp. 176ff.

empire."[9] They had only to pay their new taxes to new lords. In a sense, therefore, the Christian landscape in the Near East was less drastically disturbed than appeared at first.

The Final Breach Between East and West

For the Byzantine Empire itself, however, the Arab conquests signified an essential shrinking. Almost stripped naked and deprived of its eastern provinces, it was reduced to Constantinople, part of Asia Minor, Greece, some islands, and parts of Italy. It kept a bridgehead in Ravenna to give protection to the papacy, until the Lombards took the city in 751 and forced the pope to look elsewhere for new protectors. Those protectors were no longer to be the emperors of Constantinople but the Franks: Charles Martel and, above all, Charlemagne. With this move, the West in general definitively turned northwest, a telling symptom that the parting of the ways between East and West had become irreversible.

What were the determining factors in the final break between the East and the West? In the 1930s, in the light of economic history, H. Pirenne proposed that the real break came as a result, not of the Germanic invasions, but of the Persian raids and, above all, of the Arab conquests—more than anything else, the Arab conquests were responsible for the interruption of the East-West trade in the seventh century. The "Pirenne thesis" has been variously criticized, mainly for its almost exclusive reliance on literary evidence. Recently uncovered material evidence (archeological and numismatic) shows, however, that Muhammad and the western tribes were not the causes of the seventh-century transformations but were rather the products of changes that had altered the Mediterranean prior to their arrival on the stage. By 600 the western empire, and by 625 the eastern part as well, had entered a period of political and economic decay. The weakening of the two Romes created the space for the emergence of both the Holy Roman Empire of the Franks and the Islamic Empire. Trade and communication then neglected the East-West axis provided by the Mediterranean, but new communications were opened or restored. The Rhine again moved to the center; trade with Anglo-Saxon England increased; the Carolingian renaissance of the eighth to ninth centuries was fed by the long-distance

---

9. Brown, *The Rise of Western Christendom*, p. 187.

trade that brought to Europe the necessary silver from Baghdad via the Caspian Sea, the Volga, and the Baltic.[10] A certain curtain fell on the Mediterranean, no longer able to be the medium of cultural unity.

Henceforth East and West represented two distinct and separate political and cultural traditions, Greek and Latin, more and more alienated from one another. After 752 popes were no longer chosen among Greeks or Syrians, while in Byzantium Latin as the official language was replaced by Greek and rapidly forgotten. In most aspects of religious life, two interpretations of Christianity were allowed to grow apart. Unfortunately, what could have continued as quite acceptable cultural and theological differences instead created lasting divisions.

Whatever can be said about the nature and causes of the East-West break, the shaking of the old Roman Empire at its two ends produced a new sociopolitical situation for Christianity. The drastically reduced eastern churches were not able to reconquer the territories lost to the Arabs, but with the conversion of the Slavic populations from the ninth century on, the Orthodox church could build a new extended constituency. As for Nestorians and Jacobites, they survived as resilient minorities in Islamic lands and even expanded toward central Asia, China, and India.

For its part, Western Christianity began looking away from the Mediterranean and leaving Byzantium to its own struggles. From Clovis's conversion at the end of the fifth century, through his descendants the Merovingian kings, to the Irish and Anglo-Saxon missions to the continent, up to Charlemagne's reforms, a momentous shift was initiated from a Christianity centered around the Mediterranean to spiritual centers in Germany, England, and north France, a shift that accentuated the rift with the Byzantine East centered on Constantinople. Outstanding Christian leaders helped advance the frontiers of Christianity in northern Europe. Soon monasteries and impressive churches punctuated northern landscapes. Powerful bishops adapted to the needs of the new Germanic rulers, instilled what Christian principles they could into their peoples, and maintained what order could be saved from the Roman past. After the failure of Justinian's reconquest of the West, the papacy emerged with enhanced authority and importance. In fact, the

---

10. See R. Hodges and D. Whitehouse, *Mohammed, Charlemagne and the Origins of Europe: Archeology and the Pirenne Thesis.* London: Duckworth, 1983, pp. 169–176.

geography of the West was taking on a new configuration under the growing impact of the church; in turn, centuries of social and political involvement were to confer on the church itself a somewhat military and legal stamp.

The Making of Europe

Those "barbarians" who, to the old Romans, had appeared as an untidy mass of isolated tribes and, to the late Romans, as forming an endless flood of migrants threatening their culture and privileges, ironically were destined to salvage, under the unanticipated auspices of the church, that very Roman past so much cared about. Bishops, many taken from among the new notables, became heirs of the Roman senatorial families and worked at enhancing the place of the church. "By 600 the Catholic church had emerged from the barbarian crisis and had attained an extraordinarily powerful position in western Europe, one which it was to retain in many countries until the French Revolution."[11] A great landowner, the church included among its members the ruling classes. It had succeeded in converting all the barbarian successors of Rome, except for the Arian Lombards and the pagan Anglo-Saxons, who were themselves converted by 680. It enjoyed the universal support of those new converts.

At the same time, all those peoples were engaged in conflicts and alliances, seizures and transactions, aiming at rearranging the home space and creating the conditions for a bearable coexistence. Indeed, what was emerging in the northwestern corner of Eurasia was the constitution of a loose entity made up of quite disparate elements and interests—the construct called Europe. Without a road map, various peoples were groping in the dark for some hazy blend of ingredients variously cherished, such as classical antiquity, Mediterranean warmth, Jewish religiosity, Christian élan, and barbarian vitality. They ended up giving birth to a uniquely dynamic civilization bearing the abstract name of Europe.

Nascent Europe, however, did not wait long before turning on itself and embracing a certain isolation: Turning north had a freezing effect. The "Holy Roman Empire" of Charlemagne did not recognize

---

11. J. N. Hillgarth, ed., *Christianity and Paganism 350–750.* Philadelphia: University of Pennsylvania Press, 1986, p. 3.

the Byzantine emperor as Roman emperor. Indeed, it cared little about an eastern empire. Seldom were the Carolingians willing to consider the Byzantine emperors as co-emperors; more often they preferred to view themselves as their true heirs.

Moreover, Charlemagne in the West and Irene in the East did not see themselves as the dwarfs they really were when compared with the Islamic rulers. Then the dwarfs chose more and more to ignore each other or to quarrel. When in the eleventh century the final separation occurred between the Roman church and the Eastern Orthodox church, the move was symptomatic for the two societies at large and represented merely the last act of a century-long drama that had seen mutual neglect grow into suspicion and fateful estrangement.

Isolation breeds arrogance. Not only did Europe come to neglect, scorn, or ignore its eastern flank, it was also little inclined to worry much about peoples of Africa and Asia, who were of interest only to a few adventurers and traders and no longer the center of attention they had been to the fathers' church. For centuries Europe became devoted to itself, to its own beauty and cult. There developed in the end a lofty Eurocentricity that was to leave its mark on all aspects of cultural life, extending to religious dogmas and theological systematizations rashly held to have universal, even exclusive validity, a development that the future was to find hard to reverse.

Monastic Christianity in Western Territories

After John Cassian early in the fifth century had brought his version of Egyptian monasticism to south Gaul (Lérins, the training ground of herds of bishops, and Marseille), monastic life quietly spread to most of Gaul and beyond, providing the church of the fifth and sixth centuries with some of its more influential and better-trained bishops. At roughly the same time, however, a second, more active and aggressive style of monasticism appeared in the West, perhaps coming directly from the East owing to its notable resemblance to the more severe Syrian and Egyptian models, and reached the Celtic regions of the British Isles. A century after Patrick's (390–461) activity, in Cornwall and Wales and more strikingly in Ireland, an austere style of monastic Christianity captured the enthusiasm of a newly converted population and spread like an epidemic, resulting, as it were, in an overproduction of industrious monks. These monks were not only responsible for the rise of Latin culture and for artistic achievements (illuminations, metalwork) at home; their predilection for exile as a form of renunciation urged them to become missionaries and to take Christian faith and monastic life to pagan regions of the Isles and the continent. Irish monks started the assault; among them, Columba (521–597) initiated the monastic confederation of Iona in Scotland. Like a comet, Columbanus (540–615) traversed central Gaul to the Rhineland, the Alps, and north Italy, implanting an exacting rule that recalled the manners of the early eastern ascetics. Filtering down to large segments of populations, this austere Christianity found expression in the rigid Penitentials, a kind of penal code for the conduct of Christian life with detailed systems of tariffs, which were to affect important areas of medieval piety.

A third brand of monastic Christianity developed out of Italy under the impact of Benedict (480–547) and his rule, a blend of elements coming mainly from Basil, Augustine, and Cassian. An admirer of Benedict, Pope Gregory the Great in 596 sent to England a group of some forty such monk-missionaries imbued with the Benedictine spirit, along with Augustine of Canterbury. In tension with the Celtic church typified by Columbanus's harshness, there developed a more moderate tradition shaped by the religious outlook of these men. From that milieu came Boniface (675–754), who, with his Saxon background, was able to implant in Germany a form of Christianity both Roman and Benedictine. The historian Bede (673–735) chronicles with sympathy the deeds and needs of all those monks in their efforts to restore Catholic Christianity in Britain and beyond as they were coming increasingly under the influence of the rule of Benedict.

In fact, between 550 and 770 Benedictine monasticism experienced its first expansion and with it showed the first clear signs of its influence on society. Less austere, more aristocratic, and not especially oriented toward mission among pagans, it took up the responsibility of Christianizing and humanizing the regions where it was implanted, such as south Germany and Burgundy. Step by step, the Benedictine monastery became a miniature civic center for the dispensation of devotion, culture, and employment. It was increasingly felt that all monasticism in the West had to be reformed along Benedictine lines and strictly reorganized if its religious and civilizing mission were to prosper. When this was done, Celtic Christianity began to wane.

Byzantine Church and Minority Christianity

While "Romans" and Romanized peoples were thus opening new areas to Christianity in the west and northwest of Europe, the Byzantine church, severely amputated by the Islamic conquests, needed time to recover. Three series of events throughout the seventh and eighth centuries impeded the action of the Byzantine church within and without: the iconoclast controversy, the resilience of the pagan Slavs in the entire Balkan peninsula, and the repeated conflicts with the Arabs. Those retarding factors crippled both church and empire, and left them with only faint energies for the Christianization of the barbarians. All the same, by the seventh century modest contacts had been made with peoples as far away as the southern Russian steppes and the Crimea. Full-fledged missionary activity in those regions had to wait until the final defeat of iconoclasm in 843 and the work of Cyril and Methodius in the Slav world to see the church shake its torpor and expand northward. The Slavs, who had been raiding Greece and the Balkans since the mid-sixth century, were converted in the ninth along with the peoples of Bulgaria and Serbia; Russia followed suit one century later.

Thus, looking at the overall evolution of Christianity, it can be said that what it had lost in the south and southeast of the Mediterranean in the seventh century, it gained in the north and northwest. New territories replaced lost ones; a new map was being drawn. Christianity was leaving Late Antiquity and entering a new period—the Middle Ages.

As for the "minority Christianity" in prevailingly Muslim lands, it started on a distinct course. Chalcedonians (Melkites, Maronites) and non-Chalcedonians (Jacobites, Nestorians, Armenians, Copts) were able to maintain themselves; the latter, at last, found a level of tolerance repeatedly denied them by Byzantium. Jacobites and Nestorians even experienced a noticeable expansion eastward.

Rome and Latin Christianity

In Western Europe, churches (Frankish, Anglo-Saxon, German, and Spanish) rose and developed in interaction, stormy in many ways, with the church of Rome. After a period of changing fortunes due to the independent character of the barbarians and the continued threat of the Arabs, there evolved in the West not only united "national" churches under Roman obedience but above all the lasting, overarching entity of the Latin church. Highly centralized as to the authority of Rome and resting on various centers of education, the Latin church was ever more engaged on a path leading away from Byzantium. Through tortuous episodes, Western princes and nations in the end bowed to the church authority. Rich landowner and universal provider for his people, the pope was more and more perceiving himself as successor to the imperial power and leader of Western Christendom—to be sure, under the protection of the Franks, yet exalted above all civil powers, a claim that later princes were to find hard to live with. His temporal power enhancing his spiritual power, the bishop of Rome was well on his way to becoming the touchy tenant of the papacy that the Middle Ages were to know.

Judaism, Christianity, and Islam Around 800

The overall religious situation of Europe and the Middle East at the end of the Patristic Period evidences, therefore, a mounting segregation of mentalities reflected in complex and unsettled geographical carvings, specific bodies of literature, and entrenched loyalties.

The Christian world is now made up of three Christianities that have reached a state of considerable alienation from one another. Eastern Orthodox (Byzantine) Christianity, drastically reduced in the wake of the theological strife following its reception of the council of Chalcedon and by Islamic inroads, holds to a tradition close to the patristic sources of the first eight centuries and to the first seven ecumenical councils. There it finds nourishment for its life and piety. Integrated into society, the church tends to be subordinated to the secular rulers, who are, however, assumed to be faithful believers. Much of its future is linked with the fate of the Slavic nations. Latin language and concerns have long ceased to be understood in Constantinople.

Oriental churches (mainly Monophysite and Nestorian, better called "church of the East") survive as "protected minorities" within mostly Islamic states. Monophysite Christianity has penetrated leading families in Syria and Iraq—mainly the federated Ghassanids—and the nomadic tribes under their control; Nestorian Christianity had done the same through the federated Lakhmids in Mesopotamia (then part of Persia) and in Arabia. Being non-Chalcedonian, they deliberately embrace a more ancient form of Christianity. Their resilience not only accounts for their survival; it also led them to expand eastward into central Asia and China. They wrested for themselves a limited degree of toleration in enclaves of various sizes scattered over three continents.

The Western (Catholic and Roman) church recognizes itself in the Chalcedonian faith, which it wholeheartedly embraced. It has gone through a period of remarkable expansion that culminated in the time of Charlemagne. At this point, the alliance of the state with the papacy played a central role. Monks and church leaders might have taken Christianity into forays, cultural and religious, alien to the fathers' concerns and to the eastern traditions. In fact, the Western church yields to Eurocentricity and strikes its own course in growing ignorance and neglect of the Eastern Orthodox and Oriental churches. Nevertheless, a first Christianization of the realm had taken place. Teaching and preaching intend now further to eradicate ill-formed beliefs and to secure a deeper penetration of the faith.

Judaism seems to have been bypassed by imperial and religious developments. Definitely dispersed in small pockets throughout two empires, the religion of the rabbis upholds the faith of their people and provides a rationale for their separate existence. Conversions to Judaism are few and far between. At the time of Byzantium's conflicts with Persia, Jews were of divided sympathies and doubtless many were pro-Persian. At least the rabbis of Mesopotamia enjoyed protection from the shahs and were able to compile the Babylonian Talmud. But after the Islamic conquest, toying with any idea of a common front with Persians became pointless. The diaspora situation is there to stay, confirmed and so to speak redoubled, and Jewish communities variously accommodate. One can speculate how different the world around 800 and after would appear had Judaism yielded to the two historic temptations it confronted to come to an understanding, first, with Christianity in the first centuries and then with Islam in the seventh. What did happen is that every kind of alliance was firmly rejected and Jews consistently opted for a faithful and, as well, fateful parting from those overly aggressive cousins.

The Islamic Empire gained a foothold in the Near East and moved into Asia, Africa, and Western Europe. It suffered only two major checks: outside Constantinople in 717, and near Poitiers in 732. The religion of the prophet unifies remote regions like cement, combining the force of a religious movement and its scripture with the bonus of sociopolitical entitlements. A new civilization has emerged from Cordova to Samarkand, where educated people would soon communicate in classical Arabic. John of Damascus could present Islam as a Christian heresy in order to discourage conversions or to allow polemics. Muslims did not take him seriously and went their quiet way, undisturbed. Perhaps their way was not always quiet, though. Perhaps there were cases of forced conversions to Islam—but nothing in Islamic history can be compared to what was to happen to Jews and Muslims at the hands of Christians in fifteenth-century Spain. There were also mass conversions to Islam, as there had been to Christianity, but less to escape the poll tax than to avoid social discrimination in an Islamic state.

Mutual relations between Jews, Christians, and Muslims, seldom correct, were regularly poisoned by unfounded accusations and the suspicion that the other played into the hands of Satan; the other was regularly viewed as the infidel and often treated as subhuman. There was around 800 scant hope that such prejudices would soon be wiped out. Slim as the hope was, though, no educated Christian coldly wanted to discourage it; the Christian masses, for their part, needed help if they were ever to entertain such simmering hope. In other words, the three religious communities, at the onset of the Middle Ages, seemed to be tacitly resigned to pursuing separate careers.

READINGS

D. A. Bullough	*The Age of Charlemagne*. London: Elek, 1973.
F. M. Donner	*The Early Islamic Conquests*. Princeton: Princeton University Press, 1981.
G. R. Evans	*The Thought of Gregory the Great*. New York: Cambridge University Press, 1986.
J. Fontaine and J. N. Hillgarth, eds.	*The Seventh Century: Change and Continuity*. London: Warburg Institute, University of London, 1992.
M. Gervers and R. J. Bikkazi, eds.	*Conversion and Continuity: Indigenous Christian Communities in Islamic Lands*. Toronto: Pontifical Institute of Medieval Studies, 1990.
J. Haldon	*Byzantium in the Seventh Century: The Transformation of a Culture*. New York: Cambridge University Press, 1990.
J. Herrin	*The Formation of Christendom*. Princeton: Princeton University Press, 1987.
J. N. Hillgarth, ed.	*Christianity and Paganism, 350–750: The Conversion of Western Europe*. Philadelphia: University of Pennsylvania Press, 1986.
R. Hodges and D. Whitehouse	*Mohammed, Charlemagne and the Origins of Europe: Archeology and the Pirenne Thesis*. London: Duckworth, 1983.
W. E. Kaegi	*Byzantium and the Early Islamic Conquest*. New York: Cambridge University Press, 1992.
R. MacMullen	*Corruption and the Decline of Rome*. New Haven: Yale University Press, 1988.
H. Pirenne	*Mohammed and Charlemagne*. London: G. Allen & Unwin, 1939.
P. Riché	*Education and Culture in the Barbarian West*. Columbia: University of South Carolina Press, 1976.

D. J. Sahas   *Icon and Logos: Sources of Eighth-Century Icono-clasm.* Toronto: University of Toronto Press, 1986.

A. Schimmel   *Islam: An Introduction.* Albany, N.Y.: State University of New York Press, 1992.

J. S. Trimingham   *Christianity Among the Arabs in Pre-Islamic Times.* London: Longman, 1979.

11

Conclusion

Centuries of life and thought left Christianity at the end of the Patristic Period with a set of open questions and typical problems that continue to worry its adherents and constitute a permanent agenda for ever-renewed reflection. In briefly reviewing some of those problems, it will appear that Christianity cannot indeed claim them as exclusively its own. Most religious traditions have to come to grips with the same or similar fundamental issues, familiar to students of world religions. But early in its history, concern with those issues attracted in Christianity a degree of attention and industry that singles it out among historical religions.

Faith and Conversion

Over the centuries, the questions "Why believe?" or "Why convert?" have received sophisticated answers dealing, mostly at the individual level and in theological terms, with the nature and genesis of faith, the grounds and meaning of religious conversion, the obstacles to faith and its rewards, the conditions of growth in faith, and so forth. The answers given are striking in their constant need of further theoretical refinement. The central question can, however, be formulated in a manner that calls for a more descriptive answer: Why become a member of the Christian community? Relatively easy to answer for the period when Christianity had become established in the hearts and minds of the Mediterranean world, the inquiry encounters greater difficulties when directed to the period prior to Constantine. Yet, at all times, the account is bound to be complex and to embrace a mixture of reasons.

The motives for converting and embracing a new way of life, as well as a new view of life, may be reduced to four groups. First there are elevated motives, of spiritual and religious nature. Appeal is made to the action of God's grace that opens one's eyes and causes the "knowledge of faith." This explanation rests on a nonverbal proof that declines any objective justification but has compelling subjective force. To this group of motives belongs the explanation in terms of one's experience of release from a powerful bondage, or in terms of reaction to preaching and teaching that, owing to the implied thought content and moral direction, turns out to make sense of one's life. Suddenly an ideal becomes attractive to minds and hearts either because, in a given society, changed values and ways of life make it relevant, or because the new ideal offers a deeper wisdom and interpretation of existence, or because the discovery of the strong personality of Jesus invites to discipleship, or even because the fame of miracle cures and feats is assigned to a divine intervention and generates intimate conviction.

Second, there are practical motives, of pragmatic nature. Convention or conformity can play a role here, making one join the Christian community because most people turn to it—it is the thing to do. In the first centuries the step might have been aided by the appearance of a forceful trend within a given social network, by the lesser appeal of paganism and religious alternatives, by the promised fulfillment of psychological needs, or by the current vogue of irrationality and the general enticement of superstitious modes of behavior. Coercive pressure may be counted among the practical inducements.

Third, there are disreputable motives, of self-interested and egotistical nature. Converts may look for personal advantage, material gain, mundane convenience, or social promotion. Imperial legislation, without a doubt, encouraged pseudo-converts who, without personal conviction, were eager to avoid the antipagan measures, special taxes, or social discrimination and to join the unburdened majority. Close to these are, fourth, erroneous motives, made up of misinformation and illusory objectives. Wrongly anticipated power, delusive flight from involvement in the human condition, evasion of responsibilities, though alien to religious conversion per se, may play an obscure role in the decision to join the community.

All of those motives have been propounded by theologians, philosophers, historians, and social scientists. Their variety cannot fail to confer on the process of Christianization its multiple meanings. Their endless multiplication indicates that reflection on this topic is not closed; the identification of the real reasons for accepting Christianity and, generally, for holding to a belief is an enduring subject not only of soul-searching, but also of empirical research.

Christian Discourse

Having embraced a new religious vision and moral code, the first Christians very early took to writing; they felt compelled to find words to express what they stood for and, eventually, to proclaim their faith to prospective believers. Various articulations of the faith are encountered from the start of the Christian movement: Paul, the gospels, the Apologists, all represent early modes of account. They aim to make people see what the authors have seen but their hearers or readers had not seen before, taking them into a new realm of perception and experience. The main tenets of the faith are here arranged into a story or plot in which the narrative element taken from the life of Jesus and rhetorical devices borrowed from the surrounding culture combine to turn the message into an understandable discourse. At all times scholars raised fundamental questions as to the adequacy of the instrumental language used by the first writers and their followers, the reliability of the constructed discourse, and the legitimacy of privileging particular categories of thought in the communication of a message that claims to be universal. The problem reached its full acuity when expanding Christianity opted for the vehicle of Greek Hellenistic culture.

Faith *(pistis)* Seeking Understanding *(gnosis)*

What the many writers encountered in the previous pages had in common, reacting to and shaping the historical situation, was a sustained desire to hearken to Peter's injunction to "be ready to give the reason *(logos)* for the hope that is in you" (1 Pt 3:15) and to explain who the Christians really are. From Justin to Augustine, a typical manner of providing such an account was worded in a theoretical mode, becoming increasingly systematic. According to this manner, the account is constructed by means of mainly Greek and Latin categories, concepts, and ideas, and aims to transpose the biblical narrative into those schemes, in order to make it understood in the respective situation. Once articulated, those notions serve to define intellectually what a Christian is and stands for: A Christian is one who, on the basis of normative scriptures, holds certain beliefs concerning God and Christ, has definite ideas regarding the world and the human situation, and advocates a consequent way of life made up of prayer, moral obligations, and observances.

A second, more practical manner of providing the account was based on the outsider's view: A Christian is one who practices certain rituals (baptism, Eucharist), properly observes certain festivals (Easter, Christmas, saints' days, Sunday), and follows the right calendar (for dates of festivals, Sunday instead of Sabbath). In a second step, the outsider would try to see how those practices were grounded in authorities, scriptures, and creeds, and resulted in particular moral conduct.

Whatever the type of notion constructed to give a valid account of Christian hope and faith, the working out of the notion became encapsulated in Augustine's reading of Isaiah 7:9, "Believe in order to understand."[1] It was a matter of understanding the faith or of "faith seeking understanding," a program taken up by the patristic writers, brought to its consummate application by Anselm of Canterbury in the eleventh century, and still inspiring much of today's theology. We must recognize, however, that the fourth- and fifth-century literary productions gave to that program a signal impulse. Whether the prophetic saying was taken to mean "believe, so that you can understand," or "understand in order to believe," or even, a little forced, "believe that you can understand," in all cases the fundamental program was set for theology: Theology has to do with understanding what one believes, interpreting the content, import, and embodiment of faith in varying historical conjunctures.

There were times when advanced knowledge *(gnosis)* tended to prevail over simple faith *(pistis);* or, on the contrary, when thinking and reflection were sacrificed on the altar of obedient submission to the authoritative word. Christianity comes into its own when the right balance is struck between faith and knowledge. The fourth and fifth centuries offer many instances of successful performances in that respect. But the ideal balance is never found for good; it constantly has to be reinvented and reformulated.

Literary Petrifaction and Developments

After the brilliant output of the fourth and fifth centuries, a period of, if not literary decline, at least a certain petrifaction of the literature seems to set in. On the one hand, religious language becomes "technol-

---

1. Letter 120 in Saint Augustine, *Letters 83–130. The Fathers of the Church,* vol. 18. Washington, D.C.: The Catholic University of America Press, 1953.

ogized,"[2] codified, and standardized, leading to a definite formalism. On the other hand, we enter the golden age of *catenae* (chains of quotations) and *florilegia* (anthologies), preserving excerpts and fragments that can be used as shortcuts in the vindication of a given position. They sometimes constitute valuable sources, given that the original works are lost.

Above all, from the sixth century on, we move into a period of faithful repetition and conscientious appropriation of the Christian tradition. It is not that a "general softening of the intellect"[3] can be observed, but times have changed and, with them, the needs of the people. The literature is becoming less elitist; it is now addressed to all: simple believers, women, and slaves. The period witnesses the birth of a rudimentary biblical culture among monks, clergy, and people; biblical narratives mix with miracle stories and "lives" of holy persons, all trying to strengthen the faith of the people and to call them to virtuous life.

In more intellectual circles, clerical and monastic, the elucidation of the Christian message is buttressed by the "patristic argument," which is on the rise and experiences a growing popularity. Quotations of the fathers are sought and found in order to be put to work, isolated from their context, in the shoring up of a thesis or doctrinal position, the process leading to collections of statements, sayings (in the form of chains and anthologies), and *sententiae* (opinions). The same method is developed and applied in "dogmatic exegesis," with the difference that here the hunt is for biblical quotations that can be put to use in support of theological preferences. In both cases the resulting formalization means a noticeable stricture of the literary resources.

A new departure in literary and "scholastic" activity took place at the time of Charlemagne. The reform of education contributed much to the elaboration of a sound curriculum and to the preservation of ancient culture, pagan and Christian. However, the study of the patristic writings for their own merits and in their integrity, and knowledge of the authors for their own sake and disinterested attention to their achievements, had to wait backstage for many centuries. To all intents and purposes, the dawn of the modern period was to coincide with the

---

2. See A. Cameron, *Christianity and the Rhetoric of Empire.* Berkeley: University of Calfornia Press, 1991, p. 23.

3. A widespread opinion, criticized by A. Cameron, *The Mediterranean World in Late Antiquity.* New York: Routledge, 1993, p. 138.

rediscovery of patristic literature as made up of works like any other works requiring study as integral wholes and constituting a literature of world scale deserving the scrutiny of the best scholars.

Inculturation

It is beyond question that much of the ancient culture and ideals might have gone into oblivion with the fading of the western empire had it not been for the trusteeship of the church. Church leaders gradually took over the functions of the Roman elite and made sure that the achievements of Late Antiquity would survive. In fact, bishops and monks did more than preserve the past; they spread its ideals to populations until then untouched, and interpreted them to new audiences. By implanting Christianity in particular times and places, they helped it assume new cultural forms, a development perceived to follow directly from the belief in an incarnate God who had adapted himself to the human condition.

In the process, the point was made that religion not only is a tolerant friend of culture, but positively needs it in order to express itself and find its necessary embodiment. Since the Apologists of the second century, the typical alliance with philosophy and culture has been viewed as required by the very nature of Christian faith. Inculturation could not be dispensed with. Christianity had to interpret itself in terms of the cultural particularities of various peoples and become rooted in contemporary and local idioms. The process of adjustment was bound to affect both Christianity and the respective cultures. Thus the first inculturation of Christianity with the Jewish and Greek Hellenistic traditions brought about transformations on all sides. In particular, it left second-century Christianity with a specific language, innovative liturgical forms, special church structures, theological representations, and artistic expressions, all marks of its early venture into the world.

The difficulty was then for Christianity to grow out of its first inculturation and, further, out of its subsequent ones. How could Christianity move ahead of its fourth-century "establishment" or go beyond the theological "settlements" following the trinitarian and christological controversies? Obviously it could not simply strip off its former clothing and slip into a new cultural garb without losing itself and its memory. This is a daunting problem, touching the sinew of our historical predicament. At no time was there a pure essence, Christianity, independent of all culture and susceptible to being poured into ever-changing cultural molds. The difficulty is a chronic one: How can Christianity keep its identity while moving from one cultural incarnation to a new one? Can, in fact, the parallel between incarnation and inculturation be sustained?

Starting with Tatian and, to some extent, Tertullian, there were always people who rose to question Christianity's alliance with culture. Pointedly, Tertullian asked: "What had Athens to do with Jerusalem?"[4] although attention to his works reveals an answer to his question that is far from "Nothing at all" and is more of the kind "Quite a bit!" Graphically the challenge came to a head in certain aspects of the very complex iconoclastic controversy that shook the Byzantine church in the eighth century (726–780)—controversy partly based on the Decalogue prohibitions (Ex 20:4), partly provoked by a series of Arab victories seen as divine punishment for the church's idolatrous practices—and again in the ninth century, illustrating one aspect of Christianity's relation to cultural expressions. What was at stake in the debate was the capacity of anything finite to be the vehicle of divine energy and grace. The triumph of the orthodox position, first at the seventh ecumenical council in Nicaea in 787 and finally after 843, meant that, far from being blasphemous breaches of the doctrine of divine inaccessibility or the expression of an uncalled-for eagerness to catch a vision of the other world or, worse, a heretical separation of Christ's natures, iconographic depiction of Christ and the saints and the veneration of icons were wholly consistent with the dogma of incarnation and hypostatic union. It was made clear that, like any cultural vehicle, it is not the icon itself that is worshiped, but the divine reality conveyed by it; the icon simply leads to the divine, which it displays in analogy with the human nature of Christ displaying his divinity.

Clearly, however, the parallel between inculturation and incarnation has its limits: again, there is no such thing as a naked Christianity, culturally pure and preexisting its historical and cultural embodiments, which it could take over as so many garments. The Christianity exhibited by the Anglo-Saxon *Beowulf* (eighth century) and the Old High German *Heliand* is not a mere Christian varnish thinly applied to native cultures, nor is it made of a local dressing-up of a supernatural Christianity.

---

4. De pr. haer., 7.

Assimilated by a warrior nobility, the faith has been articulated with their own traditions and loyalties, and fused with them; interaction of two entities brought about a third one. In this context, the recovery of the early Syriac literature (Aphrahat, Ephrem) offers us the striking contrast of an inculturation not indebted to Greek categories.

Various pitfalls have been recognized in the debate on the interaction between Christianity and culture. One of them consists in Christianity's being buried under its cultural manifestations and silenced by cultural systems that can very well prosper without it. The result of that kind of total immersion may be one of the many forms of cultural Christianity that reduce Christianity to a function of culture, cancel its distinctive identity, and defuse its critical potential. A second pitfall resides in the absolutizing of one inculturation whereby one cultural embeddedness is deemed to have universal validity forever and needs only to be uniformly assimilated by the nations. It is not a small problem to steer clear of both cultural domination and the leveling of religious memory. That is why the problem needs further investigation.

Christianization

When seventh-century bishops and their successors in the West took up the legacy of the previous centuries of Christian expansion, they were confronted with new tasks. If conversion to Christianity had been a grassroots phenomenon during the first centuries, then with the conversion of Constantine followed by that of the barbarian aristocracies, Christianity now made its way "from the top downwards....It had been adopted as the religion of enterprising and adaptable leaders, of kings and aristocrats."[5] This was perhaps sufficient to call the empire Christian and to salute the advent of Christendom. But how Christian is a Christian empire? This raises the question of the degree of penetration of the gospel in the regions where it was implanted, and the question of how to measure the progress of Christianization. Evidently the "baptizing" of pagan realities did not always "convert" them. For instance, what has really been achieved when relics of John the Baptist have been solemnly transferred to the purged

---

5. P. Brown, *The Rise of Western Christendom.* Cambridge, Mass.: Blackwell, 1996, p. 272.

Serapeum of Alexandria, or when Sarapis himself has been revalued as Joseph the Provider, son of Jacob?

In most Western regions, "the old beliefs had barely been confronted" and rarely shaken. "They had simply been pushed to one side, in a society whose leaders had declared themselves Christian and left the rest to time." The old beliefs survived among the masses, "often associated with the lower classes of society, or with marginal figures who had always been both feared and despised, even in pagan times, such as witches and sorcerers."[6] The countryside was particularly slow in renouncing traditional behavior. The quantitative rise of Christianity was not always accompanied by the decline of magic and pagan beliefs. It did not always mean a real growth in faith, although a progressive Christianization of time and space did take place; sites, rites, and stories were either revalued or replaced by similar ones or even incorporated into Christian festivals or bluntly secularized.

At the end of our period the church in its efforts to develop a Christian culture and to promote a deeper penetration of the gospel had to mobilize much energy in order to eradicate ill-formed beliefs and habits. Preaching and teaching were expected to address that daunting task. In the end it became evident that Christianization is a never-ending process. When investigated, for instance, in the sixteenth or in the twentieth century, its advance is often the subject of quite pessimistic or nostalgic assessments. But for all the persistent fuzziness attached to the concepts of "Christianization" and "pagan survivals," the exploration of the phenomenon of Christianization in past centuries, and of its cousin of ill repute, de-Christianization, still holds high rewards for the students of Christianity.

Alliance with Temporal Power in the West

From Constantine to Charlemagne, the intimate collaboration between church and secular rulers did not lead, as the tendency was in the East, to the absorption of the church by the state; nor did the collaboration yield to the sporadic appeal of the theocracy, according to which the gospel would rule society; nor were leaders tempted by the idea of a separation of church and state, which was not an option in

---

6. Ibid.

those times. Rather, the collaboration took the form of an alliance in which the relative independence of both powers was preserved but their integrity somewhat compromised, as reflected in the tradition of political theology inspired by Eusebius's work. The alliance ended up inflecting the exercise of both powers.

On the one hand, the emperor took over the aura of divine election and sanction. His authority was seen to derive from God, not from the people, and it became uneasy for bishops and theologians to develop a critical stance toward the abuses of temporal authority—it was a little like criticizing God's ordinances. The crowning of Charlemagne by the pope, however, made clear whence the emperor got his authority and that the mediation of the church in the sanctioning of his power might one day be denied. But even in that eventuality, secular authority enjoyed religious character, a state of affairs reinforced by the Germanic conceptions of sacral kingship and by the medieval theories of the quasi-angelic character of the king, and of the king's "two bodies," the body natural and the body politic—the latter perfect, invisible, and immortal.[7] It was tempting for rulers who espoused such conceptions to want to intervene in church affairs.

On the other hand, pope and bishops from the fourth century on began to be clothed with imperial regalia and to exercise temporal functions, such as land ownership, trading activities, and capital accumulation. Political terminology and imperial ceremonial were transferred to the realm of church administration. Consequently, spiritual power not only could receive support from the temporal authorities, such as called for by the alliance, but it could also generate from within itself various forms of coercion put at its disposal by its own secular accretions. The confusion of powers that developed in the West was to plague the Middle Ages and persistently to stand on the agenda of problems to be sorted out.

History and Literature

The present study has been conducted on the pervasive assumption that Christianity is found in its history and literature. They remain

---

7. E. H. Kantorowicz, *The King's Two Bodies.* Princeton: Princeton University Press, 1957, pp. 7–9.

essential routes toward a factual understanding of Christianity and continue to require patient exploration.

Since Christianity ranks among the so-called historical religions, it is crucial to devote the most lucid attention to its historical dimension. Two facts above all are meant by historical religion here. First, as a religious movement distinct from others, Christianity rests on founding events that took place in history, the main events being the history of Israel and, rooted in it, the person and career of Jesus Christ as a divine envoy. Second, central to Christianity is a view of God revealing himself not only in nature and through the human spirit, but also in and through historical events, in the life of Israel, in the life of Jesus, and in the life of the church. Those two facts make it imperative to study not only the historical career of Jesus in its context, which is done by New Testament studies, but also the history of Christianity, paying attention to the complex ways in which Christianity developed and to the various aspects of its respective situations. For it is in the course of history that even Christianity "reveals" itself.

The Christian literature of the early centuries preserves accounts of the founding events and of the first developments of Christianity. It offers the precipitate of its early course. It also preserves the first worthy efforts at interpreting Christianity as a pattern of life and thought for people living in various geographical areas and historical times. Today's research into patristic literature is confident that it accomplishes a crucial task. It is fortunately facilitated by a better knowledge of historical contexts and by the greater availability of reliable texts. The study of writers and writings is thus enhanced; coming to terms with them guarantees solid insights into the pristine stage of Christianity.

Our assumption that Christianity is found in its history and its literature does not imply that Christianity is found only there; religious experience and the practice of Christian life would soon refute a reductive view of that kind. It remains, however, that the neglect of those two aspects is sure to make any student of Christianity miss all-important facets of the Christian movement.

It has been an ominous fact of Christian history that, from mid-second century, Christianity came to define itself in contrast with its Jewish origins and its Jewish competitors. The process not only led to the development of an anti-Jewish mood; it also deprived Christianity of a portion of its self-identity. By 800 the Jewish component of Christianity was almost totally obliterated. With it was obscured the idea of the community assembled around the Eucharist to remember and retell its founding events along with its constitutive sufferings, the whole eliciting the following of Jesus. Instead, Christianity tended to anchor itself in rational and metaphysical structures of the Greek type, and to emphasize doctrinal purity as essential to its self-definition. The rediscovery of the historical character of Christianity and of its lasting indebtedness to Judaism help reestablish the threatened balance between history and rationality.

READINGS

H. Belting   *Likeness and Presence: A History of the Image Before the Era of Art*. Chicago: University of Chicago Press, 1994.

M. Bloch   *The Royal Touch: Sacred Monarchy and Scrofula in England and France*. London: Routledge & Kegan Paul, 1973.

A. Cameron   *Christianity and the Rhetoric of Empire: The Development of Christian Discourse*. Berkeley: University of California Press, 1991.

J. Delumeau   *Sin and Fear: The Emergence of a Western Guilt Culture, 13th–18th Centuries*. New York: St. Martin's Press, 1990.

V. I. J. Flint   *The Rise of Magic in Early Medieval Europe*. Princeton: Princeton University Press, 1991.

G. Fowden   *Empire to Commonwealth. Consequences of Monotheism in Late Antiquity*. Princeton: Princeton University Press, 1993.

E. H. Kantorowicz   *The King's Two Bodies: A Study in Mediaeval Political Theology*. Princeton: Princeton University Press, 1957.

H. R. Niebuhr   *Christ and Culture*. New York: Harper, 1951.

A. D. Nock   *Conversion: The Old and the New in Religion from Alexander the Great to Augustine of Hippo*. London: Oxford University Press, 1961.

L. Ouspensky and   *The Meaning of Icons*. Crestwood, N.Y.: St. Vladimir's
V. Lossy   Seminary Press, 1982.

L. R. Rambo   "Current Research on Religious Conversion." *Religious Studies Review* 8 (1982): 146–159.

R. J. Schreiter   *Constructing Local Theologies*. Maryknoll, N.Y.: Orbis Books, 1985.

A. Shorter   *Towards a Theology of Inculturation.* Maryknoll,
                      N.Y.: Orbis Books, 1988.

D. Wood, ed.   *The Church and the Arts.* Cambridge, Mass.: Black-
                      well, 1995.

Glossary

Allegory/allegorical interpretation: See Interpretation.

Anchorites: Solitary ascetics (anchoretic ascetics) who "withdraw" from the world in order to pursue spiritual perfection. Also called hermits (eremitic ascetics) for their original preference for the "desert" (eremos).

Apocalyptic: The body of literature purporting to "reveal" secrets about events associated with the end of time. Also designates the immediate messianism that is often part of that literature.

Apocrypha: Books not included in the Hebrew scriptures but found in the Greek version of Septuagint (LXX); they are designated apocryphal in Protestant Bibles and deuterocanonical (i.e., canonical in a derived sense) in the Roman Catholic Bible. Also books excluded from the New Testament canon, the so-called New Testament apocrypha ("secret" gospels, infancy gospels, acts).

Apologists: Second-century Christian writers who attempted to offer a reasoned presentation of Christianity for the benefit of non-Christians.

Apostasy/apostate: The public denial of Christianity or of any religion to which one was committed, in favor of adherence to another religion or to a sect.

Apostles: Strictly, the first twelve disciples of Jesus, also referred to as "the Twelve."

Ascesis/asceticism: A way of life based on rigorous self-denial and aiming to achieve holiness. It is characteristic of monasticism.

Baptism: Christian rite of initiation, originally reserved for instructed adults and practiced by total immersion, symbolizing cleansing from sinful past and the start of a new life.

Bible: The sacred book containing the authoritative scriptures of the Jews and also those of the Christians.

Canon: The list of biblical books regarded as authoritative scriptures.

Cenobites: Ascetics who share a "common life" (koinos) and live in community under a rule.

Christology: Part of theology that studies the person of Christ with reference to his relationship to both God and humanity.

Church: The assembly of Christians "called together" (ekklesia) for worship and instruction.

Council/ecumenical council: Assembly of bishops, also called synod. When such an assembly represents the whole church, deals with a question of universal interest, and passes regulations binding on all, it is called an ecumenical (general) council. There were seven such councils in the Patristic Period: Nicaea 325, Constantinople 381, Ephesus 431, Chalcedon 451, Constantinople 553, Constantinople 680–681, Nicaea 787.

Creed: Concise and formal statement of the faith.

Diaspora: The Jewish population "dispersed" outside the land of Israel.

Docetism: The belief that Jesus' body was not real but only "apparent."

Dogma: First used to designate a well-grounded opinion, the term came to signify a doctrine authoritatively defined by the church.

Dualism: The belief that soul and body, spirit and matter, are entirely opposed entities. In its radical form it designates a split in the divinity between the True God and the creator, or between good and evil.

Encratism: Asceticism carried to the extremes of practical and doctrinal rigorism.

Eschatology: Doctrine of the last things.

Eucharist: Sacrament of the body and blood of Christ under the appearances of bread and wine.

Exegesis: The science of textual interpretation of scripture.

Gnosis/gnosticism: The belief that salvation is wrought by the revelation of secret, often esoteric "knowledge"; elaboration of that belief into a worldview.

Gospel: First referring to the "good tidings" of Christian revelation and salvation, it came to be applied to the books setting forth the good news of Jesus' mission and fate.

Hagiography: The study of the life and cult of the saints; sometimes, embellishment thereof.

Hebrew Bible: The authoritative scripture of the Jews, made of Torah, the Prophets, and the Writings.

Heresy/heresiology: From its original meaning of "choice" (hence way of thought, school, party) the term took over the sense of "wrong choice" and willful deviation from a belief of the mainstream church; the study thereof.

Hermeneutics: The art and science of interpretation.

Incarnation: The belief that the Son of God took human flesh, implying that the historical Christ was both fully God and fully human.

Interpretation: Two main types of interpretation of scripture developed in the course of history: literal and spiritual, according to whether the letter or the spirit of the text is given preferred attention.
> *Literal* means also historical; in present-day scholarship it has received a widened acceptance: What the author in fact intended to convey.
> The *spiritual* sense has been variously subdivided into
> (a) *moral, psychological,* and *tropological*, the text being respectively interpreted in terms of its meaning for con-

duct, or for the constitution of the soul, or for the mysteries of salvation;

(b) *allegorical* (or anagogical), *spiritual, mystical,* and *typological*, the text being interpreted as meaning something
hidden concerning God, the soul, one's relation to God, or
the relationship of Old Testament to New Testament in the
form of foreshadowing-realization, promise-fulfillment.

Liturgy: The public worship of the church, found in the rituals of the
sacraments, especially of the Eucharist. The term also refers to the
written text of all prescribed church services.

Messianism: The belief that a messiah/savior will come to bring
redemption to the world at the end of history.

Monasticism: A way of life characterized by withdrawing from the
world in order to attain personal sanctification, usually practiced in
community with others.

Monotheism: The belief in the one, personal, and transcendent God.

New Testament (NT): The canonical books proper to the Christian
church.

Old Testament (OT): The canonical books the church shares with the
synagogue. The Old Testament includes more books than the
Hebrew Bible.

Orthodoxy: The doctrine held to be right by the mainstream church.
"Orthodox church" refers to Christianity in the East, separated from
Rome since 1054.

Pagans: "Paganus" refers either to "peasants," people of the place,
inclined to preserve the local customs; or to "civilians," those not
enlisted in the army. By analogy, it came to designate all those not
really engaged in Christ's militia out to defeat evil powers. Increasingly pagans were also called "Hellenes" because they held to past
or alien traditions and were not true "Romans."

Parousia: The return of Christ at the end of time to judge the world.

Patristics/patrology: The study of the times and writings of the Christian authors of the first centuries.

Pentateuch: The first five books of the Bible, also called Torah in the strict sense.

Pistis: The Greek word for "faith": free assent to God's revelation.

Polytheism: The belief in a plurality of divine beings.

Prophecy: The message, oral or written, delivered by a spokesperson of the deity and considered divine revelation by those who trust that person.

Pseudepigrapha: A body of Jewish religious texts written between 200 B.C.E. and 200 C.E. incorrectly attributed to biblical figures, similar to biblical books but not recognized as part of the Bible or of the Apocrypha.

Resurrection: The rising again of Jesus after his death and burial, grounding the belief that, at Christ's Parousia, departed souls will also be restored to bodily existence.

Revelation: The process by which God makes known his person and will.

Rule of faith: A brief summary of the main tenets of the apostolic preaching, normative for the early Christians and later formulated in creeds, such as the Apostles' Creed.

Rules (monastic): Compendia of guidelines and directives governing the spiritual and administrative life of monasteries.

Sacrament: A ritual action held to have been instituted by Jesus himself and to communicate God's grace.

Schism/schismatic: A deliberate break with the church, usually based on issues of practice.

Scripture: The normative books of the Bible (OT or NT, or both). The Old Testament list is different for the Hebrew Bible and the Septuagint. The New Testament is exclusive to the Christians.

Septuagint or *LXX:* The Greek translation of the Old Testament produced in Egypt ca. 270 B.C.E.

Soteriology: The doctrine of salvation.

Syncretism: Amalgamation of disparate religious doctrines and practices.

Synoptics: The three gospels (Mt, Mk, Lk) that contain a wide amount of common material and thus can be read in parallel. The common material betrays literary interdependence.

Theology: The scientific study of God and his self-revelation in words and deeds.

Torah: Strictly, the five books of Moses or Pentateuch or the written law given to Moses. Sometimes it is synonymous with the Hebrew Bible. In a still wider sense it also designates the "oral law" presumed to have been given to Moses along with the written one.

Trinity: The doctrine of God holding that there are in God three co-equal persons (Father, Son, Spirit), all fully sharing in the one and same deity or divine substance.

Typology/typological interpretation: See Interpretation.

Vulgate: The Latin translation of the Bible, mainly due to Jerome and most widely used in the West.

Appendices

The following appendices are meant as illustrative samples. They are addressed to the reader interested in going further into scholarly studies, and intended to give an idea of the kind of instruments used in researching the literature and history under study here. Starting in the fifteenth and sixteenth centuries, the renewed interest in Christian antiquity led to the preparation of new editions of individual authors and works that served specific needs and goals: correctives to contemporary distortions, critiques of contemporary beliefs and practices, defenses of given positions. The nineteenth century witnessed a systematic and comprehensive activity in publishing, most notably the *Patrologia latina* and *Patrologia graeca* edited by J.-P. Migne, which made available for the first time the bulk of Greek and Latin "patrologies"; the recent remakes of Migne's editions *(Corpus christianorum: Series latina; Corpus christianorum: Series graeca; Corpus scriptorum christianorum orientalium; and Corpus scriptorum ecclesiasticorum latinorum)* and the work of others who have updated and supplemented this work on the basis of newly discovered manuscripts and more efficiently itemized manuscript collections. Microfilm technology has helped the dissemination of all those sources and computerization is now in the process of making readily accessible to all the entire literary evidence. Cooperative ventures in French, German, and English, as well as in Italian and Spanish, are in the process of opening up the treasures of the early centuries in original languages and in modern translations. More texts in Latin, Greek, and other languages encountered between Egypt and China have been discovered. Monographs and specialized studies proliferate. Gnostic and Manichaean writings and the forgotten or lost writings of many orthodox and "heretical" authors are progressively being disclosed; recent finds are being collated and published in critical editions. The result of all this activity is that the situation has considerably improved for scholars dedicated to the study of Christian antiquity.

Appendix 1
Some Sources and Collections

The sources listed are in original languages, some with translation in a modern language. This is a sample of editions containing the primary sources pertaining to the period.

Acta conciliorum oecumenicorum. Berlin, 1914–

Bibliothèque copte de Nag Hammadi. Québec, 1977–

Codex Justinianus. Berlin, 1887.

Codex manichaicus coloniensis. Cosenza, 1990.

Codex Theodosianus. Berlin 1905– . English Translation: New York, 1969.

Corpus christianorum: Continuatio mediaevalis. Turnhout, 1966–

Corpus christianorum: Series graeca. Turnhout, 1977–

Corpus christianorum: Series latina. Turnhout 1953–

Corpus scriptorum christianorum orientalium. Louvain, 1903–

Corpus scriptorum ecclesiasticorum latinorum. Vienna, 1865–

Die griechischen christlichen Schriftsteller der ersten drei Jahrhunderte. Leipzig/Berlin, 1897–

Fontes christiani. Freiburg in Br., 1991–

Histoire des conciles d'après les documents originaux. Edited by K. J. Hefele. Translated and revised by H. Leclercq. 11 vols. Paris, 1907–1952.

Loeb Classical Library. London/Cambridge, Mass., 1912–

Nag Hammadi Codices. Leiden, 1972–1984.

Oxyrhynchus Papyri. London, 1898–

Patrologia graeca. J.-P. Migne. 161 vols. Paris, 1857–1866.

Patrologia latina. J.-P. Migne. 221 vols. Paris, 1844–1864.

Patrologia orientalis. Paris, 1897–

Patrologia syriaca. Paris, 1894–1926. Repr. 1965.

Sacrorum conciliorum nova et amplissima collectio. Edited by J. D. Mansi. 31 vols. Florence, 1759–1798. Repr. 53 vols. Paris, 1901–1927, 1960–1961.

Sources chrétiennes. Paris, 1941–

Texte und Untersuchungen zur Geschichte der altchristlichen Literatur. Leipzig/Berlin, 1883–

Appendix 2
Some Sources and Collections
in English Translation

Ancient Christian Writers. Westminster, Md./New York, 1946–

The Ante-Nicene Fathers. Edinburgh, 1867. Repr. Grand Rapids, Mich., 1989.

Cistercian Studies. Kalamazoo, Mich., 1970–

Classics of Western Spirituality. New York, 1978–

Creeds, Councils and Controversies: Documents Illustrating the History of the Church AD 337–461. Edited by J. Stevenson. London, 1989.

Early Christian Creeds. Edited by J. N. D. Kelly. London, 1972.

Early Christian Doctrines. Edited by J. N. D. Kelly. London, 1978.

The Fathers of the Church. Washington, 1947–

History of the Councils of the Church from the Original Documents. Edited by K. J. Hefele. Edinburgh, 1883–1896. Repr. 1972.

Library of Christian Classics. Philadelphia/London, 1953–1969.

The Nag Hammadi Library in English. San Francisco, 1988.

A New Eusebius: Documents Illustrating the History of the Church to AD 337. Edited by J. Stevenson. London, 1987.

New Testament Apocrypha. 2 vols. Edited by E. Hennecke and W. Schneelmelcher. Louisville, Ky., 1963, 1965.

A Select Library of Nicene and Post-Nicene Fathers of the Christian Church. Buffalo/New York, 1887–1892. Repr. Grand Rapids, Mich., 1982.

A Select Library of Nicene and Post-Nicene Fathers of the Christian Church: Second Series. New York, 1890–1900. Repr. Grand Rapids, Mich., 1961.

Appendix 3
Some Ancient Christian Authors and Texts

Athanasius *The Life of Antony.* Translated by R. C. Gregg. *Classics of Western Spirituality.* New York: Paulist Press, 1980.

Augustine *The City of God.* Translated by H. Bettenson. *Penguin Classics.* New York: Penguin Books, 1972.

————. *Confessions.* Translated by H. Chadwick. *Oxford World's Classics.* Oxford: Oxford University Press, 1991.

Clement of *Stromateis.* In A. Roberts and J. Donaldson, eds., *The Ante-*
Alexandria *Nicene Fathers*, vol. 2. Grand Rapids, Mich.: Eerdmans, 1989 [repr.].

Epiphanius *Panarion.* Translated by F. Williams. *Nag Hammadi Studies.* 2 vols. Leiden: Brill, 1987, 1995.

Eusebius *Ecclesiastical History.* Translated by K. Lake and J. E. C. Oulton. *Loeb Classical Library.* 2 vols. Cambridge, Mass.: Harvard University Press, 1926, 1932.

————. *Life of Constantine.* In E. C. Richardson, ed., *A Select Library of Nicene and Post-Nicene Fathers of the Christian Church: Second Series*, vol. 1. Grand Rapids, Mich.: Eerdmans, 1952 [repr.].

————. *Preparation for the Gospel.* Translated by E. H. Gifford. 2 vols. Oxford: Clarendon Press, 1908.

Hippolytus *Refutation of All Heresies .* In A. Roberts and J. Donaldson, eds., *The Ante-Nicene Fathers*, vol. 5. Grand Rapids, Mich.: Eerdmans, 1986 [repr.].

Irenaeus *Against Heresies.* In A. Roberts and J. Donaldson, eds., *The Ante-Nicene Fathers*, vol. 1. Grand Rapids, Mich.: Eerdmans, 1989 [repr.].

Justin *Apology.* Translated by L. W. Barnard. *Ancient Christian Writers,* vol. 56. New York: Paulist Press, 1997.

————. *Dialogue with Trypho.* In A. Roberts and J. Donaldson, eds., *The Ante- Nicene Fathers*, vol. 1. Grand Rapids, Mich.: Eerdmans, 1989 [repr.].

Origen   *Against Celsus.* Translated by H. Chadwick. Cambridge: Cambridge University Press, 1953.

————. *On First Principles.* Translated by G. W. Butterworth. New York: Harper & Row, 1966.

Tertullian   *Against Marcion.* Translated by E. Evans. 2 vols. *Oxford Early Christian Texts.* Oxford: Clarendon Press, 1972.

————. *Apology.* In A. Roberts and J. Donaldson, eds., *The Ante-Nicene Fathers*, vol. 3. Grand Rapids, Mich.: Eerdmans, 1989 [repr.].

————. *On Prescription Against Heretics.* In A. Roberts and J. Donaldson, eds., *The Ante-Nicene Fathers*, vol. 3. Grand Rapids, Mich.: Eerdmans, 1989 [repr.].

Appendix 4
Important Bibliographical Instruments and Reference Works

BIBLIOGRAPHICAL INSTRUMENTS

B. Altaner and A. Stuiber *Patrology.* Edinburgh/London, 1960, 1978.

J. Quasten *Patrology.* 4 vols. Westminster, Md., 1950–1986.

T. A. Robinson et al. *The Early Church: An Annotated Bibliography of Literature in English.* Metuchen, N.J., 1993.

W. Schneemelcher, ed. *Bibliographia patristica.* Berlin/New York, 1959–

REFERENCE WORKS

Aufstieg und Niedergang der römischen Welt/Rise and Decline of the Roman World. Berlin/New York, 1972–, especially II.16–28.

Biblia patristica. Paris, 1975–

Bibliographical Information Base in Patristics. Quebec, 1998.

The Coptic Encyclopedia. New York/Toronto, 1991.

Dictionnaire d'archéologie chrétienne et de liturgie. Paris, 1907–1953.

Dictionnaire de spiritualité, ascétique et mystique. Paris, 1937–

Encyclopaedia Judaica. Jerusalem, 1971–

Encyclopedia of Early Christianity. Edited by E. Ferguson. New York/London, 1997.

The Encyclopedia of Religion. New York/London, 1987.

Encyclopedia of the Early Church. Edited by A. Di Berardino. Cambridge/New York, 1992.

Lexikon für Theologie und Kirche. Freiburg in Br., 1957–1965.

The Oxford Dictionary of Byzantium. London, 1991.

The Oxford Dictionary of the Christian Church. London, 1997.

The Oxford Dictionary of the Jewish Religion. London 1997.

Reallexikon für Antike und Christentum. Stuttgart, 1941–

Appendix 5
Important Periodicals

L'Année philologique.

Bulletin of Ancient and Medieval Christian Literature.

Harvard Theological Review.

Journal of Early Christian Studies (See *Second Century*).

Journal of Ecclesiastical History.

Journal of Feminist Studies in Religion.

Journal of Roman Studies.

Journal of Theological Studies.

Laval théologique et philosophique.

Recherches de science religieuse.

Religious Studies Review.

Revue des études augustiniennes.

Revue d'histoire ecclésiastique.

Revue des sciences religieuses.

Revue de théologie ancienne et médiévale.

Second Century (Since 1993: *Journal of Early Christian Studies*).

Vigiliae christianae.

Zeitschrift für Kirchengeschichte.

Zeitschrift für Papyrologie und Epigraphik.

Appendix 6
Of Special Interest to Active Scholars

Proceedings of the Oxford Conference (every 4 years since 1951), published in *Studia patristica*. Louvain, 1957–

Bulletin of IAPS (International Association of Patristic Studies). 1965–

Patristics, Bulletin of NAPS (North American Patristic Society). 1968–

Bulletin of CSPS (Canadian Society of Patristic Studies). 1976–

Appendix 7
Select Bibliography

T. D. Barnes

Constantine and Eusebius. Cambridge, Mass.: Harvard University Press, 1981.

J. Beloch

Die Bevölkerung der griechisch-römischen Welt. Roma: L'Erma di Bretschneider, 1886. Repr. 1968.

S. Benko

Pagan Rome and the Early Christians. Bloomington: Indiana University Press, 1984.

P. F. Bradshaw

The Search for the Origins of Christian Worship. New York: Oxford University Press, 1992.

P. Brown

Authority and the Sacred: Aspects of the Christianization of the Roman World. New York: Cambridge University Press, 1995.

P. Brown

The Body and Society: Men, Women and Sexual Renunciation in Early Christianity. New York: Columbia University Press, 1988.

P. Brown

The Cult of the Saints: Its Rise and Function in Latin Christianity. Chicago: Chicago University Press, 1981.

P. Brown

The Making of Late Antiquity. Cambridge, Mass.: Harvard University Press, 1978.

P. Brown

Power and Persuasion in Late Antiquity: Toward a Christian Empire. Madison, Wis.: University of Wisconsin Press, 1992.

P. Brown

Religion and Society in the Age of Augustine. London: Faber & Faber, 1972.

P. Brown

The Rise of Western Christendom: Triumph and Diversity AD 200–1000. Cambridge, Mass.: Blackwell, 1996.

P. Brown	"The Saint as Exemplar in Late Antiquity." *Representations* 2 (1983): 1–25.
P. Brown	*Society and the Holy in Late Antiquity*. Berkeley: University of California Press, 1982.
P. Brown	*The World of Late Antiquity, AD 150–750*. London: Thames & Hudson, 1971.
J. H. Burns, ed.	*The Cambridge History of Medieval Political Thought c. 350–c. 1450*. New York: Cambridge University Press, 1988.
A. Cameron	*Christianity and the Rhetoric of Empire: The Development of Christian Discourse*. Berkeley: University of California Press, 1991.
A. Cameron	*The Later Roman Empire AD 284–430*. Cambridge, Mass.: Harvard University Press, 1993.
A. Cameron	*The Mediterranean World in Late Antiquity: AD 395–600*. New York: Routledge, 1993.
H. Chadwick	*The Early Church*. Baltimore: Penguin Books, 1967.
E. Clark	*The Origenist Controversy: The Cultural Construction of an Early Christian Debate*. Princeton: Princeton University Press, 1992.
G. Dagron	*Naissance d'une capitale: Constantinople et ses institutions de 330 à 451*. Paris: PUF, 1974.
H. Delehaye	*The Legends of the Saints*. London: G. Chapman, 1962.
F. M. Donner	*The Early Islamic Conquests*. Princeton: Princeton University Press, 1981.
S. Elm	*Virgins of God: The Making of Asceticism in Late Antiquity*. New York: Oxford University Press, 1994.
L. H. Feldman	*Jew and Gentile in the Ancient World: Attitudes and Interactions from Alexander to Justinian*. Princeton: Princeton University Press, 1993.

E. Ferguson with D. Scholer and P. C. Finney eds.	*Studies in Early Christianity: A Collection of Scholarly Essays.* 18 vols. New York: Garland, 1993.
W. H. C. Frend	*Martyrdom and Persecution in the Early Church.* Oxford: Blackwell, 1967.
W. H. C. Frend	*The Rise of Christianity.* Philadelphia: Augsburg Fortress, 1984.
W. H. C. Frend	*The Rise of the Monophysite Movement.* Philadelphia: Augsburg Fortress, 1984.
J. Gager	*The Origins of Anti-Semitism: Attitudes Toward Judaism in Pagan and Christian Antiquity.* New York: Oxford University Press, 1985.
J. Geffcken	*The Last Days of Greco-Roman Paganism.* New York: North Holland, 1978.
J. E. Goehring et al.	*Gnosticism and the Early Christian World.* Sonoma, Calif.: Polebridge Press, 1990.
R. M. Grant	*Augustus to Constantine: The Rise and Triumph of Christianity in the Roman World.* New York: Harper & Row, 1971.
R. M. Grant	*Early Christianity and Society: Seven Studies.* San Francisco: Harper & Row, 1977.
R. M. Grant	*Greek Apologists of the Second Century.* Philadelphia: Westminster Press, 1988.
P. Gregorios et al.	*Does Chalcedon Divide or Unite?* Geneva: World Council of Churches, 1981.
C. W. Griggs	*Early Egyptian Christianity from Its Origins to 451.* Leiden: Brill, 1990.
A. Grillmeier	*Christ in the Christian Tradition.* 2 vols. Louisville, Ky.: Westminster John Knox, 1975, 1987.
R. P. C. Hanson	*The Search for the Christian Doctrine of God: The Arian Controversy 318–381.* Edinburgh: T. & T. Clark, 1988.

A. Harnack *The Mission and Expansion of Christianity in the First Three Centuries.* New York: Harper, 1978.

I. Hazlett, ed. *Early Christianity: Origins and Evolution to A.D. 600.* Nashville, Tenn.: Abingdon Press, 1991.

M. Hengel *The "Hellenization" of Judaea in the First Century After Christ.* Philadelphia: Fortress Press, 1989.

M. Hengel *Property and Riches in the Early Church.* Philadelphia: Fortress Press, 1974.

M. Hengel *The Zealots.* Edinburgh: T. & T. Clark, 1989.

J. N. Hillgarth, ed. *Christianity and Paganism, 350–750: The Conversion of Western Europe.* Philadelphia: University of Pennsylvania Press, 1986.

R. Hodges and D. Whitehouse *Mohammed, Charlemagne and the Origins of Europe: Archeology and the Pirenne Thesis.* London: Duckworth, 1983.

L. Hurtado *One God, One Lord: Early Christian Devotion and Ancient Jewish Monotheism.* Philadelphia: Fortress Press, 1988.

W. Jaeger *Early Christianity and Greek Paideia.* Cambridge, Mass.: Belknap Press, 1961.

E. H. Kantorowicz *The King's Two Bodies: A Study of Medieval Political Theology.* Princeton: Princeton University Press, 1957.

J. Kelly *The World of the Early Christians.* Collegeville, Minn.: Liturgical Press, 1997.

J. N. D. Kelly *Golden Mouth: The Story of John Chrysostom, Ascetic, Preacher, Bishop.* London: Duckworth, 1995.

R. Lane Fox *Pagans and Christians.* Harmondsworth: Viking, 1986.

B. Layton, ed. *The Rediscovery of Gnosticism.* 2 vols. Leiden: Brill, 1980–1981.

R. MacMullen — *Christianizing the Roman Empire AD 100–400*. New Haven: Yale University Press, 1984.

R. MacMullen — *Enemies of the Roman Order*. Cambridge, Mass.: Harvard University Press, 1967.

R. MacMullen — *Paganism in the Roman Empire*. New Haven: Yale University Press, 1981.

J. McManners, ed. — *The Oxford Illustrated History of Christianity*. Oxford: Oxford University Press, 1990.

R. A. Markus — *Christianity in the Roman World*. London: Thames & Hudson, 1975.

R. A. Markus — *The End of Ancient Christianity*. New York: Cambridge University Press, 1990.

R. A. Markus — *Saeculum: History and Society in the Theology of Saint Augustine*. New York: Cambridge University Press, 1988.

J.-M. Mayeur et al. — *Histoire du christianisme: Des origines à nos jours* (esp. vols. 1–4). Paris: Desclée, 1990–

A. Momigliano, ed. — *The Conflict Between Paganism and Christianity in the Fourth Century*. Oxford: Clarendon Press, 1963.

A. D. Nock — *Early Gentile Christianity and Its Hellenistic Background*. New York: Harper & Row, 1964.

J. Pelikan — *The Emergence of the Catholic Tradition (100–600)*. Chicago: University of Chicago Press, 1971.

J. Pelikan — *The Growth of Medieval Theology (600–1300)*. Chicago: University of Chicago Press, 1978.

J. Pelikan — *The Spirit of Eastern Christendom (600–1700)*. Chicago: University of Chicago Press, 1974.

P. Rousseau — *Ascetics, Authority and the Church in the Age of Jerome and Cassian*. New York: Oxford University Press, 1978.

P. Rousseau — *Pachomius: The Making of a Community in Fourth-*

Century Egypt. Berkeley: University of California Press, 1985.

A. Rousselle — *Porneia: On Desire and the Body in Antiquity.* Oxford: Blackwell, 1988.

E. Schürer — *The History of the Jewish People in the Age of Jesus Christ 175 BC–AD 135.* Rev. and ed. by G. Vermes and F. Millar. 3 vols. Edinburgh: T. & T. Clark, 1973–1987.

A. Segal — *Rebecca's Children: Judaism and Christianity in the Roman World.* Cambridge, Mass.: Harvard University Press, 1986.

M. Simon — *Verus Israel: A Study of the Relations Between Christians and Jews in the Roman Empire 135–425.* New York: Oxford University Press, 1986.

J. Z. Smith — *Drudgery Divine: On Comparison of Christianities and the Religions of Late Antiquity.* Chicago: University of Chicago Press, 1990.

R. Turcan — "Le culte impérial au IIIe siècle." ANRW II.16.2 (1978): 996–1084.

P. Veyne, ed. — *A History of Private Life.* vol. 1. *From Pagan Rome to Byzantium.* Cambridge, Mass.: Harvard University Press, 1987.

W. L. Westermann — *The Slave Systems of Greek and Roman Antiquity.* Philadelphia: American Philosophical Society, 1955.

R. L. Wilken — *John Chrysostom and the Jews.* Berkeley: University of California Press, 1983.

R. Williams, ed. — *The Making of Orthodoxy.* New York: Cambridge University Press, 1989.

F. Young — *From Nicaea to Chalcedon: A Guide to the Literature and Its Development.* Philadelphia: Fortress Press, 1983.

Index of Names and Places

Subject Index

Bible, 5, 37, 53, 55, 66–67, 72, 80,
172, 179, 183
bishops, 17, 71, 73, 78, 81–84, 86,
88–89, 92, 95, 104, 108–9,
112–13, 115–16, 131–34, 136,
139, 141–42, 155, 160, 164,
170, 177–78, 180–81, 187,
198, 204–6, 219, 221, 223
Bogomils, 91
Buddhism, 91, 137
Bulgars, 197
Burgundians, 197
Byzantine church, 116, 139, 157,
161, 190, 208–9, 220
Byzantine empire, 117, 164, 195,
100–200, 202–4, 206
Byzantine society, 136, 181
byzantinism, 118, 174

canon, canonical, 17–18, 39, 80, 174
Cappadocians, 88, 155, 163, 173,
177–79, 190
Carolingian Renaissance, 100, 203
Cathars, 91
Celts, Celtic, 7, 206–8
Chalcedon, Council of, 88, 117,
157–63, 176, 181–82, 189,
192, 209
Chalcedonians, 161–62, 164, 202,
208, 210
Christ, Jesus, 29, 38, 54–56, 72, 82,
84, 86, 98, 107, 117–18,
128–29, 139, 143–44, 147,
152–53, 155–56, 160, 162–63,
172, 181, 190, 216, 220, 224
incarnation, 73, 155–58, 174,
176, 178–79, 181, 186, 189,
219–20
Logos, 54, 87, 98, 152, 155–57,
159–60, 172–74, 177
true God, 86–87, 89, 155–56,
158–60, 164, 174, 220

true man, 87–88, 155–60, 164,
174, 220
Son of God, 35, 87–89, 128,
152–55, 174, 179, 185
Wisdom, 152
person, 155
Christian life, 122–44
Christianity, Christians, 3–8, 11, 13,
15–21, 23–24, 26–29, 32–34,
37–38, 42, 46–47, 49, 51–53,
55–57, 60–61, 63–64, 69, 71,
77–78, 85, 93, 95–96, 101–2,
104, 106–7, 110, 112–13, 115,
118, 123–27, 130, 132, 136,
138, 142, 147, 152, 160–61,
166, 172–73, 177, 179, 192,
196, 198, 200–2, 204–11,
214–17, 219–24
Christianity, triumph of, 104,
106–11, 132, 171
Christianization, 107, 109–12, 208,
210, 215, 221–22
Christmas, 129, 217
Christology, 38–39, 70, 79, 89, 147,
155–65, 177–81, 186, 188–89,
219
church, assembly, 3, 19, 34–36, 42,
53, 56, 64, 72, 84–86, 91, 95,
107–8, 111, 113, 115, 117–18,
128, 139–40, 142–43, 172,
184, 198, 205, 209, 219,
222–25
church buildings, 104, 112,
142–43, 162, 165
church order, 17, 71, 73, 77, 82,
131–33, 204, 219
Constantine, Donation of, 115
Constantinople, councils of, 88, 95,
110, 117, 155–56, 163,
177–79, 188, 199
conversion, 35, 51, 56, 63, 93, 107,